The Lord of Cat Bow

The Lord of Cat Bow

by
Stuart B. Weeks

HOBBLEBUSH BOOKS

B
WEEKS

ISBN: 0-9636413-1-X
Library of Congress Control Number: 2003116524

Designed and composed in Adobe Jenson Pro at Hobblebush Books

Printed in the United States of America

Published by
HOBBLEBUSH BOOKS
17-A Old Milford Road · Brookline, New Hampshire 03033
www.hobblebush.com

Contents

*Dedicated to Grampy
and to all other grandparents—
near no less than far. . . .*

THE BEGINNING

Fame is a fitfull flame,
That shines awhile on John Jones' name.
Then fame puts John Jones on the spot.
And fame shines on, but John shines not.

Anonymous
Quoted in the journal
of Sinclair Weeks

THE BEGINNING

WE CALLED HIM "Grampy." I never knew why. I guess it was one of those simple affections that made him special to me as a ten year old boy. And he was special, at least to me. Perhaps because he was my grandfather. But, as I grew older, somehow it seemed to be more. And I wonder even today, as I look back over those years, if I will ever understand all that "The Lord of Cat Bow" was to me.

Some of these were my thoughts as we headed up from our home in Concord, Massachusetts to Lancaster, New Hampshire for the summer, early in June, 1963. As we rounded the last bend in the road, nestled in a grove of pines stood a sign that read:

DRIVERS TAKE CARE,
31 GRANDCHILDREN
HERE AND THERE.

Yes, there were thirty-one of us; at least that was at the last count. But, the sign only began to tell the story.

Grampy lived on a farm, as all grandfathers should, complete with cows, horses, pigs, turkeys, and one stubborn and exasperating donkey named Janie. Janie was quite a donkey. She had the audacity to lie down and go to sleep every time we hitched her up to the cart for a ride. Even Grampy, who lived and died by the old New England proverb, *When the going gets tough, the tough get going,* found the old gal more than a match for his wits. Janie's breeding was impeccable and her code of ethics unmistakably mulish. Dad swore that she was the first cousin of one of those jackasses that he had pushed up and down the Rockies during boot camp, as a preamble to the war.

For myself, I never could understand what a former bigwig in the Republican party was doing entertaining a donkey at Cat Bow Farm. *The better angels of our nature*, a Godfather once said. I reflected.... Whatever the case, we grandchildren fancied that an elephant would have been eminently more appropriate. But, even though we outnumbered the adults handsomely, a pure democracy was not the practice at the farm in those years. That issue, the Lord of Cat Bow and I would take up in time.

No, there was no getting around it. Janie was basically a hopeless case. How well I remember all those hours, sitting in the cart in front of the old barn, the reins slack in my hands, while I pleaded with Janie to get up. All to no avail. It always seemed to me that Janie was ungrateful and quite arrogant. After all, we fed her, and she had her own stall. I figured the least she could do was take us for a short ride around the barnyard. But no, a member of the loyal opposition, Janie had other ideas. And, at ten years old and eighty pounds, I couldn't very well pick Janie up. So, we had to do without those rides.

Then, there was the hayloft—the scene of countless tomato fights, games of hide-and-go-seek, and of hay castles that always seemed to be in the state of caving in. We grandchildren must have taken at least a bale of hay to sleep with us every night in our hair and clothes—that, along with numerous cuts and scratches. But, these were all a part of those wonderful summer days when children were allowed to be children, and all the worries, responsibilities, and cares of life just had to wait a few years while we enjoyed ourselves.

Yes, those cuts and scratches were overlooked by everyone except Grandma Jane. She was Grampy's second wife. Bea, his first, and Dad's mother, had apparently died of pneumonia when Dad was away at war. Dad never spoke much about Bea's death – except to say that he had plenty of time to think as he was flying back in a cargo plane from the war in the Pacific theater to attend, belatedly, his mother's last rites here at home.

Grampy said even less. The little we heard came from a later account by a devoted secretary: *When Mr. Weeks returned to the office after your grandmother's death, Mrs. Murdock and I arose and stepped forward to greet him. Your grandfather didn't say a word,* she recollected. *He just stood there silently in the middle of the office, head bowed, holding our hands.* I breathed in. So it was.

What remained unspoken had found its way into a journal entry on the evening of Bea's death. *Today is the saddest day of my life.* Grampy's words were as straightforward and yet tender. . . , susceptible as the old lord, who suddenly found himself standing before a mystery pointed to in a verse by Whittier sent by a dear friend:

> *Yet love will dream, and faith will trust*
> *That somehow, somewhere meet we must.*
> *Alas for him who never sees*
> *The stars shine through his cypress trees;*
> *Who hath not learned in hours of faith*
> *The truth to flesh and sense unknown,*
> *That life is ever Lord of Death*
> *And love can never lose its own.*

Yes, Grampy loved Bea dearly, and she had understood him well. They were a great couple; so I was told. I wasn't around then, probably not even a thought. As a result, what was such an important event to Grampy and his six children never affected me directly.

I don't remember much about Grandma Jane either—except that she fussed over our cuts and scratches. And also, she was a Southern lady—a charming belle from Nashville, Tennessee. That, in itself, would have been fine, if it hadn't been that every time Grandma Jane greeted me, she would grab my cheek and purr, *Hi, honey chil, how's ma babe?*

Luckily, in those days we kids weren't allowed in the Big House very often, as it was. You know: *Children are to be seen and not heard*—all those formalities that lingered between the generations, biding their time until we grandchildren would grow up and set things straight. So we figured. In any case, I didn't mind not being able to run in and out of the Big House whenever I wanted. The barn was not only more inviting, but more spacious still. And, if we got bored there, we always had the lake, fields, and mountains of our Northern Kingdom to engage our awakening curiosity and perpetual motion.

But, even though Grandma Jane had the rather irksome propensity to indulge herself at the expense of our cheeks, I managed to overlook that. For her arrival at Cat Bow meant five more grandchildren—and, more importantly, one my age, Wade. Yes, in the time it had taken to repeat the vows, another ten members were added to the clan, and an impromptu grafting on our staunch New England family tree was arranged, so as to accommodate the new kin from south of the Mason Dixon. The more the merrier, as far as I was concerned. With time, even Grandma Jane's indulgences became a little easier to stomach.

Unfortunately, though, the new in-laws weren't around very long. One day I was told that Grandma Jane was very sick. Dad explained to me that she had some new disease with a complicated German name, *Alzhe. . .* , that only a few people had ever gotten, and that Grandma Jane would probably never get better. I was only ten at the time, and, sadly enough, the worst thing about the whole deal was that my new pal, Wade, stopped coming up to the farm. I really liked Wade. After I got around his Southern accent and saw that he could throw the crab apples as well as the rest of us, Wade was accepted right off. Looking back, it all seemed so simple as kids.

Anyway, a little more of Grampy died as Grandma Jane's condition got worse. The only time our Grandma came out of her room was when Grampy would wheel his "Jane," her pale hands gripping her shawl, into the Pine Room during cocktail hour or into the dining room for a meal. But, Grandma Jane didn't seem interested in eating, and eventually even those visits became less frequent. Finally, Grampy set up a new room in the north wing of the house for Grandma Jane, with a fancy hospital bed and nurses around the clock.

Your grandfather did not recognize illness; for him it was a weakness to be overcome, an old friend wrote after Grampy's death. So it was. Before we would leave from a visit to the farm, Grampy would make Nat, Bea, Brad, and me go down the long hall with him and give Grandma Jane a kiss good-bye. Grampy felt strongly about us sticking together as a family and figured it made Grandma Jane feel better. But, I wasn't sure. To tell the truth, I was a little scared. When I leaned over Grandma Jane's bed and kissed her, she never said a word or even looked at me. She just stared off at the wall.

In time, Grandma Jane's shadow faded away, too. The only bride to soundly outlive Grampy was Teenie (along with her miniature schnauzer, Tippy Toes), who, in Grampy's latter years, brought to Cat Bow Farm from the West Coast a welcome California blend—along with another half-dozen game cousins. By that time, despite ourselves, we had become a pretty cosmopolitan clan, although our roots remained firmly set in the New Hampshire soil that had become a part of the family over the generations.

For some reason my most distinct memory of those years is a retiring nook in Grampy's stately Governor Winthrop desk, which filled a quiet corner of the old Pine Room. Nestled within the nook was a small, gold-framed photograph. A sunbeam glanced over the shoulder of a kindly-looking, middle-aged lady, awakening traces of a smile on her pensive face and lighting up the shades of gray that had begun to touch her hair.

We called *him* Grampy. Grandmother, Grandma, . . . smaller than Teenie, I never knew what to call Bea; I never knew her as a mortal. Summer was passing on into autumn. Poised beneath the fleeting embrace of the old elm, Bea's gaze rested silently on the camera. In the background, the field led up to the old farmhouse, before blending into the flanks of Mt. Orne that rose up—with a happy–sad melody—over our small universe:

> *All night, all day, angels watchin' over me, my Lord.*
> *All night, all day, angels watchin' over me. . . .*

No, Dad never talked much with us about his mother. It was only years later that I discovered that it wasn't pneumonia that Bea actually died of. Though Grampy got her to the hospital in time, the oxygen tent didn't work. Instead of getting air, his beloved Bea suffocated.

I also had much to reflect upon over the years, as that, too, was part of the sad reality of life that took a back seat to our exciting capers.

* * * * *

Cat Bow Farm to a ten-year-old was just about the most exciting place in the whole, wide world! Situated at the end of a long dirt road that ambled past fields, forests, and the Baker Farm—a clump of barns where Grampy kept various animals, equipment, and drowsy winter sleighs—Cat Bow nestled among the flanks of Mt. Orne.

Mt. Orne was a small, surmountable mountain that tumbled down through golden, waist-deep fields, freckled with daisies, Indian paintbrushes, and dandelions, to a friendly, refreshing pond on one side. On the other side, Mt. Orne sloped down through the timberline to Ox Bow, a dairy farm that Grampy had bought in the forties.

Apparently, Cat Bow got its name from an old deed, dating back to the days of Roger's Rangers that referred to our particular neck of the woods as "The Cat Bow Tract." The "Bow" was borrowed from the bend in the Connecticut River, which curled up to the backside of Mt. Orne, the "Cat," to the bounty of wildcats whose screams in earlier times often pierced the still nights of our Northern Kingdom. As for Ox Bow, I don't know how that name was arrived at, other than it being a suitable sequel.

The focal point of the farm was the Big House, a warm, wooden, two-storied, gray domicile (that borrowed a touch of green from the surrounding fields), with a pair of spacious wings that reached out to welcome family and friends alike in a hospitable North Country embrace. In the case of the Big House, the logic behind the name was hardly a mystery, as one glance furnished the answer. The house was, from no matter what angle viewed, very simply big! This was where the Lord of Cat Bow held court. And, if there were ever a house built for grandchildren, the Big House was it.

To start off, the Big House had three main stairways, twelve bathrooms, eight doorways into the house, six telephones, nine fireplaces, sixteen bedrooms, three attics, nineteen card tables, and between fifty and sixty closets (the estimates on this last figure are still somewhat in doubt). Cat Bow slept twenty-seven comfortably—without counting the accommodating old couches stationed about the house, to which Grampy succumbed with no reservations—but was capable of handling twice that number when circumstances warranted.

These circumstances arose regularly for a good many years in January, when the Ski & Tumble Klub Weekends commenced, and Grampy and Bea's cronies—led by our devoted 'Uncle Ned' Monroe—convened from all parts of New England to ski, tell stories, play bridge, sample the Moose Milk, and tumble through the weekend. The Ski & Tumble Klub, established in 1921 under the "laws of gravity," was a truly remarkable club, with an even more remarkable constitution, set of by-laws, and list of House Rules. Some of its more enlightening precepts read as follows:

- *Wet socks, gloves, and Klub kaps of Active Members shall have priority over those of temporary members at, near, behind, or in front of the living room stove (God Bless It!).*
- *The colors of the Klub and auxiliary shall be black and blue.*
- *During a meeting members are required to wear said colors on the body.*
- *The first 3 officers shall be elective. The office of Treasurer shall not be elective, but shall remain in the hands of the present heavyweight ski jumping champion of the Klub, so long as he shall retain this title.*
- *The women's auxiliary membership shall consist of wives, sisters, cousins (f), nieces (f), aunts, parents (f), who shall, at the time of the Annual Meeting, be in good standing with the Active Member, who, in turn, shall be in good standing himself before fastening skis to boots.*
- *Knickerbockers, while tolerated, are frowned upon by Active Members. This question may, at the discretion of the president, be settled annually by a rising and falling vote of the entire Klub when in the field.*

From what I gleaned, the Ski & Tumble Klub's antics extended beyond the slopes and Klub House. Judging by Dad's account, the grand finales were more than memorable. On at least one occasion, the first couple to depart was escorted with much fanfare out to their car—spirited buggies ranging from old jalopies to Packards and Pierce Arrows—awaiting them at the front door. Hustled into their seats, arms waved, banners flew, kisses piqued the air, as the dear departing couple turned the key and, caught up in the bruha, pressed energetically on the throttle in order to navigate a rip-roaring exit. As the wheels spun, exhaust spumed, and hurrahs mounted, . . . the bewildered passengers proceeded not an inch. Drumming on the hood, the doors were once again flung open by the club members, a renewed round of embraces bestowed, and the friends, visibly moved by the demonstrations, were hustled back into the house for a soothing shot of whiskey—while the wooden block was pulled out from underneath the back axle, and the wheels lowered once again to the road. Duly fortified, the flabbergasted couple was sent on their way.

I took a deep breath. Yes, Grampy's "Ski & Tumble Klub" was renowned, and, although I was neither a Charter Member, nor alive during its reign, I felt as if I were one of the "boys," just by listening to the stories and reading the letters, plaques, and mementos born out of the melee. The Big House was put to the test during those years and duly primed for the subsequent invasion by the grandchildren.

* * * * *

The bedrooms were some of the most memorable parts of the Big House. They came in all shapes and sizes, ranging from cozy alcoves, ideally suited for diminutive grandchildren to great, sprawling boudoirs, set aside for an esteemed visitor or occasional great aunt. During one visit, we were told, a gentleman, fondly referred to as "Ike," lay awake through the summer night, listening to the wistful call of the whippoor-will.

Many of the rooms had their own bathrooms, a number had bay windows, and all had comfortable springy beds, smoothly tucked in with a pair of elegant, goose-feathered pillows at one end and a comforting quilt folded neatly at the other. Each room had its own charm and was filled with countless antiques and relics—which made these chambers more like museums than bedrooms, with the result that getting to sleep often proved to be a rather prolonged enterprise.

Along with the fact that each bedroom possessed its own special charm, a number of them were named. Grampy's room—the Master Bedroom in all senses of the word—headed the list. It was located at the top of the stairway at the west end of the house and opened up onto a balcony porch, from whence Grampy bid the sun adieu on many a warm summer night. Besides being the most spacious bedroom—and appropriately so—the truly remarkable part of Grampy's chamber was to be found in its adjoining bathroom. Grampy had a copper bathtub! That, in itself, might have been excusable, except that Grampy was a strict proponent of showers for men. *Let the women have their tub, but what redblooded man wants to sit in his own dirt and grime!* A bathtub, in itself, was a surprise. But one of copper; that was unfathomable.

Aside from its copper bathtub, Grampy's bathroom had a number of other idiosyncrasies, which, to us as little children, were equally impressive. The bathroom had three closets, a scale—the likes of which I had only seen in doctors' offices—and, most baffling of all, the "facilities" were located in a separate compartment of their own, off the bathroom. (We were relieved to discover that the bathroom also hosted a shower, discreetly tucked away behind a beige curtain.)

Along with serving as the facilities for Grampy's toilette, the bathroom was also the scene of a number of private family "councils," which, from what we heard, frequently involved our esteemed father. One story in particular got me thinking. By Dad's account (and confession), his youthful proclivity—innocent as it was—to get his "two cents worth" in at the dining room table didn't always go down well with Grampy.

One ill-fated evening (somewhere along the rambunctious course of our father's ninth year) he went just a *little* bit too far. Rising from his place at the head of the table, "the Lord" hoisted Sinclair Jr. up by the seat of his trousers and briskly escorted his son, and namesake, out of the dining room, up the stairs, down the long hallway, through his bedroom, and into the bathroom—where hung a long-handled hairbrush, specifically improvised for such occasions. Dad's apologies, though sincere, were belated. Depositing our father in the middle of the bathroom floor, the two Sinclairs—junior and senior—squared off. Grampy rolled up his sleeves, released our father's suspenders, bent him over, and *whop! whop! whop!* Three times for good measure. The bathroom was silent, as Dad gingerly hoisted up his trousers—delicately shifting his seventy scant pounds from one foot to the other. Then, his face as red as a beet, Dad turned to his father and proclaimed, amidst the gentle gush of tears that ran down his cheeks, BOY, THAT TICKLED! Dad's rigor was too much for Grampy, who immediately broke out laughing. Next of kin, I wasn't quite sure what to make of the matter, nor of the hairbrush—none the worse for its wear—which still held sway in the Lord's bathroom.

Beyond Grampy's room, out on the north wing of the house, down a narrow corridor, and past a glass case stuffed with menacing looking fowl, was Nat's (my older brother) and my favorite room, the War Room. Upon approaching this chamber, one had the distinct feeling of entering the war zone. Hanging on the wall were two, old, wooden signs, with barbed wire on them, written in German. A peek through the keyhole revealed a First World War gas mask, and if visitors were able to muster up enough courage to enter, they were soon to discover that this room had also been appropriately named. The walls were decorated with helmets, boots were slung over wooden pegs, artillery pieces reposed in the corners, and the shelves and drawers were filled with books, diaries, plaques, and other mementos of the Great War. In quiet moments, I often glanced through the pages of the journals, coming upon an unexpected letter or two, enfolded within their worn pages, signed "Buddy" or "Sin."

Nat and I estimated that there was no finer room in the house. And many a night, as we settled into bed, with those enveloping quilts atop us and pictures of Grampy's 101st F.A. Battalion of the 26th Yankee Division on the bed boards over our heads, we fancied ourselves jumping over foxholes, crawling under barbed wire, and leading decisive charges against the enemy, while bombs exploded in mid-air all around us. When morning came, the sun would peek over the Presidential Range, spilling streams of light across the hallway and into our room. The war was over, and, as we pulled ourselves up in bed, Nat and I were relieved to discover that, except for creaky joints, we had come out of the battle unscathed. As we marched forth from the War Room, we reckoned that we had brought victory to the Allies single-handedly.

Down the hall from Grampy's room, a long narrow carpet escorted us past the legions of closets and rows of pictures—kith and kin alike—that lined the walls. I was often waylaid by one photo in particular, a vintage shot of a stern-looking elderly lady, referred to by Grampy as "Mother." *Keep it off, or wear it out. Make it do, or do without.* Of hardy New England stock, Martha Sinclair peered out at us from a thin, dark, lace veil, keeping an austere eye on the family. Posed beneath Great-Grandmother's vigilant gaze, the second and third generations lined up in silhouette across a long narrow frame. Facing one another at either end, Grampy and Bea glanced more affably over the shoulders of Frances, John, Patty, Sinclair Jr. (Dad), Bill, in descending rank, and Baby Bea; Aunt Muff's smile traced a dawning vision, which, in times to come, would find expression in a fleeting poem that brought her Ma and namesake to heart and mind:

Treasure

The earth is bathed in shining light,
But on it night will shut the door.
Not things, just their color's what matters to me.
The treasure of life is the power to see:
Violet shadows deepening on heaven's floor;
The tarnished gold of a field of wheat;
A pool, glassy green in the breathless heat;
The myriad facets of a diamond's glow;
Nature's multi-colored bow;
The cobwebs sparkling iridescence,
Lasting as a sigh,
And the bronze vermilion flames that dance
Before the inner eye.

The hallway continued down to 'Uncle Bobby's Room,' so named because this was where General Robert Cutler, a dear friend of Grampy's, head of President Eisenhower's National Security Council, and faithful visitor, put up his feet. 'Uncle Bobby's Room' overlooked the circular pebbled driveway and was connected to Dad's former room by a normal bathroom, with a shower!

Dad's room was not much different from 'Uncle Bobby's,' except for one thing. As a boy, Dad, in one of his more remarkable—but less calculated—fits of creativity, cut a peephole in his door—so as to better observe his visitors before committing himself. The idea (adapted from a visit to Fort Ticonderoga), though really quite ingenious for a nine-year-old, was not appreciated by Grampy. And Dad's flair for woodcarving was subsequently tempered by a (less dramatic) heart-to-heart conversation with his father.

Across the hall from Dad's room was one of the numerous guest rooms that always had an open door. In Grampy and Bea's early years, when Prohibition was not only in effect in the old U. S. of A., but, (due to Bea's vigilance) at Cat Bow Farm, this particular room was known, among discreet circles, to serve also as an improvised North Country Saloon. 'Uncle Ned' Monroe, who provided a lively focal point for such circles, recalled a related ritual that wasn't uncommon during the '20's, when Grampy's old Battery B mates, who also happened to enjoy a good drink, convened at Cat Bow. In 'Uncle Ned's' words:

> *Much fun and good humor went into devising ways of getting around the liquor edict set down by the lady of the house, your grandmother. In those years as these, it was the custom that guests gathered in the Pine Room before the meal for a social hour. Hard-pressed to find any libation on the premises, other than a cranky old glass of cider, I and the other male guests would exchange civilities for a few minutes, before, one by one, excusing ourselves from the social hour and discreetly hightailing it upstairs to the guest room.*

Barring the door to all but the initiated, 'Uncle Ned' and his associates would produce a makeshift bar from the closet, bottles of whiskey from the depths of the fireplace, and, sprinkling a light smattering of sawdust over the floor, lift their glasses to Uncle Sam. "Live Free or Die" was the New Hampshire state motto that "the boys" took dearly to heart.

Meanwhile, Grampy, who, by this time, was the only gentleman within eyeshot of Bea, would grow more and more edgy, until finally he announced that he was going upstairs to make sure everything was all right. That was the last Bea saw of any of them until dinner was served, and down the stairs they came, marching into the dining room with big grins on their faces and a "shot" or two under their belts. Apparently, the good-natured fun was contagious, and, from what 'Uncle Ned' recounted, eventually even the lady of the house (reconciling herself to her stern Puritan forbears) learned to enjoy a light sip before dinner.

Down the hall toward the east wing of the house, our steps led us to Mina's Room, as tidy as her small desk, which peeked out of the window on her far wall. Mina was Grampy's house-factota, secretary, and clan-organizer during the years when Grandma Jane's health was declining. A stalwart friend to us all, Mina's enthusiasm and good spirits injected a sense of life into a house that was haunted by a fading shadow for a dozen years.

On the east wing of the house lived Dora and Cynthia. Sweet and sour, these ladies handled the domestic and culinary chores, keeping things lively in the kitchen, and were adopted Grandmas during the interim periods when Grampy was alone. Looking back, I have not a single recollection of Dora and Cynthia that is not adorned in apron strings and those neat white dresses that, I realize now, went with the job.

In quiet moments, I used to love to follow my steps through the rooms and examine the pictures and hangings that graced the walls. From nature prints that escorted us through the seasons, to more momentary snatches of wit and wisdom, each frame offered an inviting window into the life of Cat Bow and its New England Lord, Grampy. One tapestry in particular I returned to often over the years: a small hand-stitched garden scene that had found a still spot beside a mirror in one of my aunt's former rooms. In the center of its colorful flowery border rested an altar of roses that reached up to enwreath the following words:

> *There is no friend like an old friend,*
> *Who has shared our morning days,*
> *No greeting like her welcome,*
> *No homage like her praise.*
> *Fame is a scentless sunflower*
> *With a gaudy crown of gold,*
> *But friendship the breathing rose*
> *With sweets in every fold.*

Beyond Cynthia's and Dora's room was the playroom—the locus of the majority of our indoor activities. Most of the wing was a huge room with sloping eves, retired furniture, dusty old chests, and a tremendous assortment of toys and amusements with which to while away the rainy days. A swing had been set up in the middle of the floor and was seldom in repose. A herd of rocking horses danced under the far eves, and a ping-pong table rested against one of the walls, its surface overflowing with games that spanned the generations. The playroom was the perfect rainy day retreat. For hours upon end, we would pursue our fancies, while drops of rain danced upon the roof-top overhead.

From the playroom, the carpet followed a wide, white, winding, wooden banister down the backstairs. To the right, the hallway continued out through the kitchen door, into the wood shed and garage—the

scene of The Succulent Steaks Snafu, a rained-out–smoked-in bar-
becue, during which the Weeks family had the honor of being served
sizzling steaks by the thirty-forth president of the United States. So the
story went, memorialized by another aunt, Frannie: *'Twas the 24th of
June in the year '55, when Cat Bow hummed like a busy beehive. . . .*

To the left, the hallway caught up with itself in the kitchen, before
proceeding into the pantry, the sun porch (where on glistening morn-
ings we gathered for breakfast) and dining room. These rooms were
integral to the well-being of Cat Bow and were the focal point over the
years of many a protracted family parlay.

Grampy's seat marked the head of the dining-room table. Behind
it, above the fireplace, a print of a still morning landscape rested on
its hook. Drawn by the gently sloping hill, my eyes often followed the
broad path down to a rude, wooden bridge, under which a peaceful
spring stream flowed seaward.

Across from Grampy's seat at the foot of the table and against the
far wall, a stalwart pine hutch gazed down over the proceedings. A
universe in its own right, the lower half of the hutch hosted a succes-
sion of drawers, which stored place-settings and utensils galore for our
dining pleasure. In the center of the hutch, a highfalutin' ceramic hen,
sporting a gallant red soup ladle for tail-feathers, brooded away on the
baseboard. The old gal, in turn, was flanked by coasters, salt and pepper
shakers, and an alert silver bell, before three more shelves, replete with
plates, platters, and pewter, climbed above our youthful visions to the
crown of the venerable old heirloom. On either side of the hutch, gray
wrought-iron candle holders, each a good five feet high and tendering a
bevy of candles, reposed in the corners.

Often in the evenings, members of the family would strike a match
to the candles and convene around the dining room table for a few
rounds of Jenkins Up—a family game that had been passed down
through the generations. With John Paul Jones, Mr. Martin van Buren,
and other obscure notables, gazing out of their frames over our shoulders, two teams of players would congregate on each side of the long
maple table and take turns shuffling a quarter into expectant hands,
fumbling among the laps. After one team had had time to deposit the
quarter in a chosen palm, the other team would call: Jenkins Up! At
the command, an array of closed fists, small and large alike—one con-

taining the concealed coin—would arrive back on the top of the table. With hands clenched tightly and countenances straining, the defending team would proceed through a series of commands, issued by the other team, which were designed to reveal the precise whereabouts of the quarter.

Creepy Crawlers found the team with the quarter grimacing, as they quickly unfolded their fingers from closed fists to palms flat on the table. Hanging Gardens was a skillful maneuver that had the defenders holding their breaths, as they waved their hands upside down in the air, the quarter tucked into one of the palms. Venetian Blinds presented itself as a deft reversal of Hanging Gardens (fingers this time up and apart), complete with an array of aerial acrobatics of its own. And last but not least, Grand Slam climaxed the round with a mounting drone that exploded when the team with the quarter slapped their hands together in mid air and, then, flopped them, palms once again down, onto the table.

Everybody took a deep breath, before the searchers, listening carefully for the sound of clinking metal and eyeing the hands for a protruding coin, attempted to eliminate every hand, *except* the one covering the quarter. If the guess was wrong and the quarter prematurely uncovered, the defending team would get a point and another try. Jenkins Up! So it went. The dining room was a forum for many such family games, often as busy after a meal as it was during.

From the dining room, the route split. A left turn took us to the hallway and back door, a right turn to the entrance room, vestibule, and front door. The former corner was as bright as the latter areas (due to their small windows) were dark. Aged, pine floorboards and paneling were set in around a large stone hearth, emblazoned with a circular copper medallion that added a warm glint to the entrance room. Around the fireplace, a pair of broad straight-backed love-seats basked in the gentle glow of the hearth, while above, a silent owl peered down from its permanent perch atop the corner shelf.

The hallways converged once again in the living room, the halfway point between the dining and Pine Room. Often, after a big meal, the adults would convene in the living room with their coffee, instead of continuing on to the Pine Room. The living room was cozy and warm, with an accessible fire, numerous tables, strewn with pre-dinner rummy hands and colorful disjointed puzzles, and a sofa, comfortably edged with cushions. These soft asides offered further glimpses into the life of Cat Bow—one in particular customarily finding its way onto Grampy's lap. Embroidered across its fluffy face were two red-threaded bovines, nose to nose. Between the pair—bull and heifer—a gallant heart gently interposed itself, while in the background a country lane faded into the pillowy sunset, aglow with the words: *Cattle crossing, please go slow. This old bull is some cow's beau.*

Off the living room was the Summer Porch. This room was the least used of any in the house and, in fact, was boarded up for most of the year—an apt testimony to the stamina of the northern New Hampshire summers. The Summer Room was actually more closely akin to a screened-in porch and had a definite exotic flavor to it. In the middle of the floor stood Grampy's throne—a stately wicker chair that extended itself hospitably in all directions. Between its footrests, various cubbyholes, and plume back, Grampy was able to entertain nearly a dozen grandchildren on and about his lap. Spread out around this room were other smaller versions of this Polynesian grandiosity: a North Country crossbreed between a couch, davenport and divan (which swayed back and forth to the New Hampshire breezes) and colorful Indian wall hangings.

The living room continued on into the hallway, lined with six, white, wooden closets, each bearing the initials of one of Grampy's children and our, his grandchildren's, parents. Nat, Bea, Brad, and I quickly deciphered S.W. as being our familial root to the source and allowed that that one closet we could thoroughly acquaint ourselves with. A revelation it was. Glove, fishing rod, sombrero, kit and caboodle. . . . Needless to say, we were delighted to discover that old Dad, too, had once been a child!

Off the west wing was a small greenhouse that harbored Cat Bow's floral arrangements. Grandma Jane had a fertile green thumb, and, in her earlier years, she spent a good deal of her time bestowing generous amounts of T.L.C. (Tender Loving Care) on her plants. There was hardly a windowsill in the house that wasn't sprouting cheerful colors.

Directly off the greenhouse was the Telephone Room—a small but consequential alcove, stuffed with more pictures and plaques, a closet pregnant with knickknacks, and a tall, bronze, cylindrical stand, complete with swords, canes, walking sticks, rods, batons, and other angular oddities, . . . as well as a small desk and telephone that serviced the west end of the house. Above the telephone on the wall of the alcove hung one of a number of framed testaments to our grandfather that kept me guessing for a good while.

SOMETHING FOR NOTHING

Dear Mr. Sec,

My friend, Jones, received a check for $1,000 from the government for not raising hogs. So, I am also going into the not-raising-hog-business. What I want to know is what is the best kind of hog not to raise. I would prefer not to raise Razor-backs, but if necessary will just as gladly not raise Durocs or Poland Chinas. How much will you pay me for not raising 100 hogs? And will the same rate apply if I increase my non-raising capacity to 1,000? Also, will you pay me for not raising 10,000 bushels of corn, which I will not feed to the hogs which I am not raising? Please answer soon, as this looks like a fine year for not raising hogs.

PS. Can I actually raise a couple of hogs on the side, so we can have a little ham and bacon to eat?

Continuing on, the halls provided endless runways. Countless nooks and crannies afforded us perfect hiding places for our numerous games (including hide-and-go-seek from the parents). Shelves and books captured our attention for hours upon end. And, it was a rare closet we found our way into without bursting out, attired in some swashbuckling outfit, brandishing a sword—feigned or otherwise.

At the entrance to the telephone room, stood a venerable old "gent"—a good seven feet high and three broad, with a sterling Westminster tone and striking countenance, who whiled away the hours with Grampy. Encased in a seasoned mahogany frame, the grandfather clock—as far as we could tell—had been ticking as long as our grandfather. Morning, noon, eve—the watches of the day and night took their bearing from this enduring (and endearing) timepiece.

At the telephone room, the hallway branched three ways: down the corridor past a spacious guest room to Grandma Jane's quarters on the north wing of the house, back up the stairway to Grampy's room, and on into the Pine Room—a universe in its own right. And the circuit was completed.

* * * * *

When the sun was shining, its beams filled the Big House, brightening up its assemblage, past and present, and drawing us grandchildren outside.

From the front step of the Big House, one had a commanding view of Cat Bow Farm. The driveway wound leisurely around the circle—a swath of grass, edged by slate slabs and punctuated by an island of roses—across from the front door. From there, the drive continued, alongside the stone wall and column of stately elms, up to the barn—a sizable structure itself, with two wings of its own which returned the Big House's hospitable embrace. The road paused in the barnyard, before continuing up to Ester and Bill Rines', the farmer's house, and then climbing further up a steep hill to our cousins, the Bill Weeks' house, which overlooked our North Country domain.

Beside the barn were an old screened-in turkey coop (a constant flurry of squawks and feathers), the woodshed, a few catch-all sheds, and the pig sty. Of all the animals on the farm, the pigs were the object of my most fervent adulation. These jovial slop-mongers—second cousins to the hippo, indiscriminate and voracious gourmands, and surely God's best intentioned, but least inspired, creation—captured an indelible spot in my youthful heart. Many a summer day, I spent hours hanging over the fence, showering lavish praises upon these tremendous porkers, as they wallowed to their hearts' delight in New Hampshire's finest mud-baths.

From the woodshed, a narrow path passed under two crab apple trees, over a small bridge, and through a freckled glade, which led up to our main hangout—the playhouse. When Grampy was entertaining politicians, leaders of the military, or business tycoons in the Big House, we were holding court ourselves in our own miniature rendition. The playhouse, although one-third the size of Grampy's bathroom, was a real, live house. It had four walls, a roof, three windows (which guaranteed against sneak attacks), a door that both opened *and* closed, various haphazard pieces of furniture and utensils, a small porch complete with two, rickety, wooden stools, and, most importantly, an electric light for our strategy sessions that lasted well on into the night. The playhouse seated five—*uncomfortably!*

Along with having a strategic view of the Big House, the playhouse overlooked Cat Bow's agricultural and horticultural concerns. The apple orchard and garden spread out in a small field that rolled down to the Big House—Grampy's main hangout. These choice acres, along with providing the Lord of Cat Bow with fresh fruits and vegetables in season, were our ammunition dumps, and a ready supply of crab apples and tomatoes was stashed in the playhouse in order to ward off any intruders.

To the right of the Big House was a well-traveled lawn, the sight of our quintennial family photos—remarkably staged productions, which, over the years, pretty nearly exceeded the photographer's old wide-angle lens. Perfectly groomed, the carpet of grass was interrupted only by a tall white flagpole—with Old Glory atop, waving to the New Hampshire breeze. The lawn meandered around the back of the house to a terrace, before disappearing into the hayfield, which stretched on down to the boat house on the lake—an old Hodgman House that had made the trip up from Cape Cod in the early thirties on the back of a large flat-bed truck. Across the waters, on the opposite shore, a path led up to the Sugarbush, set back into the woods, and to the southwest boundary of the farm.

The terrace was one of the nicest spots on all of Cat Bow. Tidy, gray, picket fences skirted the edges of summer flower beds that blossomed with the bright colors of geraniums, lilacs, petunias, violets, and roses. Bird feeders rose out of the shrubs or dangled among the ivy from hooks on the house, and at either end of the garden a fountain spilled water onto the green carpet below. Two drowsy elms spread their boughs over corners of the lawn, casting shadows about the terrace, and stone slabs announced a path from the back door to the chairs and lounges.

In the midst of the terrace, a sundial faithfully marked the passages of its heavenly orb, lifting our gazes, in more reflective moments, beyond Cat Bow's worldly confines. The dial was a gift from Grampy's former associates at the old United Carr Fastener Corporation. Presented to the Lord of Cat Bow with a poem, its aspiring meter was a fitting expression of his business colleagues' fondness for their host—if not, admittedly, the gentlemen's poetic verve and verse:

TO SINCLAIR WEEKS

In the soft gray hush of the evening,
When the sun has gone to rest,
And the good fellows gather at Cat Bow,
That's the time we like best.
The memories will always be with us
Of Weeks and his work on the farm,
Of clam bakes, of horseshoes, of cards, and good cheer
Of the lake, of the house, and its charm.

To us, these spring meetings stand out all alone
As highlights throughout the year.
We try to express our thanks and our thoughts,
But somehow they are not so clear.

So please accept, Sinclair, this token (sun dial) we send,
To stand in the rain and the sun,
On top of the knoll that we all love so well,
To tell how the day's hours will run.

It will stand guard o'er hill and o'er lake,
And with it our thoughts will remain,
To a man and a host exceeded by none,
ENSHRINED IN A PERFECT DOMAIN!

So it was. The Presidential Peaks seemed to grow out of Grampy's backyard. Overflowing one's vision, they rose up in the distance, looming above tumbling green pastures and clumps of woods. Even at ten, I would stare at the great peaks in wonder. Yet, as I grew older, I was to find that I would appreciate the view even more. In the years to come, I watched the Presidentials shed their seasons. From the beautiful, flushed mosaic patchwork of the autumn leaves, the mountains retired into winter, harboring vast shining snow fields through the cold, still months. Then, as the icicles grew short on the eves, winter, too, stepped aside, and spring burst forth, quenching her thirst with vigorous mountain torrents, soon to be followed once again by summer, accentuating those rugged granite faces and warming the rolling hills and forests. And so it went, from one season into the next, into the next—the stage constantly changing. Indeed, there was no finer place on all of Cat Bow from which to sit and watch the final acts of many a wonderful day.

Just behind the Big House, stone steps led down to a log cabin that belonged to our cousins, the Basts. The Basts spent their summers on the farm and were the custodians of the horses, as well as the impresarios of the family athletic endeavors. Since the tennis court, which also happened to be surrounded on three sides by cow fields, was ten steps from the Basts' cabin, Uncle Bob and Dad's youngest sister, Aunt Muff, set up the round-robin tennis matches and generously provided refreshments between sets. These matches were tremendous productions, which often reached such crescendos that every cow on the farm would congregate in the bleachers, adding to the fervor.

Actually, the cows were as much a part of Cat Bow as most of the family, to a large degree, I imagine, because the farm was, in fact, surrounded on all sides by cow fields. At certain times, with a slight rearrangement of perspectives, this proved to be a rather disquieting realization. In any case, with as much fence as we had surrounding the property, it was not unusual to encounter these good-natured beasts at any moment of the day.

Since cows do happen to be both curious and friendly animals, when they did get loose, they often came looking for company. Poor Bill Rines, the farmer, spent more time than he cared to remember, chasing the cows out of the garden or coming to the rescue of some unsuspecting guest, who found herself cornered by one of these mobile milk-machines.

The most memorable episodes usually occurred on Sundays, when the family started upon its grand exodus down the hill to the Boat House on the lake for our picnic. It was about a quarter of a mile from the Big House to the Boat House. That, in itself, was no problem—

except that this quarter of a mile covered Cat Bow's most delectable and clover-strewn grazing area. Consequently, this was where the Cat Bow herd hung out.

As noted, cows are harmless, but they are curious critters, and traversing the field often resembled the game Red Rover, Red Rover, Come Over, Come Over. The adults knew the cows were good-natured. But, no amount of coaxing could make me or any of my younger compatriots believe that these monstrous creatures, complete with a hard set of horns, had any but the most fearsome intentions.

We would start down the hill, our hearts in palpitations, as we clung to our parents. No sooner had we committed ourselves to the field than the cows made their move. Getting wind of our approach, one of the old gals would lift her head out of the grass, and, her curiosity getting the better of her, lumber over to us, chewing her cud and swishing her tail. At this point we would start to panic, as the herd bore down on us. Our options were two-fold: Stay and fight with the adults, or retreat. The choice was a clear one. Calculating the distances, we hightailed it to the nearest fence, hollering at the top of our lungs. *When the going gets tough. . . .* Yes, in those years, the Lord of Cat Bow's proverb, allowed, we reckoned, for liberal interpretation.

It wasn't until a few more seasons had passed, and I had mustered up the pluck to stand up to these beasts, that I discovered, when approached, that they were, in fact, quite timid. But, the discoveries didn't stop with the cows. As I grew older, my small universe began slowly but surely to unfold.

SUMMER

What a glorious afternoon, clear, blue, and not a cloud in the sky. The sun shines, warming up this old North Country Kingdom. Took my lady down to watch Jim spreading manure onto the field—she still hasn't got a hang for the aroma. Afterward, Janie and I kicked up our heels together in the barnyard; that old donkey has got a mind of her own. The family should be arriving soon. Another summer begins.

Sinclair Weeks, Diary, June 4, 1963

I

HEADED TO THE FARM

AS THE CAR ROLLED up under the bounteous embrace of the old elm and into the driveway, the excitement of arriving at Cat Bow for the start of summer vacation was nearly unbearable. From the back seat, Nat, Bea, Brad, and I urged Dad to hurry—to no avail. Secure at the helm, our driver smiled at us through the rearview mirror. Yes, Dad was a steady soul, having, as we were fond of saying good-humoredly, two speeds—slow and stop. I don't doubt, though, that Dad was excited to be here, too. After all, Cat Bow was the place where he had spent many of his summers as a child. But, you know, being an adult, he couldn't show it.

As the car stopped, Wildcat, Grampy's low-slung, loyal basset hound, perked his head up from the cool of the garage and ambled over to greet us. Grampy had a soft spot in his heart for dogs and took a particular liking to Wildcat, who, it always seemed to me, was most inappropriately named. Wildcat couldn't have gone two rounds with his own shadow. Poor fellow, try as he might, he just never made it as an intimidating character. His long ears were a constant menace to his sense of balance and dignity. As a pup, any acceleration into high gear was disastrous. Time and again, Wildcat would come running down from the barn to Grampy—ears, tail, and tongue awaggin'—only to end up sprawled over the ground at his master's feet, rightfully forlorn over the matter. Now, as Wildcat got on in his years, he had resigned himself to his plight. God had cramped his style, and consequently his

24

welcomes were less than spectacular. But, we loved Wildcat, just the same.

We piled out of the car, converged upon Wildcat and waved to Cynthia in the kitchen, before running (which we were *not* supposed to do) into the Big House.

Cynthia, as mentioned, was one of a distinguished line of cooks who concocted at Cat Bow. Her predecessor, and the most impressive of all, was a tall, strapping, Bible-reading, fun-loving, Jamaican named John Crawford. Along with preparing the victuals, John lent a hand with the children when Dad was a boy, and, in his strong and yet compassionate way, reached out to Grampy after Bea's death.

Despite the obvious differences that appeared to separate the Lord and his good cook, the two men shared much in common—smiles as well as tears. Dad mentioned that a number of times, in the weeks following Bea's death, Grampy's searching steps carried him out to the kitchen, where he and John shared some heartfelt words around the old kitchen stove. Yes, John's faith was a deep and abiding one, which Grampy drew upon on such occasions—although he never spoke about these talks with members of the family. I always regretted that John didn't stay to welcome us at Cat Bow. Though his connection to Bea was a fine one, the relationship was apparently more strained when Grandma Jane arrived from Nashville. Grampy wasn't given to speaking about that chapter either—despite the fact that John's absence was clearly felt on the farm.

As children we were told that, as a young man, John had built the Panama Canal pretty much single-handedly. Dad recounted that John had so many muscles that he could lift a sixteen-pound sledge hammer by the handle, hold it at arm's length, and, with the strength of his wrists, lower it so that the head of the hammer touched his nose, . . . and then, *slowly* bring it back up again. Amazing! In those years, Nat and I together had a hard enough time hoisting the sledge off the ground.

Apparently, old John also had a lighter touch and was equally proficient with horseshoes and matchstick poker. Often after dinner, he would take Dad and his brothers up behind the barn and give them a lesson in these disciplines, as well. We were told that John, with his Jamaican English, was a great one for making up words. In the evenings, Dad would frequently come upon John in the kitchen, stirring his kettle.

Dad's curiosity getting the best of him, he would ask John about his recipe. *John would glance down at me,* Dad related, *and say in a deep, muffled voice: 'Why, don't ya know; that's fluk-a-steria!'* From what we could make out, the brew was heavenly.

Yes, the cooks at Cat Bow were real characters, and Cynthia had her delicacies, too. If John's specialty was fluk-a-steria, Cynthia's was cookies—butter crunch, oatmeal and chocolate chip. We were devoted to them (as Cynthia well knew), and she could count on one of our first stops being the kitchen, in order to pay our respects to the cookie jar. The odds were that it would be full. Although, before we were able to sample the contents, formalities were in order.

Arms propped on her waist, Cynthia would aver, with a perfectly straight face, that she had no idea we were coming up to the farm and how *terribly* sorry she was, but Grampy had just finished off the last dozen cookies (a feat by no means beyond our grandfather's powers). We were aghast at the prospects of an empty cookie jar, but, as our smiles sagged into frowns, Cynthia would chuckle and glance over to the counter. Reassured that she was kidding, one of us would slip over to the jar, pop open the lid, and we were in business. But, even cookies had their proper place. First we had to present ourselves to the Lord of Cat Bow.

We ran through the dining room, and, hearing Grampy's infectious laughter, figured that friends and family had gathered on the back terrace. Pausing in front of the screen door, our gazes fell upon our sire, surrounded by flock and friends and framed, in all his *living* splendor, by what he matter-of-factly asserted was the finest view in the Northern Kingdom. Adorned in rose-red granite, white clouds, and clear blue sky, Washington, Adams, Jefferson, and Madison—resolute as the ages—gazed down upon our mortal scene from their heavenly peaks atop the Presidential Mountain Range.

This old farmer was raking hay in the middle of his field when a city slicka drove up.... We had not arrived a minute too early. Sidestepping the march of seasons, for the moment *Grampy* had the floor:

> *Stopping his car, the visita glanced about the countryside, before his gaze settled on the old timer. 'I beg your pardon,' the driver leaned his elbow out of the car window, as he called to the farma, who*

continued on patiently with his work. The city slicka's gaze passed again over the countryside. 'Don't you ever feel a bit lonely out here, wish you were more in the middle of things?' The farma paused from his labors, looked up at the visita, and leaned on the end of his rake: 'Well mista,' he stroked his chin thoughtfully, 'Montreal's 'bout 150 miles due North a here. Boston's 'bout 150 miles due south. . . .' He pushed his old hat up over his brow, 'I reckon Bangor's pretty near 150 miles due East a here, and Burlington couldn't be much more due West. . . .'

Grampy's North Country accent slowed the pace down, quieting those assembled. Guests and family, cocktail glasses, chips, and children in hand, leaned, along with Nat, Bea, Brad, and me, toward Grampy. Amused glances were exchanged, as traces of smiles began to awaken on the faces.

By Jesus, . . . Grampy placed his hand firmly on Uncle Bill's shoulder and, motioning toward those assembled, nodded: *I don't know how a person could be much more in the middle a things! So it was.*

The punch line spilled over into Grampy's laughter, which found a hearty resonance in all who were gathered. As amused by the teller as by the tale, Nat, Bea, Brad, and I pushed open the screen door and ran across the terrace toward Grampy. Mom and Dad, who had caught up with us, brought up the rear.

Hearing the door slam, Grampy turned to greet us, his cheeks piqued by the invigorating combination of the tale and fresh New Hampshire air. As we children hugged him, he tousled our hair, snapping *goodie, goodie!* Grampy was in fine health, having retired as head of the U.S. Commerce Department in the fall of fifty-eight, due to Grandma Jane's illness. His hair was sparse, which gave him an appropriate air of dignity, and he was casually dressed in shirt tails that peeked out of khaki trousers—girded by an old leather belt, lined with small silver medallions, each bearing the name and birth date of us, his grandchildren and expanding progeny. The "middle of things". . . *Eh yup!*

As Nat, Bea, Brad, and I crowded around Grampy, we were delighted to notice that summer was in his bearing. Well-tanned, a smile awoke on his lips as he gave Mom and Dad a kiss, slapping them on the back in his gentle/gruff manner. Satisfied that all were present and accounted for, Grampy passed us onto the other guests, before we were shushed off with the reminder that dinner was at six. And, with Grampy, that meant six! Off we went, our sights set on the barn, with a brief detour back through the kitchen on the trail of the crumbs!

* * * * *

As can be expected when you mix children and farms, we were late. Aside from our annual tug-of-war with Janie the donkey, our delay was due to the arrival that spring of seven new calves—which demanded the appropriate civilities on our part. Third cousins (a bit removed), we had to get duly acquainted with the newcomers and, consequently, neglected the hour. It wasn't until the cows started to serenade the barnyard, in response to Bill's arrival with the oats, that we realized, to our dismay, that it was "that time of the day." Brushing off our pants and stuffing in our shirt-tails, we raced down the hill to the Big House. As we arrived at the front door, the chime from the old grandfather clock sounded the quarter hour. Pausing on the threshold, we took a deep breath and stepped sheepishly forth.

Entering the dining room, the conversation stopped, as all eyes (including the steady gaze of an admiral) turned to us. Slipping quietly into our seats between Mom, Dad, the Ramseys, and Grandma Jane, we were painfully aware that half the turkey was gone. The message was clear. Yet, no sooner had we got settled, than we were off again, as Grampy, despite the obvious, inquired if we had washed our hands and combed our hair. If the query had come from Mom and Dad, we might have stretched the truth, put up a fuss, or bargained a bit. But, with Grampy, we figured it would be better just to be quiet and do what he said. When we returned to our seats, our plates were full. Emitting hungry sighs of relief and casting a grateful glance at our host, we dug in.

Turning their attention back to one another, the adults picked up the thread of their discussion: "... De Tocqueville expressed it succinctly when he said, *America is great because America is good. And if America ever ceases to be good, she will cease to be great.*"

The conversation made the rounds along with the dinner. Admiral Ramsey shared Grampy's love of history, and Mrs. Ramsey (who, earlier in her career, as Commander of the WAFS, had outranked her husband) shared our appreciation for the anecdotes and passages—some light-hearted, others less so—that were called forth.

"Listen up, children, I have something I want to read to you." Laying down his fork and knife, Grampy pulled his glasses out of his shirt pocket, a sheet of paper out of his pant's pocket, and, turning to us, inquired, "You've heard of Davy Crockett, haven't you?"

Nat, Bea, Brad, and I nodded in unison.

"Well, he was not just an Indian fighter and frontiersman, he was also a Congressman, who had a lot to say about this country of ours."

Grampy unfolded the sheet of paper, "This, children, is from a speech Congressman Crockett gave in the spring of 1830. The House of Representatives was considering a proposal to appropriate federal funds for the widow of a distinguished naval officer. As is often the case in such matters, the proposal had its resolute backers, who had just finished making a spate of impassioned speeches on behalf of the widow. The bill appeared on its way to being approved, when Congressman Crockett arose." Grampy paused to take a good drink of water and adjusted his glasses:

> "Gentlemen," Crockett began, "I have as much respect for the memory of the deceased naval officer, and as much sympathy for the suffering of the living—if suffering there be—as any man in this House of Representatives. But, we must not permit our respect for the dead, or our sympathy for a part of the living, to lead us into an act of injustice to the balance of the living.
>
> "I will not go into an argument to prove that Congress has no power to appropriate this money as an act of charity. Every member of this body knows that we do not. We have the right, as individuals, to give away as much of our OWN money as we please in charity, but as a member of Congress we have no right to appropriate even one dollar of the public money for such a purpose. Some eloquent and beautiful appeals have been made to us upon the grounds that this is a debt due to the deceased."

Grampy paused, glanced around at us: Congressman Crockett continued: "Mr. Speaker, the deceased naval officer lived long after the close of the war; he was in office drawing his salary to

the day of his death, and I have never heard that the government
was in arrears to him." Crockett fixed his gaze on his colleagues.
Grampy read on, "Every man in this House of Representatives
knows that this is not a debt. We can not, without the grossest
corruption, appropriate this money upon the pretense that it is a
payment of a debt. We have not the semblance of Constitutional
authority to appropriate it as a charity."

Grampy and Davy Crockett drew a breath: "Mr. Speaker,"
Crockett said, turning toward the Speaker of the House, "I have
said we have the right to give as much money of our own as we
please. I am the poorest man on this floor. I can not vote for this
bill, but I will give one week's pay to the object, and if every member
of this Congress will do the same, it will amount to more money for
the widow than the bill proposes."

Grampy laid the piece of paper down beside his plate and turned to
Nat, Bea, Brad, and me, "How do you think his colleagues responded?"

Shrugs were passed down the row, until Bea, buoyed up by her
blond ponytails and abounding spirit, spoke up expectantly, "They
helped the poor lady? . . ."

Grampy shook his head, "No, not one Congressman took Crockett
up on his offer."

Easing his plate forward on the placemat, Admiral Ramsey turned
to his host, "As early as 1790, Sinny, a professor of history from the
University of Edinburgh named Tytler spoke in very clear terms about
how a democracy can only exist, as a permanent form of government,
until the voters discover that they can vote themselves largess out of the
public treasury. From that moment on, the majority will vote for the
candidate promising the most benefits, with the result that a democracy
will always collapse from a loose fiscal policy and the burden of large
public debt."

Elbow on the table and chin resting in his hand, Grampy's gaze was
fixed on the admiral, before he nodded, "There is an expression, attributed to an old Chinese philosopher, that doesn't seem to have become
any less relevant over time: 'From bondage into spiritual faith; from
spiritual faith to physical power; from physical power to freedom; from
freedom to wealth; from wealth to security; from security to compla-

cence; from complacence to indifference; from indifference to weakness; from weakness to bondage.'"

Grandma Jane drew her shawl around her. Dad paused, wiped his mouth with his napkin, and looked up at his father, "This issue is beginning to come to a head with the civil rights demonstrations in the South. Now that Governor Wallace has defied the presidential order to desegregate Alabama's schools and his National Guard has been federalized, we'll see whether we really have a united states."

The pause was longer before Grampy sat forward, "We have been given this democracy on a condition. That condition is vigilance, eternal vigilance." My gaze lifted to the rude bridge that filled the frame above the fireplace behind Grampy. The spring river, . . . Grampy's words flowed on, "What we do not understand is that if we don't meet the condition, if we focus solely on our *rights* and ignore our *responsibilities* within our democratic system, then, as those who went before us realized, the loss of our freedoms is nothing less than the consequence of our crime and the punishment for our guilt." An unfamiliar tone, earnest and more, touched Grampy's voice. Grampy's glance passed around the table; our eyes met: "These and many such worldly views would be considered 'conservative' by many people today. What the critics don't often enough appreciate, however, is that what conservatives understand intuitively, often takes those of a more liberal cast of mind years to grasp."

Dad picked up the thread, as Dora brought in the dessert plates and placed them in front of us. Mrs. Ramsey added a thoughtful strand to the conversation. Mom was quiet. I turned a questioning glance to her, before lowering it to the business at hand—bread pudding.

Dinner ended with a spree in the finger bowls, which, upon first encountering, we mistook for drinking water. Yes, much there was to discover. Rising from the table, the older folks gathered up their coffee cups and retired to pursue the problems of the world. Scooping up a pack of cards—milder distractions—we followed the grownups' footsteps into the Pine Room, settling in on the large window seat sofa across the way.

* * * * *

As the adults sat back around the fireplace, the strain of politics eased back into the conversation. Leaning against a stocky cushion, Nat shuffled up the cards, as the grownups' focus shifted from the state of our union, here at home, to the international scene. I lifted my head abruptly at Admiral Ramsey's remarks about monks and nuns in South Vietnam, who had recently burned themselves to death as a protest against the mass persecutions by their South Vietnamese government.

Grampy listened intently, as Mrs. Ramsey made note of an expected troop increase to South Vietnam. Then, placing his coffee cup down on the bench in front of the fireplace, he sat forward: "Things in South East Asia aren't good. Unless we take a clear stand against the Communists, there is going to be real trouble." The tone returned to his voice.

"War?" Nat said, as he began to pass out the cards. My glance lifted from Grampy to the gallery of photos, pictures, and political cartoons that lined the walls of the Pine Room.

A photo of a spirited company of young soldiers drew my gaze. Seated in their midst on the ground, legs crossed, back straight, Captain S. Weeks held two alert drum sticks over a snare that was cushioned in his lap. The beat was nearly audible on his companions' lips, *Over there, over there, send the word, send the word over there....We're going over, we're going over. And we won't be back till it's over there.* In Grampy's words, *"One of the most formative periods of my life,"* the flush of war had not yet touched the young captain's cheeks.

Gathering up the cards in my hands, my eyes continued along the walls. Cat Bow's celebrated rogues gallery offered a glimpse of our country's other, more peaceable, pursuits—along with a lively and instructive introduction not only to Grampy's many and colorful friends and associates, but to the Lord of Cat Bow himself. I breathed out, as the strains of the adult's conversation faded before my gaze.

Above the comrades-in-arms, an old-timer, text in hand and glasses peeking down over his nose, peered out at us from the frame, as he whispered excitedly into the kindly, but aghast face of an elderly woman, who, hand over her mouth, stood speechless before a microphone. Mr. and Mrs. Charles Wilson, the man of the family had been in the automobile business.

Continuing down the wall, a dapper gentleman, surrounded by a host of friends, beamed out at the world. A bit of homework was required before I discovered that this personality was our grandfather, the newly elected "Boy Mayor of Newton," Massachusetts. *Rome wasn't built in a day*, was the slogan that fall, *AND IT WILL TAKE WEEKS TO BUILD NEWTON!* So the family history books recounted. From the pieces I put together, Grampy's hard-fought campaign climaxed the night before the election with a huge 400-car motorcade, led by a shiny, open carriage in which the mayor-to-be sat back triumphantly with his wife at his side. The only vehicle preceding the carriage was a giant truck, flamboyantly decorated and loaded to the brim with Grampy's American Legion comrades—each one of them, in particular a certain Benny Lane, in full voice. From what Grampy related, Benny's vocal power was legendary, rivaling in both depths and decibels the bellow of a fog horn. All the way through, across, and around the outskirts (and inskirts) of Newton, Benny's inspired chant could be heard: *HERE he comes . . . Here he comes . . . Look him over . . . Look him o-o-ove . . . EV-ry move a PIC-ture!*

Apparently, the parade was Benny Lane's show as much as it was Grampy's. Be that as it may, the two were to team up again, a few years down the road, in a rip-roaring campaign that pitted Grampy, Henry Cabot Lodge Jr., and a group of young Republican stalwarts, against Boston's legendary boss, "The Purple Shamrock," James Michael Curley. With Grampy as Chairman of the Republican State Committee, Cabot Lodge became the only Republican candidate in the country during the "New Deal" years to replace a Democrat in the United States Senate—a feat about which we were to hear more in the years to come.

A neighboring photo caught the Lord of Cat Bow on the terrace of the Big House in more familiar and informal attire, pipe in hand. Gathered around Grampy, in what I later found out was a North Country political huddle, were three other men, Governor Harold Stassen of Minnesota, Senator Styles Bridges of New Hampshire, and Wendell L. Willkie, president of Commonwealth & Southern—in Grampy's words, "a fine figure of a man, who radiated magnetism, intelligence, and a rugged sort of competence."

Grampy and his colleagues (who were in the process of encouraging Willkie to join the Republican race against F.D.R.) had been impressed by the way Willkie had taken Roosevelt to task for the president's suggestion that the government build and run the Tennessee Valley Authority—to the tune of $40,000,000, when all was said and done, plus another $88,000,000 of interest to the financiers for their services. Private enterprise, Grampy and company staunchly agreed, could not only do the job more efficiently, but at less expense to the government—while generating a good bundle of taxes, as opposed to fees, in the process. Willkie was game, and, with Grampy and a small band of colleagues at the helm, one of the most exciting primary races of our century was soon to begin. Willkie won the Republican nomination, but, to Grampy's chagrin, Roosevelt, once again, took the grand prize.

Further down the wall, my eye was caught by a picture of the Lord of Cat Bow in conversation with a real live Queen (by the name of Elizabeth), adorned in satin and topped off by a demure gold crown. If Grampy's presence hadn't been unmistakable, I would have sworn that the scene was out of a modern-day fairy tale.

With the following picture, the plot thickened, as Grampy, America's chief spokesman for free enterprise, posed with a no less alive and animated Communist, Marshall Tito of Yugoslavia. Despite their considerable differences in ideology, both men apparently had a pragmatic bent, sharing one thing in common—a dislike of Hitler and The Führer's aspirations for world-wide domination. My glance returned for a moment to the adults. The drift of the conversation had shifted to more worldly affairs—business, big and small alike.

In the midst of the highbrows, a side-kick of Grampy's poked his Basset Hound head out of a dilapidated dog house atop a piece of stationery. The expression on the downcast creature's face matched his humble abode. The logo belonged to THE SONS OF BUSINESS, and the message on the letter lamented, *Sin, I thought you should know about this organization. The way things are going, this is likely to be the largest club in the U.S. We SONS OF BUSINESS must stick together.* At the bottom of the page, a parting postscript bayed, *Nothing happens in this country until somebody sells something!* So it was.

Interspersed among the assorted faces and scenes, my gaze lingered on a number of political cartoons, which, upon first encountering, threw us grandchildren for a loop. To find our esteemed grandfather, along with a fellow named Dulles, peering sheepishly out of a coliseum dungeon onto an embattled scene was a specter with which we were unfamiliar. In the center of the arena, a hefty, scornful legislator, brandishing a hatchet above his head, triumphantly ground his first victim, a beleaguered Cabinet head, into the dust with his foot, while our progenitor awaited his turn. Above the spectacle, equally picturesque members of Congress reveled in delight, their thumbs turned defiantly down as they roared, *Bring on the Foreign Aid Bill!*

Apparently, Grampy survived the debacle. The neighboring cartoon showed a considerably more sanguine Cabinet head, "Sec. Weeks," playing a merry tune on a cash register that recorded *prosperity* at its top. Casting us a wink over his shoulder, Grampy prominently upstaged a disgruntled bird, perched silently above the proceedings, in a cage that bore the letters, PEACE. The cartoon's refrain was a fleeting one: *A couple of cheerful notes from the bird would help.*

The cartoon that astounded me the most depicted our grandfather transfigured into a soothsayer, complete with a long flowing robe, elegant curved slippers, and a gem-studded turban atop his head. Leaning over a crystal ball that held sway on an ornately cushioned table, Grampy was busily at work, fingers spread apart, conjuring dollar signs out of the crystal's dark interior. In the background, a familiar donkey looked on skeptically, gesticulating toward Grampy with one hoof, while his other held a newspaper that bore the headlines, *I see no profit in that prophecy!* A picture is worth a thousand words. So it was. Years passed, along with many viewings, before I gained a fuller appreciation for the drift of these depictions.

My sights settled on an old, framed, newspaper clipping that had found a prominent niche among the proceedings. *Ike Signs Treaty at Weeks' Farm.* The paper's bold headlines went on to describe how Austria's struggle to win back its freedom from Russia at the close of World War II was sealed with President Eisenhower's signature at *Weeks' rambling North Country home.*

Beside Grampy's desk, the assemblage concluded with a last photo. A friendly looking man, dressed in simple attire, stood at ease. The words John J. Pershing were penned at the bottom of the picture. Stepping up behind us one afternoon as we scanned the gallery, Dad told us that Black Jack, as Pershing was referred to by his countrymen, was the head of the A.E.F. (American Expeditionary Force) during World War I. At the victorious gathering at Versailles, Dad went on to recount, all the allied commanders arrived regaled in their military splendor—uniforms, medals, ribbons. The last to appear was the man who had led

them all. Entering the hall dressed in a simple uniform without deco-
ration, General Pershing silently acknowledged the startled applause.
Black Jack had worked closely with Great-Grandfather, who ended his
own political career as Secretary of War under Presidents Harding and
Coolidge.

Grampy's earliest and most incisive political lessons were learned
from his father. Starting out as a farm boy in Lancaster, Great-Granddad retained an appreciation for his simple beginnings, to which
Grampy often referred over the years. Atop Grampy's desk, set off by
a docile herd of miniature elephants, my glance passed over a number
of valued remembrances, including a framed epistle from Senator John
Wingate Weeks that offered free fatherly advice to a son, who was
embarking upon his first elective office as alderman. That letter, I also
returned to over the years, as my steps began to take me on out into the
world.

January 3, 1923

Dear Sinclair,

*There are two or three things I want to impress upon you as it is
your first experience in a legislative body. Success in such a place,
more than in almost any other, depends on knowledge. A man is
a leader, legislatively, when he knows more than those who are
serving with him. He does not need to be an orator, have wealth or
any other qualifications than to have the facts; and therefore you
ought to take some part of the work, perhaps all of it if you have
time, and know all about what is going on.*

*Study the rules that are used, so that you will be entirely familiar
with them. Attend committee meetings, so that you will be entirely
familiar with the work of the committee, and, above all things, do
not attempt to speak unless you know exactly what you are talking about.*

*There is no place in the world where you get sized up quicker
than you do in a legislative body. If you are on your feet every
few minutes talking about something which all the others know
as much about as you do, you do not acquire but lose influence.
If you get the reputation of knowing what you are talking about,
then everyone will listen and will be likely to accept your views.*

Do not get into the habit of quarreling with men who do not agree with you. They are entitled to their opinions as much as you are to yours. The thing to do is to convince them that they are wrong, and that will apply in general politics as well as in the Newton Board of Aldermen. The way to cure a communist is not to suppress his speech but to argue him out of his position. If you cannot argue him out of it, he may be right and you wrong.

Above all things, because you seem to be an opposition alderman, do not disagree unnecessarily with the mayor. Personally, he is an agreeable man, who has been mighty nice to you in the past and during the last campaign. Agree with him when you can, and when you cannot, tell him so frankly and the reasons why.

You are in an unusual position which will attract attention. It is of advantage in some ways and a handicap in others. Fortunately or unfortunately, you have a father who is conspicuous. That will make it incumbent on you to try to live up to a standard and will cause you to be criticized if you do not. And then there are others, who are not favorably disposed to me, who will criticize you because you are my son.

Do not get the idea into your head that you are working for the future or for future political preferment. That will take care of itself, if you make good in the present. I am certain that people will say to you that you will be something else, you will follow your father's course, or things of that kind. Let such remarks go in one ear and out the other. If you are fit and wish to have them, you will be given higher political honors. But, they will come not because you are scheming for them or dreaming about them, but because you impress yourself sufficiently on others to lead them to follow you and to want you to have such honors.

So, in the final analysis, you have to make good on your own account. That I am sure you will do if you follow the above precepts and any other which your commonsense will indicate. Good luck to you.

> *Affectionately,*
> *Father*

Great-Grandfather's letter found a thoughtful postscript in an accompanying precept, off to the far side of Grampy's desk, penned by a godfather of sorts, Abraham Lincoln:

> *If I were to try to read, much less answer, all the attacks made on me, this shop might as well be closed for any other business. I do the very best I know—the very best I can; and I mean to keep doing so until the end. If the end brings me out right, what is said against me won't amount to anything. If the end brings me out wrong, ten angels swearing I was right would make no difference.*

* * * * *

"How's Jane's health?" The adults' conversation touched delicately on more human affairs, as the evening wore on. Glancing up from my cards, I noticed that, eyes closed, Grandma Jane's head was resting against her lord's shoulder. Grampy placed his hand tenderly over hers, which had released its grip from the shawl, "It's hard to say. . . ." He sought for words, "She's not herself. We've got an appointment with the doctors next week." An awkward silence filled the room.

Grampy eased Grandma Jane gently back upright, before leaning forward and, as the old grandfather clock sounded the ninth hour, patting a yawn. In unison, the two gents had become well tuned with the years. "Come on, children, time to turn in," Grampy said, glancing over at us.

Gathering together our cards, we concluded our game of War and rose with the adults. As I said good night to the Ramseys and gave Mom, Dad, and Grampy a kiss, my glance rested on Grandma Jane, whose eyes had opened and were watching us silently. I paused a moment, and then turned and followed Nat, Bea, and Brad upstairs. Our destinations were new bedrooms and an open window, which made the heavy quilts and comfortable mattresses just that more inviting.

Climbing into my pajamas, I checked under my bed to make sure I was quite alone. Then, hopping in, I pulled my knees up to my chest, my blankets over my ears, and, emitting a deep breath, reviewed the galaxy of faces—birds and beasts, friends and foes, lords and ladies that filled the nooks and crannies of the Big House—as I lay my head back, my sleepy gaze came to rest on the picture of the old frontiersman, coonskin cap, moccasins, and rifle in hand. As old Davy took his seat in the House chamber, I nodded silently off to sleep and to a dream that began to stir within me: *America is great, because America is good. . . .*

2

SPLASH!

SPLASH! SUMMER BEGAN with the launching of the raft—a baptism in which I had enthusiastically taken part ever since I had first managed to wriggle out of my mother's arms and make my way to the water's edge. And so it was, the launching not only of our beloved raft, but of another summer in all its resplendent North Country glory.

As Dad gave the raft its last push from the public landing with the old Ferguson tractor, Nat, Bea, Brad, and I, along with our assorted cousins and pals from around the lake, splashed aboard her swarthy planks. Pant legs rolled up, and a colorful repertoire of paddles, oars, and poles in hand, we headed out into the wild blue yonder, churning the water with our paddles and dodging as best we could the enveloping spray. The raft was all ours, as long as we could keep her on course to her mooring in front of our cabin, a good 200 yards up shore.

Attracted by the melee, Chuck Balch and Sam Bell headed across the waters toward us in their canoe and rowboat from opposite shores, eager to throw us a line and add to the horse power. The more the merrier. Led by a self-appointed cox' in, who straddled the diving board, home-made rudder in hand, we spirited our strokes with rounds from the *Volga Boatsman*, "Ho, heave ho . . . Ho, heave, ho." A sight we were! By the time our flotilla had arrived at our destination, the raft was anointed, and we were ready, one and all, for a swim. Summer had officially begun.

From the raft, a commanding view of Martin Meadow Pond, all of one mile long, one-half wide, and a good five fathoms deep, opened up before us. According to tradition, the pond took its name from a trapper, with a "roving disposition," by the name of Martin. No one seemed to know from whence the gentleman came or whither he went, but the official town record suggests that the meadows around the pond, teeming with beaver dams as much as five feet high and fifty rods long, were at least one stop along Mr. Martin's route.

A certain Honorable James W. Weeks speculated in the town history that the trapper's appearance in this particular neck of the woods must have well preceded the first settlers. For, when they finally arrived on the scene in 1761, "they found the beaver dams somewhat gone into decay and the meadows covered with grass as the waters had receded." Whereas the beavers had attracted Martin, the meadows, with their vast quantities of hay, were the lure for the first party of settlers in the area. So it was, *Martin Meadow* Pond.

To the right and up shore from the public landing, an inlet drifted into the last fluent remnant of those bygone days—a quiet haven, which we unofficially named Beaver Valley, that hosted beaver lodges, dams, and many a water-logged tree, along with deer and an occasional moose that made its way to the water's edge. Beyond Beaver Valley, the pond followed the wooded shoreline into a cove, overseen by a tall angling pine, which, in the years to come, was to host the pond's rope swing—an exhilarating seventy foot flight up, up, and away,...upon which only the most elevated of souls ventured forth.

At the far end of the cove, the shoreline continued down the lake to the Balchs' cabin. The old wooden abode housed not only our friends, Chuck, Jimbo, Cindy, and Winna, but, above its fireplace and along its walls, as impressive an array of antlers to which any of us youngsters had lifted our gazes. In the evenings, our visits often coincided with that of the local raccoon families, whose nocturnal outings included a stop at the Balchs', where the fare ranged from home-cooked popcorn to crawfish à la pail. Beyond the Balchs' cabin and nestled in a small inlet, Camp Mayo looked out onto the lake, the yellow letters of its name spilling over into a gilded trim that enlivened its rustic demeanor.

The Vashaw's cabin followed fifty yards further up shore, stone slabs leading down to a dock that was moored at its far end by a pair of large wagon wheels—a precipitous dead end for some bygone landlubber? At the edge of the clearing around the Vashaw's cabin, a windward loon, carved out of wood and stationed atop an old weather-beaten post, flapped its stalwart wings. At the mercy of even the slightest breeze, my heart went out to the poor creature, which, despite his ardent exertions, never managed to get into flight. The shoreline continued on another few hundred yards before reconnoitering with our second cousins', the Davidges, boathouse (a more recent and contemporary addition to the lake), whereupon, the shore blended into the hayfield below the Big House.

The tides gathered at Grampy's dock, an old weathered gangway that waded a good twenty yards out into the lake. On many a summer evening, I followed my homeward steps down through the field to our canoe at the dock's end—the happy/sad melody, that Mom played for us on her grand old accordion, rumoring about my lips: *Day is dyin' in the West, angels watchin' over me, my Lord . . .*

As the sun began its descent over the far reaches of the lake, my gaze would rise with Grampy's, aloft on the balcony porch, to mark the orb's timeless course. Imperceptibly, the shades of dusk settled over the waters, bringing with them a hush that deepened with the years. Lingering in the twilight, I frequently sat down beside the swimming ladder and dangled my feet over the edge of the dock. Slowly, ripples from my toes spread out across the still surface of the lake, gently inundating the tides of sunlight that quickened the waters with a wake of shimmering colors. Leaning into my reflections, as the echoes of the day faded away, other sounds, barely audible in my youth, rose up out of the depths, parting the ebbing veil of silence.

From Grampy's dock, the shoreline once again retired into the woods, jutting out to Smith's Point, and around into a larger and more secluded cove, where the busy currents of the lake were stilled in the shallows. An old abandoned raft languished away its last days among the bulrushes—a welcome landing for the Great Blue Herons, who, in the summer months, built their nests and tip-toed for frogs and minnows among the reeds.

At the far end of the cove, civilization again touched the shoreline in the fleeting guise of a simple one-room cabin—no bigger than Grampy's bathroom—whose inscription above the door became part of the unofficial lore of the lake, *Here Pa and Ma shall Rest*. A peacefulness enveloped the sylvan abode, often staying my paddle a few yards out from the small dock that hugged the shore. We never met the Marshalls, though we availed ourselves of the path that led through a pine grove behind their house and up the hill to Cat Bow's Sugarbush.

The shoreline continued down to a group of eight cabins, that were carved out of the woods, each as original and inviting as their proprietors: the Eastmans', the Kendalls' cabin (which more closely resembled the looming prow of a ship), the Sullivans' and Bergerons', Mc Cartons', Doctor and Mrs. Ferguson's cabin, the Christis', Cranes', and Aunt Em's old log boathouse, which leaned out into the shaded cove across the way, before ending up at the big rock below our cabin—the jumping-off point to the raft and many a wayward excursion. Such was the bounded horizon that we looked out upon through the summers of our youth.

* * * * *

Once secure, the raft was the dry-dock for a wide variety of water escapades, including a homemade sortie into the art of water jousting. That Mom ever allowed us to try our chivalric hands at this combat, I'll never understand. I do not remember who is to be credited with the idea. But, one sultry August afternoon, Nat emerged from the pump house with two long bamboo poles, each topped off with one of Dad's prize boxing gloves from college days. Always businesslike and mum when onto a good idea, Nat headed straight for the canoes at the end of the dock. Not a word needed to be said. Jud, his Kendall contemporary, Harry, mine, and I perked up and immediately swung into action, steadying the canoe while Nat loaded the equipage.

The sparkle in Nat's eye lit ours, until Jud hopped into the canoe with Nat. As the two older brothers paddled off toward the raft, leaving the smaller of the two poles in our hands, Harry and I knew that the challenge had been issued. Ours was to respond. We stood quietly eyeing our weapon. The glove I was familiar with, having gone a few memorable rounds with it in the past. Its good arm's-length to the end of the pole was another matter. Before Harry and I had decided on the recommended course of action, Nat summoned us to the contest, Jud's taunts his "second."

Our feet already wet, I stripped off my shirt, as Harry angled the bow of the canoe away from the dock. The older brothers clearly had the advantage of height, but, as Nat delicately mounted the prow of his canoe, pole in hand, we, God bless, hovered closer to the center of gravity. With Harry doing his best to steady our vessel, I gingerly negotiated my way from the canoe seat up and onto the prow, one foot on either side of the boat. Once as secure as I deemed I was going to be, Harry passed the pole to me, glove first. Receiving it under my arm, I proceeded carefully to adjust it vertically, turning it into an improvised mast, which, to my relief, afforded a semblance of stability as we embarked.

Confident of his assumed advantage as originator of this tryst, Nat took no precautions and lustily hailed his compatriot to cast off. As the gap slowly closed between us, I hoisted my "mast." Harry took a deep breath, I took aim, and then, as our poles came within striking range, ducked! Expecting a more resilient target, my brother was caught both unaware and off balance. The last exclamation I could make out, before Nat catapulted into the pond, taking Jud and the canoe with him, was a curse to high heaven. Ours was a jubilation, as we let the canoe slide on into the raft.

When the older siblings came up for air, they immediately demanded a second match, citing undeclared rules that we had evidently breached in this novel enterprise. We would hear nothing of it and, declaring ourselves the official Martin Meadow Pond Water Jousting Champs, steered our watery steed toward calmer waters and a sedate old bull frog or two to practice upon.

* * * * *

Come mid-June, the pastures behind the Big House had become waist-deep fields of green, topped off by the bounteous summer sun and edged by lapping shores of blue. The first crop of hay was ready to be cut, and our center of activity shifted back to the farm for a good dusty week. By that time, other members of the clan—the Hallowells, Sherrills, Robinsons, Bill Weeks, and Basts—had arrived and taken up their respective abodes in and around the Big House, where Grampy had helped his flourishing offspring build their cabins, to accommodate the summer overflow.

Haying was one farm chore toward which we grandchildren could make a *constructive* contribution. And glad we were to pitch in—from the beginning till the very end when the last bale had been snugly stashed away in the sprawling loft of the barn. The cousins assembled, we congregated in front of the tractor stall, as Bill Rines climbed onto the Ferguson and backed her—and us children up with him—out into the barnyard. Alerted by the commotion, Grampy grabbed his old straw hat from the vestibule hook and, flanked by his sons, decked out in old khaki pants and t-shirts, started up the drive to join us. Haying was a family affair, and every able-bodied male in the ranks, including the Lord himself, rolled up his sleeves.

The adults herded us together, as Bill shifted the tractor into second and, wheeling her and the long sharp-toothed cutting rake around, headed for the large field below the Big House. Grampy allowed Bill to get a good start, before lowering his arms and sending us off into the cloud of dust. Whooping and hollering, we hightailed it after the tractor, as Grampy and our fathers climbed into the truck and followed us, with the hay wagon in tow.

Jim Mosher, who helped Bill look after the place, was waiting for us with the bailer in the shade of the pine grove. Arriving flushed and out of breath, we waved to Jim, who quietly nodded in response. All of five-feet-five in height (overalls and all) and pretty nearly the half that in breadth, Jim was a mainstay at Cat Bow. A modest and reliable soul, who hailed from across the river in Vermont, Jim went easy on the words—though he seemed to enjoy tilting an ear to others. By the time Bill started into the field, the sun had climbed high into the heavens, taking with her the last drops of morning dew from the grass. It was perfect haying weather—warm, dry, and not a menacing cloud in sight.

Jim waited until Bill had cut one long row of hay down to the pond, before he cranked up the old bailer and started after him. Half of the grandchildren contingent followed Jim's churning trail, swarming over the field to herd the bales together into large piles, as they were regurgitated from the bailer. The rest of us, members of the reception committee, piled onto the hay wagon and brought up the rear.

A sight it was! Hooping and hollering, the younger cousins would flop down on a bale, their eager hands fishing for the twine. Then, while some pushed, others pulled (not infrequently in opposite directions), the rambunctious crew did their best to steer their beleaguered catch in the direction to the hay wagon. Meanwhile, in other corners of the field, my gung-ho cohorts and I paired off to harvest the crop from another—we reckoned, more promising—angle. Stooping down at either end of the bale, we grabbed it in a bear-hug, before, 1 ... 2 ... 3!, hoisting it aloft. Hay spewing from our mouths, we guided our momentum toward the hay wagon, swerving around Nat, Rob Bast, Chris, and Gerry Hallowell, who were feeling their (own) oats.

In the prime of their youth, the older cousins followed valiantly in the footsteps of their sires, grabbing a bail by its twine and half shuffling, half side-stepping their way to the hay wagon. In this business it was not uncommon to bite off more than one could chew. At regular intervals, an older brother would square off over a bale, take a deep breath, and, securing a firm hold, swing it up onto his shoulder. For a few split seconds the action stopped, as the bale tilted forward ... and, then, back ... precipitously. Fancy footwork was required before the equilibrium was re-established, and bale and brother triumphantly set forth.

And so it went, up and down the field, through the rest of the morning, into the afternoon, and on into the early evening, Bill cutting, Jim bailing, and the Lord of Cat Bow and his faithful following, hoisting the bales on high, till the wagon—full to teetering—pulled out of the procession and slowly made its way back up to the barn to deposit its load.

As the afternoon wore on, the breaks were a welcome relief—the one-man bales requiring a doubling up among the older cousins and, finally, an additional push, *all-e-up*, from a nearby uncle. Spaced out at approximately forty-five minute intervals, the breaks also heralded the high point of the day—the towering, aluminum conveyor that indefatigably cranked the bails up to their cozy berths in the loft.

Before Grampy turned the conveyor on, the heartier among us were allowed to scale her heights into the loft, while those that remained carried on below. Digging in at the top of the wagon, the harvest was passed down, bale by bale, to Grampy, who carefully tilted it onto the conveyor. One by one, the metal guides would wheel around the bottom of the frame and, clanking away, escort the bales up to our ready grasp in the loft. And the cows were in business!

As the afternoon drew to an end, Grampy pulled the truck up into the shade of the pine grove and gave her a rest, his pooped progeny trailing behind. A kind aunt had brought down a pitcher of lemonade, and a proper break was in order.

Taking off his straw hat and resting it up against the windshield, Grampy cast his eyes down across the field, "In the olden days, children, it was even more work." He took a big swig of the lemonade and wiped his mouth with his hand, "We didn't have this kind of machinery. Rather, horse power was the mode of operation. One team, large and lanky, pulled the mowing machine, a hulking contraption with a broad vibrating blade, which was guided by its driver perched on high. Depending on the dampness of the hay, another team of horses hitched to the tedder was engaged. The rest of the job was done by hand, man power. One group followed the mower, raking the hay into long columns called windrows. Another group, pitchforks in hand, joined in. Breaking up the windrows, they gathered the hay into piles, which were then thrown up onto the old hay wagon drawn by a third team of horses."

A recollection awoke a smile on Grampy's face, "In the thirties, I spent a good part of my summer break in this field with a scythe, practicing for a hay-cutting competition that had been arranged for the Lancaster Fair between me and a local farmer, John Beatty. Some of the folks in town weren't sure a week-day politician knew how to work up a good sweat."

Our fathers joined us in the shade, Dad and Uncle Bish, angling over to the pitcher of lemonade on the hood of the truck, Uncle Bill mopping his brow with an old towel, Uncle Bob stooping down beside us to catch his breath, and Uncle Woof, sweat covering pretty near every inch of his rugged six-foot-three frame, draping his arms over us as he settled himself down square in our midst. Nods and smiles accompanied Grampy's story.

"Well," Grampy went on, "I had a point to prove, which was for me something of a matter of honor, . . .and I made sure I was prepared. When Labor Day came around, a good crowd was gathered, and the bets were made. Beatty was a man who cut hay for his living. I was someone who, supposedly, just made it." Grampy reflected, "We'd both sharpened up our scythes, rolled up our sleeves, and were ready to go when the whistle blew." We took a breath along with Grampy, who put down his glass, "I don't remember who won. All I know is that grass was flying, and that the folks were mighty surprised—as were Beatty and I, who collapsed in each others arms, laughing and gasping for air!"

Grampy couldn't have had a more devoted audience. One thing that hushed us up, as he well knew, was a good story. Uncle Bish (whose childhood antics—before he swapped his overalls and bear-skin coat for the cloak and collar—often involved Dad) called over to Grampy, asking if he remembered a certain greased-pig contest, which also drew quite a crowd at the fair. Grampy's smile returned, as his gaze sought out Dad. "It's a shame, your Uncle John isn't here. He's the one who deserves to tell the story." Our prodding was short; Grampy's memory, on such tales, long.

"To my recollection, you and your brother, John, signed up one year for the greased-pig contest ..." Dad was silent on this one. Grampy turned to us, "The way it worked, children, was pretty simple. A pig was greased up slick, from tail to snout, and any youngster who considered himself quick on his feet was invited to jump into the ring..."

"Which was pretty wet after the rain the night before," Uncle Bish interjected.

Grampy nodded, "Yup. As soon as that pig was set free, squealing to high heaven, the boys took off after her, one and all."

Dad lifted his glass to Grampy. The story we knew well. Apparently, the rainfall the night before had discouraged all but the most stalwart souls, because Dad and Uncle John were among the few who were still on their feet five minutes later. Stopping to catch his breath, one of the older boys (who apparently had been in the ring before) stepped back to reassess the contest, while Dad, Uncle John, and a couple of the other youngsters continued to throw themselves at the terrified pig, each time just barely missing their catch, but succeeding in transferring the grease from the poor creature onto themselves. Finally, well into the melee, the pig took a sharp turn, avoiding the last desperate grasp by Dad—by this time nearly unrecognizable in the mire—and shot by the older contestant, who, having stepped back to catch his breath, reacted even quicker. Scuttling the pig in mid-flight between his legs, the young man reached down, secured a good grip on its weary hide, and lifted his squealing prize out of the mud.

After the story, and a long hot day in the field, we were ready for a good swim. Traversing our freshly mowed path down to the lake, we slipped into the boathouse to don our suits and headed for the water, which received us buoyantly. When we had cooled off, the party broke up—Grampy, Uncles Bish, Bob, Woof, and Bill, heading back up the field with their troops, Dad, Nat, and I, climbing into our canoe and turning its bow toward our cabin at the far end of the lake.

As we paddled along, a Great Blue Heron rose out of the shallows and, skimming the surface of the water, lifted our glances with its flight up the flanks of a nearby mountain to its stone fire tower on the top. Sharing the summit with the fire tower was a mountain home, with a beautifully sloping roof and steps that led up to a broad, stone, encircling terrace. In the latter years of Great-Granddad's life, as his sights turned from a busy life in the nation's capitol back to his boyhood home, John Wingate Weeks had built a gracious house atop Mt. Prospect, with his and his wife's, Martha Sinclair's, retirement in mind.

As dusk settled upon the lake, my thoughts lifted to the spacious upstairs room in the mountain home and to a great gray-brown portrait that gazed down from on high above the stately stone fireplace. As a child, I looked often into the face of that man whom I came to know as Great-Grandfather. Above and between the gentleman's eyes, lines gently etched a patient brow and balding head, but for wisps of gray hair trimmed neatly around his ears. Full cheeks, a strong—yet—harmonious nose were drawn gently down over a gray mustache, turned faintly up at the corner of John Wingate Weeks' mouth. Below, a firm, full chin was set. With the words of his biographer deep in mind, my eyes rested in Great-Granddad's gaze—steady, thoughtful, still in all it beheld.

> *Whose life in low estate began*
> *And in a simple village green;*
> *Who breaks his birth's invidious bar,*
> *And grasps the skirts of happy chance,*
> *And breasts the blows of circumstance*
> *And grapples with his evil star;*
> *Who makes by force his merits known*
> *And lives to clutch the golden keys,*
> *To mold a mighty state's decrees,*
> *And shape the whisper of the throne.*

* * * * *

The first crop of hay tucked away for the summer, we tackled a few mountains, with our cousins and pals from around the lake. These were carefully planned expeditions, which required extensive preparations that generally commenced the night before. Laying our knapsacks on the bunkroom floor of the cabin, we equipped ourselves with walking sticks, compasses, canteens full of lemonade, insect repellent, Band-Aids (for those inevitable cuts and scratches), our jackknives, extra shoelaces, a store of apples, nuts, and M & M's, and, last but not least, a roll of "bum-wad" for an ill-timed emergency—not to mention one or two other essentials that we invariably managed to forget.

After our knapsacks were loaded up and tied down, we unfolded the map of the White Mountains and spread it out across the bunkroom floor. Then, sprawling down over the peaks and valleys, we cast our sights over our Northern Kingdom, in search of a suitable outing. The nooks and crannies of White Mountains were as colorful and evocative as their names—from the heights, Black Angel Trail, to the very depths, Devil's Slide, with many a notable landmark in between.

I loved to pour over these names, imagining what might await us at any given bend of the trail: Imp Brook, Thunderstorm Junction, Alpine Gardens, Ammonoosuc Gorge, Last Chance Springs, Forks of Israel, Cathedral Ledge, Bridal Veil Falls, Goose Eye, Lone-some Lake (a refreshing respite, I remembered gratefully from the summer past) before continuing on down Jacob's Ladder, The Cannon Ball, Eagle Crag, Laughing Lion, Giant Stairs, Hurricane Gap, Skookumchuck Slide, Proteus Fall, Sphinx Ravine. Yes, worlds beckoned.

Having taken our bearings, we set about to decide upon a fitting route on the map for our expedition to our agreed upon destination atop the pinnacle of the Presidentials: Mt. Washington. With Cousin Sin's chin nestled comfortably in the Lake of the Clouds, Jud gazed westward, tracing the Ridge of the Cap Trail, up over Nat's elbow (which was angling off with his sights southeastwardly) to the summit of Mt. Jefferson. Cousin Kim charted our course from there. Bypassing the Six Husbands Trail, she headed off with our itinerary down the Gulfside Trail, over Mt. Clay to Washington. Meanwhile, Bea and Cousin Barbara, disinclined to follow in any but their own footsteps, were blazing a more direct route to the summit. Starting out from the eastern slope at Pinkham Notch, they carefully followed the Tuckerman Ravine Trail, by the Crystal Cascade and up (between Bea's ponytails) to the junction of the Lion's Head Trail and link to the Boot Spur. At the Hermit Lake Shelter, their path came to an abrupt end, before Sam Bell's extended palm, which engulfed Tuckerman's Ravine.

Having scanned the territory, Nat offered an alternative route. Shifting his elbow, along with his gaze, over Desolation Pond, Isolation Trail, and Mizpah Springs, he proposed a southerly ascent from the base of the Crawford Path—a good eight miles, and hours, from our summit. Taking a deep breath, I swapped drowsy glances with Sin, before my sights rose north, over the summit of Mt. Washington, to the top bunk and my sleeping bag, which enfolded the horizon. Whatever route it was to be, we clearly had a good hike ahead of us the next day.

One trip in particular I doubt I will forget. Mr. Kendall, Harry's father, headed up the expedition. Braced by the fresh mountain air, our paternal guide put on a little show for us, as we started up Mt. Star King. Pretending that he was King Kong, Mr. Kendall waded through the undergrowth, venting his two-hundred-plus pounds of feigned wrath on any likely tree. We were delighted by his production. Mr. Kendall would beat his arms, give a few snorts, and then, squaring off in front of an old tree, gather it up in a big bear hug and tear it down. This worked well until "King Kong" confronted one particular tree—a tired old birch. Taking an impassioned breath, he gave a great roar and proceeded to wrap his arms around a bees' nest and a few thousand rather perturbed bees. Well, our fearless leader took off down the mountain, hollering and slapping at the swarm of bees, hot in pursuit, and we took off up...only to meet later after a long and careful detour. That maneuver made the trip and was a good enough tale to earn a laugh at the cookouts that summer. I'll never forget Mr. Kendall's expression, and somehow I doubt he will ever forget his little tête-à-tête with the bees.

* * * * *

Then there was the tree house, the highlight of that summer. I built it all by myself (with the help of some friends). It was a magnificent wooden structure—the product of divine inspiration and improvisation—that stood three stories high and stuck out over the lake like a sore thumb. But, despite its blatant lack of glamour, I was the chief architect and thus quite proud of my masterpiece.

In those days, when (we fancied) painted Indians roamed the countryside and lions and tigers slunk through the woods, the tree house was about the only safe place on the lake. Together, with my motley band of desperadoes, we would man the ramparts and repel one Indian attack after another, returning crab apples for arrows in frenzied battles that lasted well on to lunch. Along with being the focal point of our many skirmishes, the tree house also served as a headquarters for our war councils and as a general get-a-way from the rigors of family life. We even slept in it on a number of occasions during the summer—Harry, David Bergeron, and I—hoisting our sleeping bags, pillows, and lanterns up to the main deck, with the help of a cranky old pulley.

Those were memorable evenings. Lying back among the whispering treetops, our hands cradled behind our heads, we swapped stories as we reviewed the exploits of the day, pausing as fishermen quietly trolled by beneath us. Occasionally, an angler would slowly reel in his bait. And then, a brief pause followed, before the swish of a rod sent line and lure out again into night. Gazing up through the quilt of hushed leaves to a sea of stars that gently sprayed the heavens, I listened as the bait settled again into the waters. *Children fishing for a dream, fishing near and far. Their rod a silver moon beam and their bait a silver star. Sail, children, sail—out upon that sea. Only don't forget to sail, back again to me....*Mom's voice, accompanied by the gentle strains of her accordion, wafted down to us on evening breezes from the cabin porch, stilling our thoughts. A first song drifted gently into a second, lowering my gaze with a falling star to the Big House, tucked silently into the flanks of Mt. Orne, across the lake. My eyes rested on a lone light from the balcony porch on the west end of the house that shone out into the evening, before sleep gently gathered me up in its nocturnal embrace. . . ..*Sleep my child and take your rest, angels watchin' over me.*

Morning came, and the ripples of our dreams settled back into the watery depths. The days were spent entertaining our inclinations. We were in and out of the water—bathing suits, Band-Aids, and sunburns adorning our bodies. Harry and I spent many an afternoon hanging over the side of our old rowboat, harvesting lily pads. This fledgling venture, my foray into the realms of free enterprise, was an earnest affair. We would count every lily pad we secured, figuring that we could realize a penny on each, and dream of cabin cruisers and foreign lands. However, despite our efforts, we were never able to find a buyer. Apparently, in those days, lily pads didn't command a very large market. Undismayed, when Harry and I had collected a good pile of pads, we would trundle them up to the terrace for Mom to inspect, leaving a neat trail in our wake.

Despite the fact that Mom encouraged us in nearly all our other pursuits, she never seemed to take to our lily harvests. It's funny, mothers don't seem to appreciate those kinds of things. Instead, she would make us take the lily pads off the picnic table and put them back into the lake—them and the frogs we caught, borrowing pots from the kitchen to keep them in. No, Mom didn't appreciate that either. And, after she repeatedly explained to us that frogs didn't *really* like being stuck in a pot, we'd throw them back as well—never quite sure we were doing the right thing.

Cousin Wade was around then, too. He and I used to spend hours fishing together. We would convene at the dock, where we would assess the weather, complexion of the lake, and then go through painstaking preparations before casting off. Although even with only one fishing rod to attend to, we seldom managed to be silent or patient enough to get a nibble, we would gather every rod in sight. Then, adorned with nets, tackle boxes, and assorted cans of worms, grasshoppers, night crawlers, and marshmallows, we set out to do battle.

A sight we were! I imagine we could have given the Spanish Armada a good tussle. Apparently, though, we lacked a bit of tact and continually suffered from a severe case of overkill. Our enthusiasm, coupled with the excessive equipment and elusive oarlocks, betrayed our arrival on each occasion. Even if we had used the marshmallows, I doubt it would have made a difference. There was seldom a fish within a hundred yards of us. However that might be, finally, after much calculation—which included very elaborate and complicated measurements—we arrived at "the spot." Known only to the inveterate fishermen of the lake, "the spot" was situated horizontally across from the upper left corner of the roof on Grampy's boathouse, vertically down from the tip of Smith's Point and directly over a cool, trout-infested spring hole—so hearsay had it.

After careful maneuvers, we agreed that we were exactly "there," and, as tactfully as possible, we proceeded to heave our rock anchor overboard. (Looking back, I suspect that that was about as close as we ever came to getting a fish.) Once secure, we would roll up our sleeves, scan the water for fins, and assemble our equipment. Then, tying on the most flamboyant hullapopper we could muster, complete with a grasshopper, worm, and night crawler, we threw our lines in, fortified ourselves with marshmallows, and braced ourselves for the battle.

Wade would sit on the side of the boat, stare intently at the water, and reel in his line every five seconds, to see if he didn't have a bite. Watching Wade's maneuvers (which produced little more than sea-sick bait), as well as my equally unproductive antics, called to mind Grampy's account of the best way to catch a fish. One day, after I had been thoroughly "skunked," Grampy sat me down at the end of the dock and explained that all I really needed, in order to catch fish, was some tobacco and a good sized club.

"What you do," he said, "is chew up the tobacco good and hard. When it is well lubricated, you then proceed to spit it into the water." He paused to make sure I was following him, "Fish, as is not commonly known, are partial to tobacco and will take it in their mouths and, descending again into the depths, start to chew it. Needless to say, tobacco is not to be swallowed, and subsequently the fish are obliged to return to the surface and regurgitate. When they break water and start to unload,"—my glance turned with Grampy's, out over the lake—"grab your club and knock them over the head!" I looked at Grampy in wonder, as he nodded, "It's as simple as that."

I believed every word Grampy said and would have taken his advice, if it hadn't been for the stipulation that the tobacco had to be well chewed in advance. Grampy covered his stories well.

In any case, regardless of either the truth or the efficacy of Grampy's approach, Wade had not yet mastered the technique. I suggested he give the fish time to see the worm before he reeled in the line, but I could not succeed in making my pal believe that there wasn't a fish under the boat with his mouth open, waiting for the worm. Wade would assure me that this was the way it was done in Nashville, Tennessee. So, what could I do? Never having been there, although a bit skeptical, I would sit out on the lake—rain, sun, or hail—braving the elements, while Wade waited for the fish to close its mouth.

Many a summer day came to a peaceful end with a cookout at the Indian Fireplace, an old stone hearth tucked away in a pined knoll in the woods, just down from our cabin. Friends and cousins were often invited, bringing along with them offerings—both raw and burnt—which included a rustic smorgasbord of hamburgers, hot dogs (replete with catsup, mustard, and assorted relishes), bulging bags of chips, corn on the cob, and often a pail or two of crawfish, minnows and frogs—legs and all, for the showing. Mom threw in a fresh garden salad, watermelon, and pitchers of lemonade, and we children contributed any spare marshmallows that we could conjure up.

The best thing about the Indian Fireplace was getting there—down a narrow wooded path, covered with pine needles, that skirted the shore on one side and hugged a small forest cliff on the other. As the crew gathered, Mom loaded us up, on one end of the path, with the trays of provisions that had been set out on the kitchen porch. At the other end, Dad, who was stoking up the fire, relieved us of our burdens, as, one after another, we stumbled down the path, doing our best to navigate the legions of roots and rocks at our feet, before coming out into the clearing. Broad, rough-hewn, wooden benches, weathered with the seasons, formed a semi-circle around the old stone hearth.

Food, family, and friends assembled, we struck up some songs around the fireplace, while the meat was laid out on the blazing grill and the corn-on-the-cob set to boil. There Was an Old Woman Who Swallowed a Fly. The tune had as many verses as our imaginations were able to conjure up. So it was. Over the years, we had pretty well immortalized the heroine. "There was an old woman who swallowed a fly," I started off. The others joined in, *I don't know why she swallowed the fly. Perhaps she'll die.*

"There was an old woman who swallowed a spider," I glanced about before motioning to cousin Francie Weeks, who, taken aback by the proceedings, frowned as she searched for the words, "That wiggled and jiggled and diggled inside her." Francie took a breath, "She swallowed the spider to catch the fly." The chorus provided a temporary relief for both good souls, *I don't know why she swallowed the fly. Perhaps she'll die.*

"There was an old woman, who swallowed a bird." I pointed to cousin Bengy, always on his toes. "How absurd!" Bengy's expression matched the words perfectly, "She swallowed a bird. She swallowed the bird to catch the spider, that wiggled and jiggled and diggled inside her. She swallowed the spider to catch the fly." We all sat forward, *I don't know why she swallowed the fly. Perhaps she'll die.*

Rascal climbed up onto Bea's lap. "There was an old woman who swallowed a cat." Bea and my glances met. I nodded. She smiled and, gathering her kitty tenderly into her arms, purred, "Think of that; she swallowed a cat! She swallowed the cat to catch a bird. She swallowed the bird to catch the spider, that wiggled and jiggled" (along with Bea) "and diggled inside her." Bea's smile lit others, "She swallowed the spider to catch the fly." Bea sat back. We joined in, a melancholic tone momentarily weighing down the chorus, *I don't know why she swallowed the fly. Perhaps she'll die.*

"There was an old woman who swallowed—Sin—a dog."—"What a hog!" Sin shot back, a smile of defiance on his face, "She swallowed a dog." Sin's momentum carried him on, less assuredly, "She swallowed the dog to catch the cat. She swallowed the cat to catch the ...bird. She swallowed the bird to catch the spider that wiggled and jiggled . . ." Sin wiped his sleeve over his mouth, "And diggled inside her. She swallowed the spider to catch the fly." Patting Sin ceremoniously on the back, his older brother, David led us into the refrain: *I don't know why she swallowed the fly. Perhaps she'll die.*

"There was an old woman who swallowed a pig." Groans made the rounds. It was David's turn. I tapped him on the shoulder. Legs calmly crossed and his gaze focused on the ground in front of him, Dave nodded, "She did a jig and swallowed the pig." The rest of the menu was consumed with a characteristic flourish, "She swallowed the pig to catch the dog. She swallowed the dog to catch the cat. She swallowed the cat to catch the bird. She swallowed the bird to catch the spider." We took a breath for David. "That wiggled and jiggled and diggled inside her. She swallowed the spider to catch the fly." Sin returned his brother's pat on the back. David nodded sedately. *I don't know why she swallowed the fly. Perhaps she'll die.*

Cousin Barbara edged her way to the back of the bench. "There was an old woman who swallowed a *sheep.*" I opened my arms to her.

"What!" Barbara was aghast. The song hung in the air. "We haven't had that one before." Nat broke out laughing. The rest of us egged her on, as the poor old lady gasped for air. "She . . . let . . . out . . . a. . . ." Barbara's word was almost a whisper, "Peep?" We cheered and gave her a boost, "And swallowed a sheep." On her own again, Barbara proceeded cautiously, "She . . . swallowed the sheep to catch the *pig*. She swallowed the pig to catch the *dog*. She swallowed the dog to catch the *cat*. She swallowed the cat to catch the *bird* . . ." Becky gave her younger sister a nudge forward on the bench. "She swallowed the bird to catch the *spider* that wiggled and jiggled and tickled,"—"*Diggled!*" Barbara squirmed, continued, "Inside her. She swallowed the spider to catch the fly." We came to her rescue. Barbara sat back, relieved *I don't know why she swallowed the fly. Perhaps she'll die.*

"There was an old woman who swallowed a goat." I cast my eyes about the circle of benches. Wade, Nat, Margy, Robby. . . . His sister Kim was following intently Our gazes met. Kim took the cue, "She opened her throat and swallowed the goat." Kim's quick start almost caught her off guard, "She swallowed the goat to catch the . . . Sheep!" Fixing me in her gaze, she continued, "She swallowed the sheep to catch the pig. She swallowed the pig to catch the dog. She swallowed the dog to catch the cat." I nodded; Kim was back in swing. "She swallowed the cat to catch the bird. She swallowed the bird to catch the spider, that wiggled and jiggled." Her eyes lowered for a instant. "*Diggled,*" Rob whispered. Kim nodded, carried on, "She swallowed the spider to catch the fly." We finished the verse off with Kim. *I don't know why she swallowed the fly. Perhaps she'll die.*

"There was an old woman who swallowed a mule." Cousin Margy leaned back; Wade sat forward, a look of concentration settling over his face. He had the floor. "She needed some fuel and swallowed a mule." His older brother, Bengy, guffawed beside him. Resolute, Wade carried on, ignoring Bengy's quiet braahs, "She swallowed the mule to catch the goat. She swallowed the goat to catch the sheep. She swallowed the sheep to catch the pig. She swallowed the pig to catch the dog. She swallowed the dog to catch the cat." Wade's voice lowered as his lungs emptied, "She swallowed the cat to catch the bird. She swallowed the bird to catch the spider." He took a deep breath, "That wiggled and jiggled and diggled inside her." Replenished, Wade finished off the rest of the course, "She swallowed the spider to catch the fly."—*I don't know why she swallowed the fly. Perhaps she'll die.* The end was approaching. I glanced over the rest of the crew, my gaze resting on Rob. "There was an old woman who swallowed a cow." Rob motioned to himself. I nodded. He shrugged his shoulders, "I don't know how, she swallowed the cow." Glancing around, Rob lined up the herd, "She swallowed the cow to catch the mule. She swallowed the mule to catch the goat. She swallowed the goat to catch the sheep. She swallowed the sheep to catch the pig. She swallowed the pig to catch the dog." Rob hesitated a moment. Sister Kim nodded intently. Her older brother went on, his eyes resting on Rascal, purring contentedly in Bea's lap, "She swallowed the dog to catch the *cat*. She swallowed the cat to catch the bird. She swallowed the bird to catch the dog . . . *spider*." The tune had disappeared, but Rob held onto the words—most of them, "That wiggled and jiggled and diggled inside her. She swallowed the spider to catch the fly." *I don't know why she swallowed the fly. Perhaps she'll die.* We all joined heartily in. Baahing, bleating, chirping, mooing, . . . the menagerie laid the old gal to rest—almost.

"There was an old woman who swallowed a horse." Nat gently eased young Margy forward. We turned to her silently. "She died of course?" We cheered; Margy sighed, a smile of relief passing over her face. And the song came to a sad but fitting end.

* * * * *

Having momentarily exhausted our powers of rendition, we stretched for a moment, refreshing ourselves with the lemonade and casting a glance over the grill, before Nat took up the baton. His lanky legs crossed and a big grin on his face, Nat struck up a tune that had become a mainstay of our cookouts, though, to this day, I'm not sure any of us were able to follow him through all of its generations. With the lapping of the evening tides on the shore, we settled back down on the benches.

> *Many, many years ago, when I was twenty-three,*
> *I was married to a widow, who was as pretty as can be.*
> *This widow had a grownup daughter, who had hair of red;*
> *my father fell in love with her, and soon the two were wed.*

So far so good. Nat took a breath before continuing:

This made my Dad my son-in-law,
and changed my very life.
For my daughter was my mother,
for she was my father's wife.

To complicate the matter,
even though it brought me joy,
I soon became the father,
of a bouncing baby boy.

My little baby then became,
a brother-in-law to Dad.
And then became my uncle,
though it made me very sad.

For if he were my uncle,
he would have to be the brother,
of my wife's grown-up daughter,
who, of course, was my step-mother.

Rob and David swapped a dubious glance. Barbara appeared sympathetic, if a bit dismayed by the affair; Becky disaffected. As for the rest of us, we were not quite sure which end was up. Nat's grin broadened, as he sang on:

My father's wife then had a son,
who kept him on the run
and he became my grandchild,
for he was my daughter's son.

That made my wife, my mother's mother,
and it makes me blue,
because although she is my wife,
she's my grandmother too.

Now if my wife is my grandmother,
then I'm her grandchild.
And every time I think of it,
it nearly drives me wild.

For now I have become the strangest
case you ever saw,
the husband of my grandmother,
I'm my own grandpa.

That much we concluded! We all joined heartily in, *I'm my own Grandpa. I'm my own Grandpa. It sounds silly, I know, but it really is so. I'm my own grandpa.*

The hot dogs and hamburgers were done, and so were we—for the moment at least. Stepping forward, we lined up with our plates in front of the fireplace. The grill was a sizzlin', and so was Dad, as he adroitly scooped up the franks and burgers and deposited them snugly into our rolls and buns, sampling a bit and piece along the way. Stepping over to the broad bench, we surrounded the chips, salad, corn, and condiments, which we piled on the meat, before returning to our seats.

Our appetites were hearty, and quick work was made of the main course, before we pulled out our jackknives and, retrieving branches from the woods around us, set about carving sticks for the marshmallows. The roasting of these delicacies was an ancient backwoods craft, one that increased in complexity with each contestant around the fire. Elbow room was scarce, and often as many as a dozen marshmallows vied for the choicest coals. A steady hand and keen eye were needed in order not only to turn the right marshmallow, but to achieve the desired texture—a delicate, golden brown on all sides. Once accomplished, we would carefully draw off the outer skin of the marshmallow, pop it in our mouth, and angle our stick back into the flames for a second go—our prize becoming smaller but tastier with each turn. The Bast's contribution to this finale of our cookout was a memorable one— marshmallows and Hershey squares, sandwiched between Graham Crackers! "S'Mores," they were called. And so it was. The combination was appropriately named.

After the last of the marshmallows had been roasted, and the flames of the fire had died down, Dad pulled a stump up beside the hearth. Twilight began to descend over the Indian Fireplace, and a story was in the calling. As we settled in with the shadows, a chorus of frogs and crickets rose up out of the silence that gently engulfed us.

"In the early days, children, Lancaster was almost one unbroken forest," my gaze rested on Dad, the left side of his face lit by the flames. He leaned forward, "There were a few settlers, but their clearings were small. At times it seemed to James Weeks as if there were more wolves in residence than human beings." A hush settled over the Indian Fireplace:

The full-grown wolf, as I knew him, was the most formidable animal that ever inhabited this region. His lean, lank body, his big legs, large head, long and erect ears, with jaws capable of crushing the back or neck of a deer as if they were sponges, would have made him, but for his cowardice, extremely dangerous. His long-drawn howl, when bringing his pack together, can be heard for miles and is something fearful. But when half a dozen wolves are together and in their tantrums, one would think the spirits of the infernal regions had broke loose.

Generally hunting in packs, the wolves would kill sheep every night, often a dozen or more at a time....During the hay season on Prospect Farm, a storm was coming up, and I worked in the field till it was entirely dark. Now milking was in order, but my brother William, a boy of seven or eight years old, who was to look after the cows, had let them go off on the road.

After the usual lecture an older boy would give a younger one on such an occasion, I took William with me and started after the cows in the direction of Mr. Brackett's. We had got to the height of land where the old schoolhouse stood in District Number eight, when in the field, not fifty rods from us, the wolves set up a ululation that would have done credit to fifty devils from the old school. I knew what the sound was; William did not, but was particularly desirous to find out. I did not tell him, but took him by the hand and said to him that we could not find the cows if we went farther. It was getting dark, and we would see how quick we could go home. After we had gone a little way, I told William what it was. Two boys never made better time.

We squeezed closer together on the benches, filling in the spaces. By this time, it was difficult to make out the storyteller in the shadows:

At another time, when about sixteen years old, I had gone with my two sisters, younger than myself, and two or three of their girl friends to a little pond south of Mt. Prospect for lilies, which used to grow there. After obtaining what we could, we returned home. We had hardly reached there when the wolves opened their infernal concert at the very place we had left half an hour before. One would have thought bedlam broke loose. Someone who was there a day or two later said they tracked over half an acre, running every way, tumbling and rolling as if their noise was but a small part of their exercise. They had evidently been aware of our presence all the time when we were at the pond, and when we had gone they came out to look the ground over, swear, carry on, and talk large like other cowards.

The shadows crept closer; the voice grew less distinct:

One morning, while sitting at breakfast we heard the wolves again. The question was quickly asked, 'Where's William?' The reply was, 'Gone for fir boughs for a broom.' Stepping to the door, the woods toward Whitefield seemed full of the infernal creatures and almost precisely where we knew William had gone. I, without hat, seized the first thing I could lay hands on and started upon a run down the Whitefield Road. My father, more deliberate, took his gun and ammunition from the hook near the door and followed at a quick pace. After a few moments that seemed an hour, we saw William very leisurely climb over the fence into the clearing with the fir boughs under his arm, and, in the most deliberate manner, straight as a ramrod, march up toward the road. When he had gone a little way, he turned and looked back, the wolves still keeping up their howl and moving away. When we reached him, he was white as a ghost and said that the wolves were so close to him that, after one of their long-drawn howls, he could hear them draw in their breath. . . .

The voice was silent. We all sat still as the story receded into the sounds of the night—suddenly heightened by the quiet all around us. Breathing in, my eyes rested on the embers of the fire that glowed deep in the ashes of the hearth. Moments passed before a familiar melody arose. I glanced around silently at the circle of cousins . . . and then lifted my gaze, with the kindling sparks, up through the branches of the great pines overhead, to the universe of stars that now filled the heavens:

> . . . *All night, all day, angels watchin' over me.*

Grandmother Bea—mortal/immortal—returned with the melody to heart and mind, as the evening drew to an end.

3

LABOR DAY WEEKEND

AS JUNE LANGUISHED into July and July on into August, the summer sun began its descent. Labor Day Weekend approached, a lovely hyphen between the seasons and occasion for any in-laws who weren't present and accounted for to drop everything and head north to Cat Bow.

The ranks had swelled considerably over the last five years. Cousins had married; new babies had arrived on the scene, and now we tipped the scales at fifty-plus. We had even reached the milestone, where, mixed in the clan, was a choice sampling of great-grandchildren. But, the Lord of Cat Bow took it all pretty much in stride. He must have stopped counting with his own six children, because the mounting offspring never fazed him. Sitting back in his lounge chair on the terrace, Grampy would matter-of-factly ask who belonged to whom, doing his best to sort out the babies as they waddled up to him, parents in tow. What our sire would have made of us had he not been well girded by his old medallioned belt (name, rank, and serial number), I cannot guess.

Even though proud parents insist that at one year of age their babies exhibit unique personalities of their own, Grampy seemed to have trouble making the distinction. I guess that after one had both seen and kissed as many babies as he had, infants were all pretty much the same. Grampy would simply hoist the newcomer up on his knee, where, to the horror of its parents, he would bounce the infant up and down and offer it a sip of his Jack Daniels.

Unfortunately, though, the confusion didn't stop with just the babies. New in-laws ran into the same problem. Not infrequently, when they greeted Grampy, he was at a loss as to who they were. This proved

64

to be rather disconcerting to the other member of the team, who would exclaim: "Grampy, don't you remember _____? He's my husband. You were at our wedding!" If Grampy happened to recognize his own grandchild (which was not to be assured), he would diplomatically salvage the situation by saying, *Oh sure*, slapping the new member on the back, and then proceed to reintroduce the newcomer to his mother-in-law! And around we went!

What an experience it must have been to break into the family, particularly for those of a slightly more liberal persuasion! Rosa, Sue, Ned—my young heart often went out to the new in-laws, as no amount of coaching was sufficient to prepare them for what they were to encounter. When someone married into the clan, they pretty much got the rest of us in the deal—for better and for worse.

On Friday afternoon, the last of the family arrived: the Rankins from Washington, the John Weeks, nine strong (not counting their own "grand" additions to the clan) from Boston and Nantucket, and our second cousins, the Davidges, from Maryland—along with an older cousin or two who had left their family fold and begun to make his or her own way out into the world. The rest of us made up the welcoming party.

The reunions were as lively as a three-ring circus. As cars pulled into the driveway, horns honking and hands a-waving, we would exit from the barn, fields, tennis court, and Big House and converge upon the party, shaking hands and swapping kisses. Everyone grabbed a bag, and in no time the cars were empty and the circle and vestibule swamped with tennis rackets, duffel bags, fishing rods, knapsacks, and hiking boots.

After a second round of hellos, kisses, and "my, you've grown biggers," the adults would retire to the terrace, while we children searched out our cohorts and disappeared back into the folds of the farm, until the next delegation arrived.

It was a joy to be together once again. Everyone—aunts, uncles, and cousins alike—was interested in how life had fared since the last reunion, and each family added a special contribution to the tableau. The Rankins brought with them the flavor of the South, sprinkling "you alls" and "chillun" in and among the conversation. The Hallowells, led by Aunt Frannie, the family lyricist, and Uncle Woof, with his crunching bear hugs, orchestrated the family's cultural affairs, from dances to song fests. Uncle Bob Bast always seemed to have a pack of cards near at hand or a magic trick up his sleeve, with which to delight and, often, baffle us. And Uncle Ben Robinson, the family toy salesman, won the admiration of every child under ten with a wide assortment of toys and games, which he produced from his voluminous pockets.

The John Weeks, notorious for their monopoly of clowns, provided the indispensable spark of humor—aided and abetted in their efforts by the Sherrills, who helped tickle the family's funny bone, with their lively combination of wit and wisdom. Last but not least, the Bill Weeks kept us abreast of the political winds, which had become less favorable over the last decade to the Republican ship of state. Names were not to be taken for granted, though "Beas" and "Sinclairs" were often a safe bet. As for the rest of the family, "cousin," "cuz,". . . or most anything would do. Amidst the hullabaloo, even old Janie contracted the spirit, condescending to contribute a ride or two in the cart, if duly recompensed for her labors.

* * * * *

The most popular event of the weekend was the *Quintennial-Cat-Bow-Farm-Invitational-Round-Robin-Tennis-Jamboree-Extravaganza*—open to any and all bona fide members of the clan, in good standing and with a secure branch on the family tree.

The event started around ten o'clock on Saturday morning, and everyone rallied—including the cows, which took up their positions in the meadow bleachers. Grampy was given the task of orchestrating the mayhem, by throwing out the first ball, before he took his place on the portable throne that had been set up on the sidelines. The tournament was even more hazardous than our family dances. In-laws, of all shapes and sizes, attitudes and inclinations, convened on the court (attired in a variety of wardrobes—from the traditional whites to bespeckled bell-bottoms and rustic cut-offs—which would have piqued a rainbow) to limber up for the event. The contestants ranged from little toddlers, barely the size of their rackets, through the gamut of hard-hitting cousins, to uncles with business elbows, and slightly awkward but enthusiastic aunts.

Finally, after Uncle Bob carefully went over the rules, the Lord of Cat Bow heaved the orb onto the court, and the contest was officially begun.

What a sight it was! Prodded by the uproar, each person took his or her turn hitting the ball, before shuffling the racket to the next in line and, then, proceeded to round the net in a variety of gaits that defied imagination, so as to preserve the rally. Uncle Bill (his sight set squarely on the ball), Bea, Aunt Kitty, Benjy, Roger, Aunt Frances, Tony, Kim, Brad, Marnie, Rob, Wade, Dave, Will, Uncle Kirk, Ma, Aunt Muff, Francie, Nat, Chris, young Sinny, middle Sinny, Dad himself . . . urged on, one and all, by the "ump" upon his throne. Faster and faster the ball would go—lobs, volleys, and line drives—until, one by one, miscalculating their shots, the rank and file would drop out and stagger over to the sidelines, where they shouted encouragement, in between laughs and gasps for air.

As the numbers dwindled, the hubbub grew louder, and the family allegiances stronger, until finally there were only two players left, with the challenging task of chasing their own shots. These rallies were brief, and a tie for first place was awarded to the two pooped, but exhilarated, finalists, who collapsed in the crowd. All took a deep breath.

Around noon the family migrated down to the Boat House on the lake for the Annual Labor Day Lobster Bake. This repast was practically unheard of in the North Country, as the nearest lobsters were to be found a good hundred miles east, off the coast of Maine.

Be that as it may, the Lobster Bake was a tradition at Cat Bow, over which Grampy presided most sumptuously.

Caravans of cars carried the lobsters, clams, potatoes, salad, corn, chips, pretzels, popcorn, and drinks down to the Boat House, where they were received by a regiment of eager helpers. The Boat House had all the character of the Big House, gathered into two good sized rooms that were connected by a corridor lined with a familiar row of closets. On one end of the Boat House were the changing quarters, which hosted four commodious dressing stalls for the adults, as well as a wide-open floor, adrift with rubber rafts and life preservers, for the children. At the other end of the Boat House was a quieter corner, where 'Uncle Ned's' old barrel bar (refurbished with the years) found its sober reprieve. Around the bar, chairs, stools, and an old wooden table or two placed themselves at the disposal of any family member who cared to step out of the hubbub and cool off.

This quiet corner I often availed myself of, lingering in front of a set of drawings, one on top of the other, that hung in a simple wooden frame on the wall beside the bar. Illustrated by John T. McCutcheon, the title of the drawings was "Indian Summer." The top sketch depicted a grandfather, leaning back against a tree into the afternoon, his rake resting between his legs, his corncob pipe in his mouth. In front of him, beside a small pile of burning leaves, stood his young grandson, dressed simply in overalls and a shirt. The gazes of grandfather and grandson alike were directed off a ways to an autumn field—its harvest of corn stalks gathered together across the pasture and tied at their tops. *Yep, sonny . . .* The grandfather reflected,

> *This is sure enough Injun summer. Don't know what that is, I reckon, do you?*
>
> *Well, that's when all the homesick Injuns come back to play. You know, a long time ago, long afore yer granddaddy was born even, there used to be heaps of Injuns around here—thousands— millions, I reckon, far as that's concerned. Reg'lar sure 'nough Injuns—none o' yer cigar store Injuns, not much. They was all around here—right here where you're standin'.*
>
> *Don't be skeered—haint none around here now, leastways no live ones. They been gone this many a year.*
>
> *They all went away and died, so they ain't no more left.*

In the sketch below, evening has cast its shadow over the field, softening the outlines of the day and transforming, before the boy's gaze, the corn stalks into teepees. Eyes open wide, the child listens attentively as his Granddaddy carries on, the smoke drifting on up from his pipe:

> *But every year, 'long about now, they all come back, leastways their sperrits do. They're here now. You can see 'em off across the fields. Look real hard. See that kind o' hazy misty look out yonder? Well, them's Injuns—Injuns sperrits marchin' along an' dancin' in the sunlight. That's what makes that kind o' haze that's every-*

where—it's just the sperrits of the Injuns all come back. They're all around us now.

See off yonder; see them teepees? They kind o' look like corn shocks from here, but them's Injun tents, sure as you're a foot high. See 'em now? Sure, I knowed you could. Smell that smoky sort o' smell in the air? That's the campfires a-burnin' and their pipes a-goin'.

Lots o' people say it's just leaves burnin', but it ain't. It's the campfires, an' th' Injuns are hoppin' 'round 'em t' beat the old Harry.

You just come out here tonight when the moon is hangin' over the hill off yonder, an' the harvest fields is all swimmin' in the moonlight, an' you can see the Injuns and the teepees jest as plain as kin be. You can, eh? I knowed you would.

Jever notice how the leaves turn red 'bout this time o year? That's jest another sign o' red-skins. That's when an old Injun Sperrit gits tired dancin' an' goes up an' squats on a leaf t' rest. Why, I kin hear 'em rustlin' an' whisperin' an' creppin' 'round among the leaves all the time; an' ever' once'n a while a leaf gives way under some fat old Injun ghost and comes floatin' down to the ground. See—here's one now. See how red it is? That's the war paint rubbed off'n Injun ghost, sure's you're born.

Purty soon all the Injuns'll go marchin' away agin, back to the happy huntin' ground, but next year you'll see 'em troppin' back—th' sky jest hazy with 'em and their campfires smolderin' away jest like they are now.

My gaze lingered on the young grandson in the sketch, before I stepped through the boathouse doorway and onto the porch. A breeze from the lake brushed my face. I perked up my ears as it journeyed on, whispering through the leaves in the lithe birch that cast its pale shadows over the shore.

In front of me, picnic tables ran the full length of the porch, edged by a thick wooden railing and topped off with a fluttering awning. From the porch it was but a hop, skip, and a jump down the steps, onto the dock, and into the water blue.

Everyone pitched in with the preparations for the lobster bake. The

ladies decked out the tables with settings of wooden plates, paper napkins, forks, knives, and spoons. Uncle Bob took charge of the cooking,
keeping a group of us busy wrapping potatoes in tinfoil, husking corn,
rinsing clams, and splitting kindling wood for the fire. Grandchildren,
too young or faint of foot for the sturdier jobs, were assigned the duty
of keeping an astonished eye on the lobsters, until the pot was steaming.
Kith and kin filled every nook and cranny.

The drinks were served by Uncle Bill, who plunked ice cubes into
glasses and poured everything from ginger ale on the rocks, for minors,
to Bloody Marys, for the adults, which he spiced with a favorite family
quip: *'Am I concerned about General Grant's drinking?'* Lincoln paused
(with Uncle Bill, who leaned out over the old bar) and gazed at Grant's
detractor. . . . The president stroked his chin thoughtfully, *'Well, I'll tell
you. I wish I knew what kind of whiskey old Ulysses drank, and I would give
it to all my generals!'* Those gathered, generations young and old, lifted
their respective glasses.

Between stories, older cousins made repeated trips back up to the
Big House to fetch essential provisions which had been overlooked in
the exodus, while every remaining able-bodied soul—who was not on
assignment or otherwise occupied—was swept along with the preparations, lending a hand where necessary. Only the Lord of Cat Bow sat
back amidst the commotion, cushioned by his years and content to
be waited upon hand, foot, betwixt and between. Shaded by his old
dilapidated sombrero, Grampy shouted words of encouragement to us
all, while he steadied teetering babies that waddled past and made sure
that the popcorn bowl didn't overflow.

It wasn't long before "the show was on the road," and all that was
left for us to do was to wait for the clams and lobsters to come to a boil.
Having worked up a good sweat, we wasted little time climbing into our
bathing suits and heading for the lake. The cameras popped out, as all
the males in the family went in—on their own volition or with a helping hand. Everyone, that is, except Grampy, who, pardon the expression,
was something of a sacred cow.

One by one, the kids would team up and chase a distracted uncle
down the dock. At times like these, there was little respect for age, and
the poor man was fortunate if he was able to shed his shoes, belt, and

wallet, before he had run out of dock and found himself—dear Uncle Bob—flying through the air. As the waters settled, canoes, rubber rafts, inner tubes, and sailboats were launched, and the ladies and younger cousins raised the second wave. Overhead, the summer sun floated in the clear blue heavens, bestowing its bounteous rays upon the day.

After most of us had flopped back onto the dock, refreshed, Grampy announced that the lobsters were ready. One summons was enough. Grabbing our towels, we eagerly headed for the porch and picnic tables—one for all and all for one. Squeezing together, we drew in our elbows, sorting out our glasses, utensils, and bowls of butter. *Rub-a-dub-dub, thanks for the grub,* Cousin Sin whispered under his breath beside me. *Yea Lord!* chimed in Wade and I wholeheartedly. Helping each other tie on the bibs, by the time the lobsters were doled out and the clams piled onto our plates, our appetites were piqued.

A messier meal it could not have been! It was difficult enough trying to secure a solid bite when you are surrounded by fifty-odd people, without at the same time having to avoid the geysers that shot across the table, as the clams were opened, the lobster claws cracked, and the salad, corn, chips, and pitchers of lemonade made the rounds, along with the conversation.

" 'I have a dream,' he said." I glanced up from my plate, as Ned White—a prospective "outlaw" in the family and a good seven years my senior—looked over at Uncle Bish: "Over two hundred thousand people, not just blacks, but thousands of white people as well—apparently the largest demonstration in Washington to date—gathered yesterday with Martin Luther King at the Lincoln Memorial."

Ned paused, as other glances lifted from their plates. " 'I still have a dream,' King witnessed—a dream, he said, that was deeply rooted in the American dream. Standing in front of the Lincoln Memorial, King spoke about the day that our nation would rise up and live out the true meaning of its creeds: 'we hold these truths to be self-evident that all men are created equal.' " A bowl of corn-on-the-cob from an unsuspecting kin gently side-swiped Ned, who, passing it on (along with a frown), turned his attention to the lobsters and clams. *A dream,* . . . the words echoed on in my depths, as my gaze passed back out to the dock and its gathering tides.

Finally, after every last morsel of lobster and clam had been extracted from the shells, we leaned back to take a breath. A New Hampshire lobster bake it had been!

The tables were quickly cleared by the grandchildren, before we turned our attention to Aunt Frannie, whose preparations for the lobster bake had been of a more literary order. Holding up a scroll, she tapped her glass with a spoon and turned to address Grampy, "We would like to invite you and the rest of the family to sit back for a moment and 'unlax.' A number of us have come up with a few tidbits of wit and wisdom for your listening pleasure."

Aunt Frannie nodded to Uncle Bish, who divested himself of his bib and rose ceremoniously to his feet. Unfolding a sheet of paper, Uncle Bish glanced with mock seriousness over the younger grandchildren, who had squeezed together on the benches, "Well, ladies and gentlemen, I did come up with a couple of lines that I managed to extract from the family files, which I believe have some redeeming value." Uncle Bish held up a letter, "This is the concluding paragraph, short and sweet, from a note to Grampy, written by a gentleman from the Midwest named Hutch." Uncle Bish glanced at Grampy, who nodded attentively. Then, adjusting his glasses, Uncle Bish cleared his throat and, as a slightly pious Eli (Yale) grin snuck up on his face, started in:

> . . . *I see by the papers, as Mr. Dooley was wont to say, that your colleague, Gasoline Charlie (Wilson), has decided to relinquish the baton of power and join the ranks of the unemployed. Personally, I find it a beatific state. But he, like the Boston Brahmin, who, after going to Milton, Harvard, Harvard Law School. . . .*

Uncle Bish eyed the Crimson (Harvard) ranks spread out around him, before continuing:

> . . . *at an early age found himself a partner in one of Boston's leading law firms and a member of the Somerset Club; but in the way of all flesh eventually presenting himself at the gates of heaven heard St. Peter remark, "Well, there's no reason why you can't come in, but I don't think you will like it here!"*

Amen!, Uncle Bish's nephew-in-law (and fellow Yale grad), Ken White, exhorted. Laughing heartily, Uncle Bish leaned over to pass the passage on to Grampy, before relinquishing the floor to the next speaker, Aunt Frannie, who, adjusting her sun bonnet, unrolled her scroll, "I found an article in the Cat Bow archives, which I thought would give you all a little chuckle. You'll see that it is a little more down to earth." The twinkle was in Aunt Frannie's eyes, as she cleared her throat:

WASHINGTON SCENE
By George Dixon

Republican Weeks, in 1829 Really Spent the Dough
(reprinted with permission)

Aunt Frannie started in amidst smiles and chuckles:

Secretary of Commerce, Sinclair Weeks, submits that inflation is not as modern Republican as some administration critics would have you believe. He has just unearthed an old family diary, which shows it costs a "pillar" of the Federal Government more to get to Washington in 1831 than it does in 1958. The author of the musty record was a certain John Wingate Weeks.

Glancing down at us grandchildren, Aunt Frannie paused and reflected, "Your great-great-great...."

"GREAT,..." Uncle Woof nudged her on.

"GREAT!" Their son, Gerry, added a definitive postscript, as he proudly lifted his baby son, Roger, the forerunner of the next wave of Weeks, above the rank and file.

"*UNCLE!*" Grampy kept the story on track.

Aunt Frannie carried on:

...who served two terms in Congress, from 1829 to 1833. Republican Weeks spent more money, including a Bacchanalian outlay of 90 cents for liquor, to make the journey from the old Weeks home in

Lancaster, New Hampshire, to the nation's capital, than his more abstemious descendant does today.

The speaker motioned to the Chairman. Grampy received Aunt Frannie's recognition with an amused nod, before she continued:

It took Republican Weeks ten days, by stage and boat, to make the trip and cost him $44.33. The Secretary of Commerce now makes the trip, nearly every other week, in three and a half hours, at a cost of $34.87.

Of course, the current Weeks does not stop off at Lincoln, Plymouth, Concord, Nashua, Boston, Worcester, Middletown, New Haven, New York, New Brunswick, New Jersey, Philadelphia, and Baltimore, to belt down nearly a dollars worth of booze. Nor is his charitable heart so wrung that he bestows 7 cents upon a "poor boy" and another 12 cents upon a "poor girl." In fact, if he distributed alms with the lavish hand of his ancestor, a beneficiary might truly be referred to as a "poor girl."

The laughs were more subdued.

The Secretary of Commerce found the ancient diary in a storeroom in the old Weeks' place and was kind enough to turn it over to me. He said he believed it was just the proof he needed to reassure Americans, particularly inflation-fearing Congressmen, how much farther their money takes them today.

When his great-great uncle was serving the people, members of Congress were paid $8 a day for every day Congress was actually in session, as opposed to a flat $22,500 a year now. A Congressman was lucky if he totaled $1,000 a year. It cost old John Wingate Weeks $1,176.28 to maintain himself in Washington for the first session of the 22nd Congress, which lasted from Dec. 5, 1831 to July 16, 1832.

There are a few items in his accounts that are something short of self-explanatory. Take for instance these: "For slave's freedom $1" and "Siamese Twins 25 cents."

Aunt Frannie raised her eyebrows; Grampy stroked his chin thoughtfully, as he gazed out over the lake.

Today, few members of Congress are ever called upon to spend their own money on either slaves' freedom or Siamese Twins.

Rep. Weeks paid $6.19 for "blackening boots." Were he in Congress today, Weeks could get his shoes shined in the House barber shop for 15 cents. As further proof of the runaway inflation of the time, the Rep. paid $15 for a shawl for himself. A Congressman today would think twice before wearing a shawl that costs anything like that.

Aunt Frannie cast her eye about the family ranks:

In one respect, the old gentleman professed to feel the same about Washington as many do today. He wrote Gov. J. W. Williams of New Hampshire: "Any honest man is to be pitied whose service is required in that Fountain of Corruption, Washington City. Its name should be changed to Babylon."

There was a stir in the assemblage. Aunt Frannie raised her hand, "Hang on; it's a happy ending."

But Rep. Weeks' illustrious great-great nephew has no such depressing views about Washington. Secretary of Commerce Weeks, the Eisenhower Administration's "Cheery Outlook" man, constantly avers that things here are pretty good and due to get better.

Grampy glanced over the text, which Aunt Frannie handed him graciously. Cousin John Weeks, whose ears had perked up at the familiar mention of the name of the gentleman in question, asked Grampy if the piece had, indeed, been reprinted with permission.

Grampy looked up, "Yes, and it bears a careful re-reading. The subject of inflation aside, there are a number of valuable lessons that one can learn from your ancestor, who, though not a saint, was, indeed, a well-respected citizen in his day around these parts. Not least of those lessons is the fact that, apart from his political leanings and propensity for a good drink now and again—which, given the condition of water in those days, was shared by many—your uncle kept precise records of his expenditures....*And,*" Grampy directed his gaze to the future generations, "even though he didn't mince words in his criticism of the state of affairs in Washington, he nevertheless did his part—at considerable expense and inconvenience to himself—in serving his country."

Roger, who had settled again onto his father's lap, seconded Grampy's motion with a hardy hiccup. Grampy sat forward, "I happen to have a little something for the occasion, as well." He drew an envelope out of his shirt pocket and, opening it, held up an old newspaper article, well worn with the years. "This was written about another John Wingate Weeks, my father, and about a close friend of his named Henry Cabot Lodge. There is much in it that is instructive for the younger generations." Grampy put on his glasses, before inviting us to sit back:

BOB WASHBURN SAYS

Massachusetts probably never has had a stronger team in the Senate of the United States than Henry Cabot Lodge of Nahant in the county of Essex and John Wingate Weeks in the county of Middlesex, from 1913 to 1919.

They were both strong types, yet each distinct from the other, and yet each complementing the other. While all the virtues were to be found in neither of these men alone, in both together there was very much to be found. Nevertheless, neither were very responsive to what may be called the forward element of the party. "Progressive" is a tired term, which should be abandoned. Neither were they very responsive to those who looked upon political problems with altruism and from other than political and business angles only.

Grampy paused and lifted his head, glancing at us over his glasses:

Each of these men has now been gone long enough to be estimated exactly as he was, without that touch of generous emotion which belongs to those who are recently dead. So now, where did these two men diverge?

Mr. Lodge was a product of Beacon Hill, from its innermost sanctuary, of the sort of which it likes best to boast. Mr. Weeks was the product of a country town, Lancaster in New Hampshire. He symbolized the substantial qualities of a state known throughout the country for its enduring granite.

The first of these men was born with an advantage well before the tape. Mr. Weeks began life nearer the scratch line. Everything was made easy for the development of Mr. Lodge, an ancestral snow plow clearing the way. But Mr. Weeks himself pretty much cleared his own path. The first sight which doubtless caught the eye of the baby Cabot was a frock coat. While the first spectacle which stirred little John was probably overalls. The genealogist would find the Lodge dynasty a blazed trail, while he must set out on the Weeks tree more in the spirit of a pioneer. More people can name the mother of Mr. Lodge than the father of Mr. Weeks.

I listened with interest as Grampy read on:

Mr. Lodge prepared for college at the most de rigueur school in Boston. Its membership was carefully filtered through a close meshed sieve. He taught at Harvard College. Mr. Weeks began in the little red school house, peopled with boys in patched pants. There later he taught. He pitched hay on the farm.

My glance lifted to the field. Grampy nodded:

From both hay and farm, Mr. Lodge had a continuous alibi. Mr. Weeks completed his education at Annapolis. The liveliest of imaginations could not picture Mr. Lodge in uniform. He saw more seas than he sailed. He never led a company of cadets on the common, as did Captain Weeks.

Mr. Weeks went into business, the last of terminals for Mr. Lodge, who was to be found in the Harvard library, to gratify a taste for books, always saturated, never satiated. It is a good guess that Mr. Weeks read few books, except when in search of concrete facts to back up his practical researches, and then the job was delegated to a secretary when possible. He was at his best in a mass of figures showing the condition of some investment. It was the Senate which had brought them together in close contact, the one a scholar, the other a man of business, as the Weeks bridge at Harvard binds its academic and commercial branches.

The table was quiet. At the far end, Uncle John, his hands folded in his lap, glanced thoughtfully across at his father. Beside him, Aunt Kitty leaned back against the porch railing, cradling Bobby, the youngest of the brood, in her lap. Grampy took a drink before continuing:

Then they were elected to public office. Mr. Lodge became a state representative. Mr. Weeks became a mayor. Nothing could have tempted Mr. Lodge to the office of an executive, for he preferred the legislative branch. He respected the Constitution, which divorces the two. Mr. Weeks, when elected mayor, was as coy toward office as an old-fashioned maiden toward marriage. But Mr. Lodge was as receptive as the young woman of today. When the voice of the people was heard at the front door, Mr. Lodge was in the front hall, but Mr. Weeks was in the back parlor....Mr. Weeks was always a stranger to worry, fatigue and fear, like a Newfoundland dog; when the steam orchestra stopped, he could go to sleep, while Mr. Lodge kept on smoking, figuratively and literally.

Mr. Lodge was ruffled often, like a rivulet. Mr. Weeks was placid always, like a mill-pond. The former was angry often, the latter never. Mr. Lodge used to say, "'When I am angry, which is often, I go to Weeks, who soothes me....'"

Mr. Lodge has not succeeded in loving his neighbor as himself, but Mr. Weeks has made much progress in that direction. The scriptural words: "'Bless them that curse you," had small charm for Mr. Lodge. But Mr. Weeks forgave everyone, with only two exceptions, and they, too, are now dead....

Grampy reflected a moment before reading on:

...Weeks was a stranger to envy, hatred, malice and all uncharitableness.

In their speech, they were most divergent. It was Lodge's great ambition to make a great speech. It was Weeks' ambition to do a great piece of work, whatever it was. It was on the platform that Mr. Lodge thrilled, but it was in conversation that Mr. Weeks best drew one toward him. Mr. Lodge appealed first to the intellect. Mr. Weeks above all to the heart. In this respect, Mr. Weeks was the essence of simplicity, as modest as a maiden and moreso than many. Mr. Lodge was in essence a superb mental machine. In the estimate of many, with or without reason, Mr. Weeks was essentially a materialist.

Grampy pronounced the word sparingly:

In the Senate, questions of national policy appealed first to Mr. Lodge, business and financial questions first to Mr. Weeks. The responsibility for the party patronage, Mr. Lodge was glad to assume, and Mr. Weeks glad to release. They were very sympathetic. Mr. Weeks was in closer touch with his colleagues, for he was the more humanly pliable of the two. The defeat of Mr. Weeks for the Senate in 1918, Mr. Lodge took hard.

"There is a touching story to be told there." Grampy rested the article on his plate a moment, before picking up the thread:

Mr. Lodge had an imaginative and poetic nature. Mr. Weeks was neither. He neither thought nor wrote poetry. In his busiest days, Mr. Lodge maintained a huge correspondence filled with philosophy and literary allusions. Mr. Weeks wrote only when it was necessary and only what was necessary, and then he stopped. He was vital and to the point, but he thrilled no more than a fire escape, which is also vital.

Grampy smiled. Then, glancing at us, skipped a page:

Mr. Lodge was content with his seat in the Senate, but there was no horizon to the aspirations of Mr. Weeks. He was a candidate for the presidential nomination before the process became popular in Massachusetts.

In the scope of their social affiliations, Mr. Lodge was happy with quality only, but Mr. Weeks with quantity also. This was as to be expected, for Mr. Weeks, in life's crescendo, had lived with all sorts of people . . . . It was harder to say, Cabot to the first, then John to the second. And yet, Mr. Lodge had a sentimental side, to which Mr. Weeks was a stranger. Both were sincere, but with Mr. Lodge it was subcutaneous, while with Mr. Weeks it stuck out.

Mr. Weeks went out of office in full political bloom. Mr. Lodge died under the setting sun of popular favor. He stood by the bonus, and for this reason, and for others more sordid on the part of others, he was pilloried. He could have done nothing else, as a man of honor. When the lion falters, the jackals love to feed!

"The article ends on a note you will appreciate, Reverend Sherrill." Grampy glanced at his son-in-law and, then, back down to the pages:

Of such they were, the one a scholar, the other a man of affairs, and both statesmen. Blending here and separating there, each was vital to the Senate. They did much, but they could have done more. What a superman Providence could have shaped out of these two, their failings filtered here, their virtues toned there, urged on by the conception of grand idealism, which is the aspiration of the church.

The family was quiet. Grampy took off his glasses and, casting his eyes over the generations, added a postscript, "The author, Washburn, it should be noted, was a close friend of my father's. Though his background was more similar to Lodge, he may, in fact, have understood John Weeks better." Grampy reflected a moment before concluding, "None of us, however, can recount the full story of another's life. No matter how close we feel we are to a person, there are always aspects that elude us."

My gaze rested on Grampy, as a last hiccup rose from the ranks. Our clam bake came to a slightly sober end.

* * * * *

Monday morning was devoted to preparations for the family photo—that moment during the Labor Day festivities when all loose ends were tied together. Following a quick breakfast, the family convened on the side lawn, above the tennis court. The metamorphosis was striking! Ties and coats—like father like son—replaced t-shirts; long trousers stood in for shorts, and even the parts in my cousins' and my hair were uncovered and bestowed a good lick. After the parents had given us the once over (for the third time), we squeezed into place in and around the benches that had been set up and did our best to contain ourselves.

We must have presented quite a picture when viewed from the other end of a wide-angle lens. The Lord of Cat Bow sat back in the middle of the throng. Dressed up for the occasion, his lady, Grandma Jane, sat silently beside him, her hand held in his. Grampy and Grandma Jane, in turn, were surrounded on either side by their daughters and daughters-in-law, who were flanked by their husbands—chests up, shoulders back, and a smile or two among the stiff upper lips. The rest of us, too big for laps and too small for the back row, sat on the ground at our parents' feet, amid an array of pigtails, cuffs, tweed, plaids, hair bands, and a demure silver heart that hung down from cousin Caroline Rankin's youthful neck. Despite appearances, there was a system to it all.

Finally, after the count had been taken, and Grampy was satisfied that all who belonged had been flushed from the woods, tennis court, hayloft, and rest rooms, we all took a deep breath and turned our attention to the camera, to wait for instructions.

Such settings brought to mind the story that had made the family rounds about a letter Grampy had received during his years in the Commerce Department from an associate in the Census Bureau, who had followed with particular interest the proliferation of his boss's progeny. Though nobody seemed to recall the entire contents of the letter, its good-natured conclusion (after another grandchild had been ticked off on the great population clock that held sway in the lobby of the Commerce Department) was that, if the flood didn't ebb, some thought would have to be given to starting a new sub-race. In a letter to an intimate, Grampy was more matter-of-fact, *Birds and bees aside. I have six children, who, at last count, have twenty-five of their own, plus two stepchildren who've added six more to the pot. The first wave I can account for. How the rest arrived on the scene, I wouldn't speculate.* Young Billy Weeks, legs crossed and bow tie askew, flashed a gaping, unabashed, four-year-old smile out at the world.

Birds and bees aside, the photographer appeared to have his hands full, fitting us into the same frame. Motioning from under the black cloak that was draped over the camera, he squeezed in the ends, drew forward the flanks, and did his best to elevate the slouch that had fallen upon us younger members of the ranks, spread across the front row. Finally, all in focus, the gentleman lifted an arm: 5, 4, 3, 2, 1....The camera managed to catch most of us looking, if not smiling, at the same time. And flash! We belonged to posterity. The consensus being that all in all, considering the circumstances, the shot was as good as could be expected, we children were excused. A sigh of relief rippled through the younger ranks. No one dared imagine what five more years would do for our pose.

The rest of the morning was spent bidding farewell to the farm. This involved a final surveillance of the hay forts, soon to be grist for the Cat Bow herd, adieus and parting tributes to the animals (with the exception of old Janie, who had lapsed back into her former obstinate state), and a visit to the playhouse and apple orchard. Summer had presented her offerings; now the time had come for autumn to ripen the fruits.

Around noon, Mom and Dad called us down to the Big House. Other families with longer drives ahead of them were getting ready to go. All good things must come to an end. Such was an enduring lesson of those years. Swapping kisses and fond farewells—a major part of those long-drawn-out good-byes, which always seemed to end up with the departing ones stopping halfway out the driveway, while a cousin skedaddled back into the Big House to retrieve a toothbrush or sundry item—the party slowly began to break up.

Considering the numbers and logistics, Grampy orchestrated a remarkable departure. Doling out missed kisses and slaps on the back to children, grandchildren, great-grandchildren, alike, The Lord of Cat

Bow positioned himself amid the island of roses in the middle of the driveway. *Come on now; if you are going to go, go!*

Looking down on the proceedings from a grassy knoll beneath one of the apple trees in the orchard, I was struck by something in Grampy's voice—an undertone that filled me for a fleeting moment with a deep and inexplicable sadness. I listened; Grampy was saying two things. I looked at him. A tiredness accentuated the lines on his face, relieved for a moment by a searching smile that passed across Grampy's lips, as his offspring waved good-bye, before settling into their cars, into the trip. Behind the smile, deep within, I glimpsed a tear. *If you are going to go . . .* Bea, his first wife; Grandma Jane, his second—led back into the Big House, down the long hall to her room, more unfamiliar with each passing day . . . *go!*

August, Labor Day, September. The leaves of the old elm were turning, colors changing....We were going. I looked at Grampy, surrounded by the fading circle of summer roses. Clouds touched the sky above Mt. Orne. Only ten years old, I realized for the first time that my grandfather was struggling, struggling, amidst life's festivities, to remain true to something that, I sensed, was larger than, and yet no less a part of, himself.

My thoughts went back earlier in the week, to a surprise visit Grampy made to us one evening after dinner at the cabin, before the rest of the clan arrived. This was not customary, as it was generally we offspring who presented ourselves at Cat Bow. Mom and Dad hurried about to perk up the old abode, prevailing upon us to set aside our pursuits for a few moments and help.

When Grampy drove up, Nat, Bea, Brad, and I ran out to the field in our pajamas to greet him. An autumn chill touched the air. At first I was surprised that Grandma Jane wasn't with Grampy, but Grampy's warm smile and affectionate embrace dispelled all concerns. Taking our grandfather in hand, we led him down the path and into Mom's and Dad's arms at the door.

The sun was setting at the end of the lake, and the sky was ablaze with blues, light reds, paling yellows, and oranges. Stepping into the cabin, Grampy paused on the porch and looked out silently over the lake for a moment through our large picture windows, while Dad brought in the drinks and Mom shushed us off to bed. As I settled under my covers, the unease I had felt in the field returned. I didn't know where it came from, but I sensed something different in Grampy's mood. For what seemed like long hours, I lay awake, the quiet conversation of the adults on the porch, filtering indistinctly into Nat's and my room, until a screen door quietly closed outside our window and steps returned up the path. With the picture of Grampy silhouetted in the evening sunset, I closed my eyes and drifted off to sleep—and to a dream that stirred within me.

Apple in hand, I arose, as Dad called us down to the car. The rest of the family had left. It was our turn to say our good-byes, before we returned to the cabin to gather up our belongings. As I started down the bank from the orchard, bits of the conversation earlier in the week returned to mind, *No one seems to know much about this disease, except for the fact that it is now taking Jane away from me, too.*

As we piled into the car, I turned and watched Dad give his father an affectionate kiss good-bye. Grampy put his hands on Dad's shoulders a moment and gazed into his eyes, "Come back soon." Dad nodded; they embraced, tenderly–gruffly, before Dad returned to the car. We waved to Grampy, amid the flush of roses, and followed the others out of the driveway.

Summer drew to a crisp end. Alas, school was coming. What an injustice, never mind a waste of valuable time, when there were marsh-mallows to roast, woods to explore, and a certain indignant donkey still to be prodded into gear. But, all in all, it had been a pretty good summer, even if it didn't stick around long enough!

AUTUMN

Overnight, the wind took most of the leaves down from the old elm. Fall has set in. Patty and her tribe left after breakfast. Otherwise, spent most of the day alone, walking and reading and keeping profitably busy, I hope. Not much else worth spelling out. Folded up early tonight.

Sinclair Weeks, Diary, October 3, 1966

4

ALZHEIMER'S DISEASE

Up where it's nine months of winter, Jane,
And three months of fall,
They don't grow cotton and the sun's kinda small.
Folks don't eat possum; there's no rabbit pies,
Baked beans and codfish win the weekly prize.
And when the mercury starts a droppin',
An' your joints start to stall,
You'll have to hurry up (Jane) your southern drawl,
And after tomorrow, it's 'you' not 'you all'
Let's get these changes made by fall—
These changes made by fall. . . .

Wedding Verse for Sinclair Weeks and Jane Rankin

JANE. . . WHO'S JANE? Grandma Jane sat abruptly forward. Grampy lowered the book he was reading and looked across at her on the Pine Room sofa. The smile on his lips wavered, as his wife cast her eyes anxiously about, *What's gotten into me!*

The leaves from the old elm that stood sentinel before the Big House settled down over the driveway, lawn, and circle, with a parting flush of colors. Autumn came, a first and then a second. And with the passing of the seasons came changes, noticeable in Grandma Jane's condition, less so in Grampy's. The fond memories of the middle-aged couple's new beginning—baked beans, codfish, and rabbit pies—faded, along with the once enchanting bloom on Grandma Jane's face, into the backdrop of the seasons.

*In 1906, Alois Alzheimer identified a clinical, non-heredi-
tary condition of presenile dementia, the onset of which is
insidious and subtle. In the early stages of this fatal disease,
the patient suffers emotional disturbances and odd, unpre-
dictable quirks of behavior. As the illness progresses, for as
long as ten to fifteen years, unless brought to an end by the
effects of advanced age, the patient gradually reaches a state
of total helplessness and requires institutional care.*

Grampy closed the book.

These words about Alzheimer's Disease were just that: words, a definition. The disease itself, in its all too-distinct symptoms, had been Grandma Jane's companion during the last years, slowly pushing Grampy out of the picture and claiming his lady for its own. Grandma Jane, too, had little say in the matter. Even an article about Alzheimer's, discovered under her bed, resulted in little else than familiarizing our grandma in the beginning with exactly what it was that had "gotten into her." From 1963 on, the north wing of the house cast a shadow over Cat Bow and its increasingly lonesome lord.

When Grandma Jane first became ill, I didn't understand what was happening. At first, I gave little thought to the empty place across from Grampy at the dining-room table. But, as the gap grew with the years, it became clear that something was wrong. Often, to our dismay, Grandma Jane would break into tears in front of us. At other times, shrill cries from her room at the end of the hall would disturb the deli-cate peace of the Big House.

The ripples spread out over Cat Bow. As the years passed, our new cousins—first, the Rankins and, then, the Robinsons—stopped coming up. Grampy frequently appeared preoccupied, both welcoming our vis-its and, yet, at times, distant. And, although no one said a word, it came to be understood that the north wing of the house was off limits to us grandchildren. The undertone that I had first sensed two years earlier at the conclusion of our Labor Day celebration became more pronounced with the advent of the autumn season.

So it was. In the beginning of Grandma Jane's illness, no one seemed to know exactly what was wrong. Grandma Jane had one of the early reported cases of Alzheimer's Disease. When Grampy walked her into the Pine Room for cocktail hour, it was hard for us children not to stare at her. Grandma Jane would sit there among us, silently gripping the quilt that lay across her lap. And yet something about her was distant, veiled, missing, as if drawn into another world. It was difficult to find the words to express, never mind understand, the change that slowly came upon her.

Grandma Jane's illness began innocently enough.

> *Dear Adele,*
>
> *Thank you so much for sending back my boots. I really have been wondering all winter where I left them and have missed them very much. You were sweet to do this, and I appreciate it. Remember me to Charley,*
>
> *Love, Jane*

At the outset of the illness, Grandma Jane simply forgot things— boots, her purse, her shopping bag, and now and again her name, ... her self. With time, those slips of memory became both more frequent and disturbing. On a visit to some friends, Grandma Jane just couldn't remember where she was. She kept excusing herself and walking around the house, upstairs and down, opening and closing doors, until Grampy, increasingly upset, excused them both and took her home.

As visits to friends became increasingly difficult, Grampy tried taking Grandma Jane to the movies, a distraction to get both her and himself out of the house. But Grandma Jane didn't do much better in public. Although Grampy managed to keep her in her seat, he was unable to restrain her from blurting out responses to what the actors were saying on the screen. They left, turning instead, over the long winter evenings, to the television set, which, in the beginning, they were able to enjoy together, sharing laughs and simple remarks.

Bearing the painful memory of Bea's illness and tragic death, Grampy sought out the best medical help available, turning to his close friends, Dr. Charles Lund and Francis "Mook" Boyer, an old army buddy, who later became the president of Smith, Kline, and French. Mr. Boyer responded to Grampy's queries by offering to provide experimental drugs for the treatment of the new illness, which was coming to be known as Alzheimer's Disease.

Along with the drugs, Mr. Boyer suggested that Grampy contact Dr. Wilder Penfield in Montreal, one of the leading neurologists of the day. Grampy did, and he and Jane began regular trips north. Though there was little understanding of the cause of the illness, the symptoms were becoming clearer. At the conclusion of their first visit, Grampy was told to keep regular and careful notes about Grandma Jane's progress:

> While sitting out on the terrace before dinner, she got up from her chair and said, "I'm going to pick my bleeding heart." Startled, I watched her walk over toward the flower bed and was greatly relieved when I understood that she was speaking about a flower.

Flowers in hand, at times there appeared to be a reprieve to the illness, and for precious moments Grandma Jane was her old, charming self. She was present and attentive to Grampy, as well as to the family and guests, both speaking up and listening with interest to the conversation. Even though Grandma Jane's memory wasn't perfect, Grampy made particular note of her comment one day, on the way home from shopping, about forgetting the cherries. Grandma Jane *had* remembered that the cherries were on the list—even if she overlooked the fact that she herself had picked them out. During these phases, Grampy's spirits were lifted, as the whole affair seemed to be nothing but a passing nightmare. Mentally, Jane seemed brighter, Grampy noted. The wonderful sparkle was still in her eyes, and she was always glad to see him.

> We embraced and kissed, Grampy wrote, like the old days. Most of the time she is in a good mood and often very cute about things. When Mrs. Ramsey helped her into her bed for her nap, she was a little restless, and Mrs. Ramsey said, "Lie back and close your eyes and think nice thoughts." Jane

looked up at her with a most impish look and said, "All right,
but what about your thoughts?"

As the disease progressed, these spirited entries into Grampy's journals gradually became fewer. Slowly but surely Grandma Jane settled into her dream world in the north wing of the house.

In response to Grandma Jane's slow withdrawal, Grampy tried different approaches to engage her. In the early days of the illness, he often brought us in to visit with Grandma Jane, as Grampy felt she enjoyed the distraction that we grandchildren, indeed, presented. Afterward, Grampy noted in his diary that our visit elicited more of a response from Grandma Jane than she had expressed over the day. We were unsure. Grandma Jane seldom talked with anybody except herself, and she would turn to us with a confused look on her face when we offered her some mints from the bowl that sat on her table. Unsure of what to do, we would put the treat into her hand, adding a quick and uncertain word. In time, we learned to bypass Grandma Jane, as the offerings invariably ended up in the folds of her robe or on the floor.

When we or our cousins were not at the farm, Grampy was left to his own searching devices:

> *I have tried to talk less and let her talk. Any talk I initiate, I*
> *try to be as sure as possible that Jane will understand. I have*
> *held all conversation very short. The meal times have been*
> *very leisurely, and I have tried not to watch Jane at all, as I*
> *find it makes her nervous if she thinks she is being watched.*
> *She talks much better when she is relaxed; consequently she*
> *talks better when she starts the conversation, as she has done*
> *her thinking before she speaks.*

Despite Grampy's efforts, Grandma Jane's condition continued to decline. It wasn't long before she had to be fed, and her walking slowed down to the point where she could only go about fifty yards before she would lean awkwardly forward and seem to lose control. These developments bothered Grandma Jane as much as they did Grampy, calling forth at times pained and searching expressions. At the conclusion of one of their trips to Montreal, Grandma Jane turned abruptly

to Grampy. "I want to know exactly how I am!" Grampy could give
no answer and had little success in explaining to Grandma Jane that
nobody knew much about this disease. "Except that it is killing me," she
declared. Grampy's gaze, always firm, steadfast, direct, wavered before
Grandma Jane's fixed expression.

Grampy kept regular contact with Drs. Lund and Penfield, revealing, in the process, something of his own progress with the disease:

> I don't suppose you have turned up anything new, which
> might give some hope of at least a slight improvement. If
> you do turn up anything, I assume obviously that you will
> let me hear from you.
>
> Jane doesn't give any indication of pain. Dr. Lund
> and I exchanged some correspondence with Dr. Cameron
> about some RNA from France. He told me that he had
> sent the information to you, and I suppose that even if
> it does amount to something, that it will be very slow in
> development and probably be too late to do us any good.
> However, a drowning man keeps reaching for straws....

The visits to Montreal became more frequent, and, as Grandma
Jane's condition continued to deteriorate, Grampy found himself making the long trip back alone. The drug treatments became more intensive, and it was requested that Grandma Jane stay on for observations:

> Although Mrs. Weeks is about as helpless as a mortal can be,
> she looks very well in the face, and it seems to me—tests or
> no tests—that there is some thought process going on in that
> brain of hers. A number of times during the day, she will say
> something that is thoughtful and to the point.

The time apart was difficult for both Grampy and Grandma Jane,
as her disorientation became more acute in her husband's absence. The
entries from the medical staff in Montreal revealed the onset of other
symptoms, which accompanied the disease itself:

> Some little depression here and there, and this time when
> Mr. Weeks went away, Mrs. Weeks seemed to be particu-

larly lonely. That evening, after having been in bed an hour or so, she sat up abruptly. When I asked her if I could get her anything, she said no, she was worrying about her husband.... After his regular evening call, she asked for him three times, before she finally fell asleep.... Also, this morning, before her bath, as we were sitting together, she had her pearl circlet pin on her nighty and kept saying, "He gave it to me." I said, "Mr. Weeks?" and she said, "yes." I said, "He loves you so much, Mrs. Weeks. He is always telling me how much he loves his Jane—and is always planning for you." She said, "Does he?" and her eyes filled with tears.

The reunions lifted both their spirits, Grampy describing how they went out to dinner at the Queen Elizabeth Hotel and danced for the first time since October. All things considered, Jane did pretty well, Grampy reported, and soon after he took her back to Cat Bow again with a new wheel chair and plans for changes in the household.

As nurses moved into the north wing of the house, life at Cat Bow settled into a routine, carefully set up around Grandma Jane's needs:

Up for an hour, sometimes more in the morning and after-noon. We wheel Jane out to the sun porch each day to have a change of scenery. She loves her garden, and often asks me to pick a flower for her. Her meals have become simpler, as diet appears to be important for her. She gets some enjoyment out of the television, although recently her gaze has tended to drift off from the screen, so that it appears that she is doing little more than listening to the program. She is best in the evening after she has had a nap and often sits contentedly beside me doing her needlework, which she still appears to have hung onto. She has taken a particular fancy to doing covers for the cushions.

The ups, as fleeting as they were precious, were followed by downs—longer, more intensive, and often anguishing, as Grandma

Jane became increasingly irritated and unmanageable. Frequently, the disquiet and confusion were accompanied by tears and would last the whole day. When we were visiting, Grampy would occasionally mention at the breakfast table that Grandma Jane had been in and out of her bed a number of times that night. Though Grandma Jane spoke less and less frequently, what she did reveal came from a bleeding heart: "What got me into this business anyway?...How long is this going on?...I wish to God I was dead!"

Grampy took a deep breath, as his diary entries became shorter and shorter—catching the precious parting glimpses that he held onto as long as he was able:

> *This evening, when we were sitting on the terrace, I commented on how lovely the view of the Presidential Peaks was. Jane looked off vacantly, and then quietly commented, "All this and heaven, too."*

One of Grampy's last entries, before the nurses took over the reports, harkened back to an old and sweet melody:

> *The other morning, a song appeared to play across Jane's lips. She announced to the nurse that she wanted to go shopping and stated that she was planning to buy two blue dresses. "Sinny and I are going to have a ball."*

A familiar tone, susceptible, tender, straightforward, concluded Grampy's duties:

> *So far nothing to be done that isn't being done.*

The last report on Grandma Jane and Grampy's condition came from an old and devoted friend, Al Lehman, at the conclusion of a letter he wrote to Grampy after his visit to Cat Bow:

> *...Sinclair, you have earned fame and fortune. But to me your attitude toward the two women of your heart is fully as praiseworthy as your great career achievements. My heart goes out to you, old friend. You are indeed a stout fellow.*

* * * * *

The branches of the old elm hung bare. September passed on into October, into November. Amidst the darkening days, Thanksgiving came; the family gathered. Grampy bowed his head at the dining-room table, paused, read:

> *Governor Bradford pointed out that they (the Pilgrims) had much to be thankful for. They had twenty acres of corn almost ready to harvest and a firm friendship with the Indians in their vicinity. The woods and rivers teemed with game and fish. They were no longer threatened by either starvation or annihilation. Instead of wondering about the advantages of Massachusetts Bay, perhaps they should all offer thanks to God for the blessings he had given them here at Plymouth.*

I folded my hands, as a bevy of candles whispered in the corners. The Thanksgiving story we had come to know over the years. The son of an English farmer, William Bradford was not only familiar with the harvest celebrations of England, but he had taken part in the annual Thanksgiving Day held on the third of October in his adopted land, Holland. After all that the Pilgrims had gone through since their arrival in the New World, Bradford inquired, would such a time of thanksgiving not be appropriate here in Plymouth, so that the small colony might "after a more special manner rejoice together?"

Governor Bradford's suggestion found ready agreement among the small colony, and preparations for the first Thanksgiving Day were soon begun. The twenty acres of Indian corn that the colony had planted had brought forth an abundant harvest—the acres of English barley and peas were more modest. It was clear to the colonists that they would not survive long without the friendship and support of the natives. Wisely, the Pilgrims concluded that their Indian allies should be invited to the festival. A messenger was immediately sent to Chief Massasoit, while the remaining men of the colony headed out into the woods fowling and to the shores to secure their catch for the table. Grampy read on thoughtfully:

> *In one day they killed enough turkeys to feed the whole company for*

almost a week. There were also eels, lobsters, and shellfish gathered from the bountiful shores of the bay. But not even this abundance seemed enough when the great chief Massasoit arrived with no less than ninety hungry men.

For a moment, even that budding diplomat Edward Winslow was speechless. Ninety braves! Knowing by now the Indian tendency to gorge as long as food was available, the colonist saw all their provisions for the winter vanishing. They did not realize that for Massasoit and his Wampanoags a harvest thanksgiving was also a customary festival.

Grampy paused to take a drink of cider. My eyes passed over the table—sweet potatoes, squash, carrots, gravy, cranberry sauce, pitchers of cider, and bowls full of stuffing spread out around the crisp wings of one of Cat Bow's prized turkeys. My appetite piqued, as my thoughts returned to the story.

Knowing what was expected of them, Massasoit sent a party of braves into the woods, who came back with five "fine deer." The game was presented ceremoniously to the leaders of their allies, Governor Bradford, Miles Standish, Edward, Winslow, William Brewster, Stephen Hopkins, and accepted gratefully—as were the fish, eels, and other sea creatures that the guests contributed to the feast.

From the household gardens, the women brought forth a bountiful harvest of vegetables: parsnips, carrots, turnips, onions, cucumbers, radishes, beets, cabbages, and wild fruits: gooseberries, strawberries, plums, and cherries, which, cooked in "dough cases," became the forerunner of the pies that I had glimpsed: pumpkin, pecan, and apple, waiting further in the wings. Wine from the wild grapes, that grew "very sweet and strong" throughout the coastal region, seasoned the meal, lifting the spirits of the Pilgrims and Indians alike.

Grampy read on, the description of the games of sport and skill, spurring my imagination:

There were shooting exhibitions with both guns and bows. Massasoit and his men were impressed to discover that some of these white men, especially Miles Standish, could handle a bow and arrow almost as well as an Indian. The red men were delighted to find that John Alden, John Howland, and the other younger men were ready and eager to join them in their races and wrestling matches.

Captain Standish entertained with military maneuvers. Choosing his best men, he marched the company briskly down the main street into the clearing where the feast was being held.

"Rest your muskets," he barked.

We younger members of the ranks sat forward. As the men "expertly thrust their pieces in the spikelike rest that supported the heavy matchlock during firing," Grampy carried on with the maneuvers:

"Draw out your match." The long match was made ready. "Try your match. Guard your pan. Present. Give fire!" The volley boomed out, to the Indians' mixture of delight and dismay.

"Bring up your musket," the captain shouted. "Poise your musket and recover your rest. Shoulder your musket."

We came to attention:

Always quick to seize an opportunity to impress his Indian allies, Standish climaxed his military parade by firing one of his cannons on Fort Hill. With the same brisk military order, the big gun was loaded (but not shotted) and the match was applied to the touchhole by the captain himself. Whoom! The Indians had been astonished by the crash of the white men's muskets. But this mighty gun seemed to steal the thunder from heaven itself. Truly, Massasoit had been wise to make peace with these people!

But the display of power was not the main purpose of this feast; by far the largest part of it was devoted to uninhibited drinking and eating and gaiety.

Gone were the fears that once made a worried Standish post extra guards against a treacherous attack. By the time this first Thanksgiving was over, the formal alliance between Plymouth and the men of the Massasoit had been cemented by strong ties of genuine friendship. Red men and white men parted, vowing to repeat the feast the following year and for many years to come.

ONE SMALL CANDLE." Grampy paused and looked across the table at us, as we settled back into our seats. "So it was on the first Thanksgiving, children. The celebration goes back to the settlement of this land by your ancestors. They realized that they had much to be grateful for." I glanced up at Grampy. A reflective note touched his voice, "We celebrate the holiday today to remind ourselves of this fact." Grampy paused, before closing the book, "Your Grandmother Bea often reminded us to count our blessings."

* * * * *

Two sterling Westminster tones sounded from the north end of the house. Rising from the table, Grampy asked if anyone wanted to join him for a walk. Dad nodded. Nat and I stepped forward, anxious to take a good breath and to digest the Thanksgiving offerings that had filled our plates.

As Dad and Grampy tucked in their scarves, we headed out the driveway and down the road toward the fields. The golden color of the pasture had paled into dark greens and browns, as the sun had dipped below the summer zenith. A cool autumn breeze stirred the air. I glanced along the trees that lined the fence, their naked branches reaching out into the afternoon, before my gaze settled on a large rock in the field that Dad called to Grampy's attention, "Do you remember the walk we took up to that boulder in 1948?" Grampy considered a moment and turned to Dad, whose voice had become more reflective, "You told me you had something important that you wanted to share with me, as we made our way up through the field and sat down on the boulder." A smile touched Dad's face, fainter on Grampy's.

"Yes," Grampy paused, "I found myself falling in love again and wanted some feedback on the thought of remarriage." Grampy's words rested in the air, before settling back into silence, into reflections. Nat and I walked along quietly beside our father and grandfather into the waning afternoon, the browns fading to the grays of dusk.

My thoughts rested with the no-longer-newlyweds, as I realized that the distress that I had come to feel for Grandma Jane was surpassed only by the silent grief that had grown in me for Grampy. Despite the embraces and affections that Grampy tenderly bestowed upon Grandma Jane, she paid less and less attention to him. Though ever faithful, Grampy's visits to Grandma Jane in the north wing of the house became shorter. The care that he gave her accomplished little more than prolonging Grandma Jane's state, beyond the few years that she had initially been given. Not even the Lord of Cat Bow's quiet bedside prayers, Grandma Jane's hand held vacantly in his, were able to rouse his lady from the deepening spell into which she was being drawn.

The road led on toward the woods, cooler, darker, strewn with damp, matted leaves that kicked themselves up at our feet. Tucking up my collar, I looked over at Grampy. The day before I had come upon him in the hallway, as he returned from Grandma's Jane's room. Startled by the handkerchief that Grampy was rubbing across his eyes, I asked him if he was okay. Grampy paused, looked down at me. Our gazes met. The hallway was silent; the ticking of the grandfather clock filled my ears—time interminable. Grampy rested his hand for a moment on my shoulder . . . and then continued on through the Telephone Room and out to the greenhouse. Tucking the handkerchief back into his pocket, he gently cupped a blossom that lingered by his side, before lifting his gaze on out into the autumn afternoon. The tear that I had glimpsed at the conclusion of our family reunion the Labor Day before last had broken for a moment through the surface, and with it returned the sadness, sudden and inexplicable, that I had felt.

I stepped back into the Pine Room, and walked quietly over to Grampy's desk, my glance settling on a small card, resting against the delicate flanks of one of the glass elephants that rose up into the spaces. *There is a time of war, and a time of peace, a time to keep, and a time to cast away, a time to laugh and a time to weep. . . .*

* * * * *

We walked on into the late afternoon, my glance rising beyond the boulder and on up the flanks of Mt. Orne. The parting rays of the sun gave way to clouds. A shadow touched a corner of my universe. I took a breath, reflected. My last memory of Grandma Jane was the most vivid. The family had gathered together at the Mountain View House in Whitefield to put on a surprise birthday party for Grampy, his seventieth. Colorful streamers, a sumptuous buffet, our swelling ranks, and a live band succeeded in lifting Grampy's spirits throughout the evening. In response to the lyrics and songs that each family composed in his honor—heartfelt and often humorous attempts to put into word, if not rhyme, all that our grandfather meant to us—Grampy delightedly extended to us a one-man standing ovation.

After the last of the family had boomed out their tribute, we all rose to toast the Lord of Cat Bow with a full chorus of "Happy Birthday." Grampy was tickled. A round of applause was followed by a wholesale exchange of kisses, before Grampy called for our attention and drew forth a written offering of his own—its source uncertain. When all were quiet, young and old alike, Grampy set his glasses down over his nose and launched forth in his most sonorous voice:

> *There's nothing whatever the matter with me,*
> *I'm just as healthy as I can be.*
> *I have arthritis in both knees,*

A hand fumbled across his knee caps, . . .

> *And when I talk, I talk with a wheeze.*

. . . rose plaintively to his chest.

> *My pulse is weak, and my blood is thin,*
> *BUT I'M AWFULLY WELL FOR THE SHAPE I'M IN!*

Leaning forward to us grandchildren, who had lined up before him, a courageous smile puckered itself up on Grampy's lips, before spreading itself delightedly on out over ours. Grampy took a breath.

> *Arch supports I have for my feet*

. . . and tenderly pirouetted in front of us.

> *Or I wouldn't be able to be on the street.*
> *Sleep is denied me, night after night,*
> *And every morning I look a sight.*
> *My memory's failing . . .*

Grampy scratched his head, searching for the words...

My head's in a spin,

...fumbled in his pockets.

I'm practically living on aspirin.
BUT, I'M AWFULLY WELL FOR THE SHAPE I'M IN!

Bolstering himself up and patting himself on the chest, the smile returned with the refrain—sheepishly on Grampy's lips, less so on ours. Taking a deep breath and fixing us grandchildren in his sights, Grampy brought the ditty to a fitting and measured conclusion:

The moral is—as this tale I unfold—
That for you and me, who are growing old,
It's better to say—"I'm fine" with a grin,
THAN TO LET EVERYONE KNOW THE SHAPE WE'RE IN!

Grampy opened his arms to the cheers, which were followed by a hearty round of embraces.

The decks cleared, Aunt Frannie motioned to the musicians, before curtsying in front of her father. Rejuvenated, Grampy steered his daughter onto the dance floor, as the band picked up the tune and played on.

Around and around Grampy and Aunt Frannie whirled, beaming at each other. A good dance Grampy loved and, in our estimation, was remarkably agile for a father, grandfather, and even great-grandfather! Spurred on by the music, the rest of us pushed our chairs aside, secured a partner, and joined in around the lead couple. It was a spectacle! Fathers and daughters, aunts and nephews, cousins and cousins and more cousins of all shapes and sizes. Every conceivable combination was tried, as we slipped across the dance floor, bumping into each other, stepping on toes, and wearing out the old box-step, polka, and waltz.

After we had exhausted ourselves, the lights were lowered, and, by special request, the band played, "Won't You Come Home Bill Bailey," Grampy's favorite. Once again the ranks parted, as this time Grampy chose a partner, his second daughter, Aunt Patty, who happily allowed him to escort her back onto the floor. Grampy's second wind was blowing gracefully as they twirled around and around, rousing a renewed wave of applause from the ranks. We all watched the couple with great pleasure, until Grampy abruptly broke away from Aunt Patty and, with arms outstretched, danced on alone—turning, sashaying, bowing.

As I followed Grampy's steps, he suddenly appeared sad and immeasurably older. I was confused and, overhearing Mom's and Dad's words, realized that Grampy was not entirely alone. Instead, he had switched partners, gathering up his invisible bride, a wilting Southern belle, whom he had summoned from her bed and transported across the spaces into his arms. Bewildered, I noticed tears gathering in Dad's eyes, as Grampy slowly waltzed on, guiding his invisible partner across the dance floor.

* * * * *

Our steps led us back to the Big House. Evening had settled over the farm. Grampy paused and scraped his feet on the mat, before opening the front door and stepping in. Dad and Nat followed him into the vestibule and entrance room. I lingered on the doorstep. The north wing of the house was dark, curtains discreetly drawn. I turned my gaze up along the stone wall to the barn, which settled back into its sleepy North Country embrace, before raising my glance through the still branches of the old elm to the darkening flanks of Mt. Orne that rose up into the enfolding backdrop of the night. All was quiet.

Dad's brief exchange with Grampy echoed quietly within me, along with a memory from another walk, one that Dad and I had taken over the summer. In response to a passing question that I had asked Dad, regarding his time in the Air Force, he shared a rare glimpse of his own mother. "Before I went off to war, my parents asked if there was anything special I wanted to do. I told them I'd love to go to Lancaster with them for the weekend, and so we set off. Toward the end of our stay, your Grandmother was moved to offer me some motherly advice. Feeling my oats as a young volunteer recruit, I interrupted her, 'Ah, leave me alone, Mother. I'll be gone before long, and you won't have to give me advice anymore.'" Dad paused, "My words silenced her. Looking at my mother, I was surprised to see tears filling her eyes." I lifted my head to Dad in time to see him glance off, as he brushed his own eyes. "That was to be the last time I would see her. The next day, we parted."

Before putting us to bed that evening, Ma filled in the picture, "Your Grandmother contracted pneumonia from your Uncle John, when she hastened to visit him in a military hospital. Your uncle had just returned home from the war wounded. The health conditions weren't good at the time, and not only was she tired, but, undoubtedly, deeply concerned."

Ma's and my gazes met, and then, as she kissed me good night, my thoughts lifted to the young officer, seasoned by his thirty-eight combat missions in the Pacific theater, flying home in the cargo plane. . . to visit his mother's fresh grave in Lancaster's cemetery. Yes, Dad had plenty of time to think on that long flight home.

I breathed in, lifting my gaze further, looking, searching . . . . Overhead, a lone star glanced down from the encircling heavens, awakening words of an old Concord neighbor named Emerson, which had delicately impressed themselves upon my young mind:

> *Wouldtst thou teach,*
> *How in each mortal*
> *Immortality reflects,*
> *Thou must penetrate the portal*
> *Where thine angel thee perfects,*
> *Learn where the departed are,*
> *Hitch thine wagon to a star.*

5

THE LORD'S COMING TO DINNER

"YOUR GRANDFATHER came into the world on June 15, 1893, at West Newton, Massachusetts and, as he often related, very narrowly missed making an untimely exit soon thereafter." Dad leaned into his reflection in the bedroom mirror as he gathered the ends of his tie. Sitting up on the bed in our Sunday School clothes, Nat, Bea, Brad, and I strained to follow Dad's words amidst the folds of the tie.

"At that time, your great-grandparents were living at the corner of Otis and Lenox Streets." Dad arched his neck, "Dr. Perkins, who was to 'officiate' at your grandfather's birth, had been a frequent visitor in the days preceding and thus wasn't surprised, when, as the story goes, he was summoned on a dark and stormy night to the bedside." Dad glanced at his visa-vi, reflected, "The doctor arrived in his familiar horse and buggy in the midst of a mighty downpour, performed his service— which was pretty straightforward in those days—and continued on his evening rounds." Draped around the bed poles, we leaned with Dad into the mirror.

"Back home later in the night, the good doctor found himself restless. Lying in bed, he finally roused himself and his wife with the exclamation, 'Fanny, I didn't like the looks of that Weeks baby.'" We exchanged uncertain glances in the mirror. "A few minutes later," Dad went on, "the doctor was dressed and out the door. Throwing the wet harness back onto his weary horse, the two hurriedly retraced their steps to Otis Street, where Dr. Perkins found the Weeks baby *in extremis* and red in the face!" I slid down the bed pole. "Not wasting a moment, the doctor threw open his bag and drew on all his means, including a touch of strychnine, for which we can be eternally grateful."

Dad pulled his tie tight, adjusted the ends, and glanced at us over his shoulder through the mirror, before turning around and rousing us from our rapt attention, "Come on it's 12:00 noon, your grandfather will be here any moment. Let's make sure everything is ready!"

* * * * *

In the kitchen, Mom was finishing up her preparation of the hors d'oeuvres when the doorbell rang. Placing the bowls of smoked oysters, nuts, artichoke hearts, and Grampy's old reliable favorite, popcorn, on the tray and popping the last olives into our gaping mouths, she gave us a quick glance—tucking, arranging, parting our hair—before shuffling us out of the kitchen in front of her. This time we were the hosts and were expected to be on our best behavior.

As Dad led our guest into the hallway, we hailed our grandfather warmly. Smiling, Grampy leaned over and gave us each a big kiss and tousle of the hair, before straightening up and passing Dad his hat. Grampy was done up for the occasion himself and appeared to us most distinguished in his "city garb." As he took off his coat, the first thing that caught our eye was a gold watch chain that dangled out of one pocket of his vest, trickled across the front of his shirt, and disappeared in the next pocket. Suspenders peeked out of the sides of his jacket, and a silver tie clip bearing his initials completed his attire. Straightening our own loose ends, Bea and Brad took Grampy by the hands as we escorted him into the living room, where he was greeted by a blaze in the fireplace

Grampy took a seat beside the fire, while Nat, Bea, Brad, and I squeezed in alongside each other on the sofa, across the way. Grampy seemed pleased to see us cleaned up and asked us questions about school, sports, and our latest escapades, which we answered in turn, surprised by the note of excitement in our voices.

Mom, who had slipped out of the room while we engaged Grampy, returned with the hors d'oeuvres and asked us to pass them around. Eager to be the bearers of good tidings, Bea and I jumped up and proceeded to do the rounds in our well-rehearsed fashion. We went up to Grampy, put a bowl of olives well within his reach, and asked him if he cared for any. Then, flabbergasted, we watched as our esteemed guest dug a large hand into the bowl and popped three or four into his mouth. After we had completed the circuit, we set the bowls down in front of us on the table and endeavored, as inconspicuously as possible, to salvage the remaining contents. The next time we were called to make the rounds, Mom noticed that we had nearly exhausted the provisions and suggested that this time we set the bowls down in front of Grampy. The bounty out of reach, we redirected our attention to the adults.

Grampy was busy, catching Mom and Dad up with the latest events of the family—a topic that appeared to know no limit. Alongside the usual swelling of the ranks, our ears perked up as Grampy went on to speak about the farm. There, too, the progeny had been prolific: "Seven new calves, five sheep, two pigs. . . ." Grampy paused, drawing us forward in our seats, "And I don't know how many turkeys, but the coop is a flurry!" A smile broke out on our faces. Between kith, kin, and Cat Bow livestock, Grampy was surrounded by devoted heirs—bar one recalcitrant jackass, as ever a stalwart member of the loyal opposition.

As Grampy took a drink, I sat forward and asked him about "Tonto?..."

"*Tomo*," Dad, who was the source of my information, corrected me.

I nodded, before turning back to Grampy, "Yes, the butler, who rushed to pick up Great-Granddad at the train station one day, when you were a little boy."

A smile touched Grampy's lips, "The story lives on, I see." Grampy reflected a moment, "Well, children, when I was your age, cars were a rare sight. The principle means of transportation was horsedrawn buggies and wagons—station wagons they were called when someone was to be picked up at the train station."

Mom passed Grampy some artichoke hearts. He took one, leaning forward to rub it in the dip, and carried on, "We had a burly coachman named James and a diminutive Japanese butler," Grampy glanced over at me, "named *Tomo*, who weighed in at about one-third of James' size. This contrast touched off a bit of comedy one day, during the five o'clock commuter exodus from Boston, that had our Newton neighbors chuckling for a good week."

Grampy continued, "Your great-grandfather had telephoned to have James meet him at the station at a specified time. Tomo took the call, but couldn't find the coachman anywhere. Finally, and somewhat frantically, the butler hurried to hitch up the carriage himself. Assuming that the garb was as much a part of the job as horse and harness, Tomo hustled into James' greatcoat and top hat and set forth in all haste to 'make the train.'"

We leaned forward in our seats, "There was a steep pitch leading down to the commuter station, and the gallant Tomo, realizing by now that he could do more or less as he pleased, took the corner 'on two wheels,' as we said in those days." A smile snuck up on Grampy's face, "Tomo's arrival was perfectly timed. As your great-grandfather and his friends and neighbors stepped down off the platform, the well-known equipage of Mayor Weeks came tearing down the grade at breakneck speed, topped by little Tomo draped in the ample folds of that greatcoat, with James' oversize topper pulled down over his eyes."

"WHOA!" I held onto my seat. Grampy continued, "The butler's reedy Oriental voice held little authority for the horses. Poor Tomo, who had enough to contend with with the outfit, never mind the steeds, desperately braced all of his five feet against the reins." Grampy shifted his weight forward; we, back. "By the time the horses were brought to a halt, everybody in the station was in an uproar, except your great-grandfather, whose only comment was, 'That surely was a train well met.'"

Grampy's smile spilled over into a hearty laugh, "Tomo, who had never signed up for such exertions, was glad to get the rest of the evening off, before turning his attentions back to the steadier domestic side of the household."

Grampy's description of Great-Granddad added a new wrinkle to the poised and venerable portrait that we looked up to above the great stone fireplace atop Mt. Prospect.

* * * * *

Grampy sat back on the sofa, "Life was a lot simpler when I was a boy." He glanced across at us, "Can you imagine, children, a world without electric lights, watches, telephones, radios, televisions, cars, and planes—to say nothing of movies, comic books, popsicles, candy bars, or cola drinks?" We looked at each other incredulously.

Grampy's smile settled into reflections of the earlier days, "None of us knew what a comfort it might be to sit back and listen to the sound of the vacuum cleaner, the automatic washer, or frostless refrigerator—not to mention the sweet hum of the automatic heater that responded to the touch of a thermostat. Our heat was piled up in the woodshed, and the bucksaw we used to get at it was powered by our elbow grease, and nothing more."

Grampy glanced at the fire, "If you wanted light or heat in those days, you had to work for it. Coal, wood, and kindling had to be lugged in, and the ashes out. On top of that, nearly every home had some sort of contraption for sifting the ashes, which allowed us to retrieve the good cinder bits, for a second burning. Fragile lamp chimneys had to be washed and polished, wicks had to be trimmed, and every so often all the lamps in the house had to be refueled from the family's gallon-size kerosene can." The world Grampy described was, indeed, a foreign one to us.

"When the time came to light those lamps, touch off the kitchen fire, or kindle Father's after-dinner cigar, we had matches, 'Portland Stars.'" Grampy smiled, "Though a good step beyond the early settlers' flint-a-steel, these 'eight-day-matches,' as they were popularly called, were the first and, no doubt, worst matches American children were ever taught *not* to play with. Those little splints of wood could raise quite a ruckus, and unfortunately they often did. I remember, a number of times in my youth, running to the window as our local fire engine, a three-horse hitch of big grays, thundered down the street at top speed, bell clanging, smoke billowing from the pamper, men and animals straining every nerve." Grampy raised his eyebrows, "It was a breath-stopping spectacle if ever there was one."

My gaze was drawn by the flames that stirred in the hearth behind Grampy, who took a drink before continuing, "Yes, life was pretty simple in those days." A smile touched his face, "Apart from the intermittent refrains of the fire alarm, the only music we had in the house was a harmonica that I lay claim to, my sister Katherine's recorder, Father's sturdy baritone voice, and the family piano, adorned with Mother's hymn book and a big brown volume of *Home and Fireside Songs*. Though a modest choir, we managed to strike up a good tune."

Dad refreshed Grampy's drink, encouraging him to tell us about the ice cubes they availed themselves of as children.

Grampy lifted his glass, "In those days, ice cubes weighed a sturdy 100 pounds. Freckled with sawdust, they came from a nearby country pond by way of an icehouse. On a warm summer's day, when our larder needed a good cooling off, Mother would put a six-inch card in the front window, and, sure enough, before long a muscular chap in a damp covered wagon, with a 'Gay Nineties Ice Cube'—all three dripping steadily—would appear at our door. Stowed away in our ice chest, the cube stoically dispensed last winter's slowly waning chill to our meat, milk, butter, and other perishables." Grampy nodded his head with mock seriousness, "And woe betide the one who forgot to empty the big collecting pan beneath the ice chest before the unrelenting drip became a flood!"

* * * * *

As we sat back in the sofa, the conversation turned to the purpose of Grampy's visit to the Big City, a reunion with his old B Battery mates of the Dugout Club, an occasion, always, of the greatest joy for Grampy. Among the many and celebrated circles that Grampy's life had lead him into, the simple but hearty ranks of his old Battery Boys had remained a true devotion throughout Captain Weeks' years. Many were the stories we had heard about how, even in the busiest periods of Grampy's career, when political and business obligations were most pressing, Grampy always found time for a Dugout mate who needed a helping hand or an encouraging word. The snatches that I had gleaned from this chapter in Grampy's life had left a vivid picture in my mind—of my grandfather chasing the notorious bandit, Pancho Villa, along the Mexican border. Dad asked Grampy about the Battery, prodding memories of earlier days.

"I'll never forget the day, children, when I won my two stripes as Corporal of B Battery, 1st Battalion of Field Artillery, Massachusetts Volunteer Militia. Among the honorary awards I've received, that was the most important and hardest earned diploma of them all." Grampy shook his head. "I still chuckle at the fact that it all started with a simple

house party at the home of a college friend named Margaret Merrill."
Grampy set his drink down.

"At the end of my Freshman year at college, I met a man who talked
so enthusiastically about Battery B of the Massachusetts Volunteer
Militia that I joined the organization the following Friday evening and
showed up at camp the next morning." Grampy reflected. "I had 'made'
all the clubs that any boy would want to make at college, but Battery
B was in a class of its own; it gave me a real workout. Field Artillery in
those days was horse-drawn. We were a mounted outfit, which, you can
imagine, pleased me, and I eventually became a member of Battery B's
'Rough Riding Team.'" A smile lit my face, as I imagined Grampy gal-
loping after Great-Granddad across the plains of Boston.

Grampy continued, "The Rough Riding Team went into the riding
ring with our horses equipped with nothing more than a bridle and sur-
cingle. The routine included dismounting and mounting at a trot and at
a gallop, both on the flat and over hurdles. Once we mastered the first
step, two horses were coupled together for the same exercises—and,
finally, three steeds with six riders, forming a pyramid. The toughest
stunt, for me at least, was vaulting off a horse and back onto the same
horse's back, facing to the rear. In this exercise, it wasn't unusual to
throw yourself over the horse and onto the tanbark." Bea winced; Nat
arched his back; Brad grimaced; I pulled in the reins.

Grampy rode on, his story taking him from New England to a barren mesa on the Mexican border—the starting point, as he later wrote,
"of that 'long, long trail a-winding' into the mud and memories of the
Allied Armies dug-in and deployed behind a monstrous battlefront of
trenches that stretched across the entire map of France."

"We drilled once a week and went to a summer training camp for a
week each year—hardly enough training to make real soldiers out of us,
but we got along and learned how to handle the three-inch field pieces
that were standard equipment for light Field Artillery of that day and
age." Grampy looked at us, "You all are too young to appreciate such
things, but I'm a strong believer in the fact that nothing would send
high-school youngsters on to college with greater maturity and appreciation of their opportunities than a period of military training with its
practical arts and sciences."

Grampy was right. We were still a bit young to understand the vir-

tues of the kind of training about which he was speaking. What caught
our eye, however, was the glamour of his battery exploits, including
his brief tour of duty during the International Workers of the World
strikes in Lawrence, Massachusetts. Imagining Grampy as a mounted
cavalry officer, riding back and forth in front of the huge Arlington
Mills, with a carbine and saber, inspired us—though we were little able
to appreciate this fact of life, as well.

With the flare-up of World War I in August of 1914, things got
more serious. In the summers of 1912 through 1914, B Battery went to
training camp on Cape Cod and, for the first time in Grampy's experience, fired live ammunition across the marshes, to the great sand dunes
to the north of the town of Barnstable. For more than a year, there had
been war maps featured and front-page war news headlined in the daily
newspaper, but that was a chapter for a later date.

Grampy fortified himself with another handful of popcorn, before
redirecting his attention to us. By this time, his three-piece suit itself
had taken on a distinct luster.

"In the springtime of 1916, there was gunfire and bloodshed down
by the Rio Grande, along the U.S.-Mexican border. Pancho Villa, billed
by some as a 'bandit leader,' had assembled enough men and munitions,
and surrounded himself with an aura of sufficient magnetism, to be
rated as a 'revolutionist' with a guerrilla-style army and a 'cause' that
gained him some fractional support in his own country—until his raids
extended across the border into United States territory."

"Overnight, Pancho Villa drew bigger war headlines than the Kaiser. Our government promptly ordered General Pershing to lead a puni-
tive expedition into Mexico, in hot pursuit of the raiders. In support
of General Pershing's movement, National Guard units from several
states, including ours, were dispatched to points along the border. The
National Guard expedition from Massachusetts assembled at Framingham. And the men of B Battery, with our three-inch light artillery and
equipment, were a part of it."

"In Framingham—and in the public press—there was a great 'to
do' about this business. Quite a number of our B Battery boys, their
courage plucked up, hurriedly set about getting themselves married. At
the station, it seemed as though the troops were outnumbered by the

mobilization of families and friends, who came to bid farewell to their soldier sons, brothers, husbands, and beaus."

As Grampy's words evoked images of the crowd, I glanced about for a young, quiet, brown-haired mother, a babe in her arms, her eyes set upon a parting husband.

Grampy carried on, "It was quite a traffic jam. By midnight we had packed up our duffel bags, bulging canvas tents, guns, and caissons and were ready to make our move. A Pullman car had been ordered for the officers, day coaches of the 1880 vintage for the rank and file."

"What about the horses, Grampy?" Bea's question was accompanied by a gentle note of concern.

Grampy turned to her, "We brought some single mounts with us, Bea, and a few mules. But, the draft animals to pull the artillery pieces were to be picked up on the border in Texas."

We journeyed on West with Grampy. "The train bumped along with regular stops to water our animals, which were accustomed neither to the fanfare nor to the mode of transportation. At these way stations, crowds gathered, flags in hand, to cheer us on, while the train whistle blew almost non-stop. Needless to say, none of us got much sleep that night. The next morning, Massachusetts, and the farewells now behind us, things were suddenly pretty quiet. A long sweltering journey lay ahead of us."

A smile returned to Grampy's face. "I recall a station in Ohio, where the train came to a halt with our day coach astride the main street of a little town and remained there, as was not uncommon in the military, for some time. It was a hot day. Every window in the car was open, and each of its passengers was giving ear to a rollicking ditty rendered in good voice by Private Dave Sigourney, famous in our Battery for his repertoire of practically every off-color song in the folklore of camp, trail, and barbershop. By the time we were underway again, I suspect the town fathers and mothers uttered a sigh of relief."

"In St. Louis, we also left a colorful impression. By that time, the heat was pretty intense, and when the train stopped, some of the troops hustled to dig up hoses, so they could not only water down the horses, but cool themselves off, as well. They gave the horses a good shower, but were only half way through their own, when the whistle sounded, and the train headed on its way once again." Dad laughed; we were agape. "It was quite a sight seeing the boys, stark naked, chasing the train down the tracks. Hanging out the windows, we waved their clothes as we cheered them on." Grampy paused to wet his whistle, "I don't think those fellows ever ran so fast in their lives." A banner of wet clothes flapped from the windows, as we continued on west, Grampy at the helm.

"Our train finally arrived at Fort Bliss, Texas—which, name aside, was about the dreariest sight any of us had seen. All around us stretched a hot, white expanse of sand, interrupted only by cacti, often knee high, and well armed with an array of disagreeable thorns. This was going to be home for the next months—a home, we were soon to discover, that we shared with a host of equally disagreeable critters, including tarantulas, scorpions, and as unseemly an assortment of bugs as any of us had laid eyes on."

Grampy directed his words once again to Nat, Bea, Brad, and me, "One of the things that army life teaches you is that you can get used to pretty much anything. Ditches and drains were dug, our tents set up and secured against the frequent dust storms, and we even managed a semblance of comfort. After we had stretched our limbs and settled in a bit, a number of us went down to a huge corral near Camp Cotton with a good 6,000 horses in it. There we were told to go on in and take our choice. Well, we did, which wasn't particularly to the liking of the horses. Some of these Western nags were still a bit wild and ornery. At one time, three of my own section men were in the Fort Bliss hospital with broken limbs and plenty of time to compose valorous, if inventive, letters from the front—recounting their exertions on behalf of Uncle Sam and their loved ones at home."

"We spent most of the day in maneuvers, drilling and firing, as we dashed across the desert, kicking up dust storms. As you can imagine, this got rather tiresome, particularly since none of us had seen neither hide nor hair of the notorious Pancho Villa." Grampy chuckled, "A couple of the boys from two of Boston's finer families, who concluded that they had better things to look forward to, decided one evening that they had enough of military life. Pressing a couple of weary mules into service, they tanked up with the local "brew" and headed for home. Well, they got fifteen miles, but not much more, before they passed out and were led back to camp the next morning, atop their mules, by a search party we had sent out."

* * * * *

Grampy sat back in his seat, his gaze turning for a moment to the fire, "The evenings offered plenty of time for reading and reflecting. As a young boy, I had developed an interest in a native son from Lancaster, Colonel Edward Ephram Cross, who was one of the North's unsung heroes during the Civil War—rendering his country the ultimate service one can give. My interest was particularly piqued, when I discovered that Colonel Cross also spent some time in the Southwest and Mexico." Though the name, Cross, had a ring to it, it was not immediately familiar to us. Grampy had done some research on his fellow townsman and went on to sing the colonel's praises.

"Cross was born in Lancaster in April, 1832. He was educated at the Lancaster Academy, before he started upon a career as a journeyman printer, his first job being as a Printer's Devil with the *Coos County Democrat*. Like many in his position, Cross's work in the printing field and his itch to travel gradually moved him into the newspaper profession and directed his gaze west."

Grampy crossed his legs, gathering up a couple of stray popcorn kernels that had settled into the folds of his trousers, "In 1854, Cross moved to Ohio, where he became a reporter and later editor of the *Cincinnati Daily Times*. The opening of the West presented the young man with many opportunities, ranging from steamboat building, to politics, mining, trapping, buffalo hunting, publishing, and stints in the military, where his greatest ability lay."

Nat and I perked up, as the story continued. "In the early 1860's, Cross had made his way farther West, moving across the border into Mexico, where he served as a Lieutenant Colonel in the Mexican Army. It was during this time that he received news of the attack on Fort Sumter and the beginning of the Civil War. Resigning his position at once, Cross returned home and immediately offered his services to the Governor of New Hampshire. Recognizing Cross's experience, Lancaster's native son was given the task of organizing the Fifth New Hampshire Regiment, whose command he assumed."

"Cross quickly earned the respect of all who served with and under him. He was an exceptional leader of men, his military skills were exceeded only by his humanity. Throughout the Civil War, the Fighting Fifth, as the regiment came to be known, was engaged in eighteen battle actions against the Confederate forces and present at five more, including the siege of Appomattox. The Fighting Fifth sustained the greatest loss of any infantry or cavalry regiment in the entire Union Army—nearly half of its 2,496 men either killed or wounded in action. Cross himself received eleven wounds in battle, before his time came in the Battle of Gettysburg."

We sat forward in our seats. "On twelve occasions, Cross's superiors recommended him for promotion. General Hancock's words expressed the feelings of the group: *The conduct of this regiment has been heroic; in the most important battles it has been highly distinguished. To Colonel Cross, much of this honor is due; he has faithfully disciplined his regiment, given it the highest tone, and always led it into battle.* Political decisions, however, appeared to hold back Cross's promotion."

Grampy's voice became quieter and more reflective, "On the morning of the Battle of Antietam, after the Fifth New Hampshire had crossed the creek, Colonel Cross halted his troops and addressed them: 'Soldiers, the Rebel Army is in front; the Potomac River is in their rear. We must whip the enemy this day, or we shall be disgraced and ruined. I expect every officer and soldier to do his duty like a man. No one must leave the ranks unless badly wounded. If I fall, leave me on the field until the battle is over. Stand firm and fire low.'"

"It was during this battle that the Fighting Fifth was credited with saving Richardson's Division from being outflanked. Cross wrote from the battle lines, 'I had been in several battles before, but they were nothing in comparison with Antietam.... If the Rebels didn't hear the Apache war-hoop that day, it was not my fault, for I yelled it until I was hoarse. My men fought nobly, gloriously; never wavered, never shrank. Not a man but the wounded and dead fell out. My officers, also, conducted themselves like heroes. As for myself, I was hit five times but not seriously injured.'"

Grampy went on, the battle line shifting to Fredericksburg. Midwinter was approaching. "December 13, 1862 was a dark day. In the midst of the conflict, a fragment from a shell knocked Colonel Cross unconscious. Another fragment brought him back to his senses when it struck his leg. The battle swept over him and then back, leaving him caught between the two sides. 'Dizzy and faint,' Cross wrote, 'I had enough sense to lay myself out, feet to the foe . . . I lay on the field four hours—the most awful moments of my life. As the balls from our lines hissed over me within a foot of my head, I covered my face with both hands and counted rapidly from 1 to 100. . . . When it became dark, some of my men found me and took me to the hospital.' "

"Cross recovered in time for the battle of Gettysburg. As he led his four trim regiments into the contest, General Hancock called out to him, 'Cross, this is the last time you will fight without a star.' The Colonel did not break stride as he responded, 'Too late, General. This is my last battle.' " Grampy paused, his gaze distant, "Cross was rallying his men around 6:00 in the evening when a mini-ball pierced his abdomen and came out near the spine. He was fully conscious throughout his waning hours and suffered much pain before he died at midnight. The last words he was reported to have said were, 'I did hope I would live to see peace and our country resolved. Thank Heaven, I have done my duty.' "

A gentle tremor touched Grampy's voice. I looked at Dad and then back at Grampy. "Colonel Edward E. Cross was brought home to Lancaster to be buried in the place where his tour of duty began."

* * * * *

Dad asked Grampy a number of questions about Colonel Cross, before Grampy returned to his own military stint, completing the chapter with an account of bullfights that the troops, disguised in civilian attire, attended across the border in Mexico; a visit to the great Elephant Butte Dam, and a lighter touch—an episode, involving another of Cat Bow's delicacies that had found its way into *Yankee Magazine*. It seemed that Grampy had put in a number of special requests home for a "care package" consisting of fresh raspberry jam, to sweeten up the rather bland prairie life of Camp Cotton. Grampy's preoccupation with the preserve apparently didn't sit well with his father, the future Secretary of War, who, after Grampy's third request, responded tersely and rather uncharacteristically with a telegram, *In the Spanish War, we thirsted for blood—not jam!*

I never found out if the jam arrived, but it wasn't much longer before Grampy's tour of duty was up, and the "winding trail" led him back home to Bea and his first-born, our Aunt Frannie. Apparently, other than breaking-in horses and the accounts of Colonel Cross, Grampy saw little action—and even less of the infamous Pancho Villa and his band of desperadoes. In a letter home toward the end of his stint, Grampy summed up his first military experience:

Though we didn't engage the enemy, we got a good taste of what this business of war is about. It's not quite as glorious as a lot of people make it out to be. Most of the day is spent on maneuvers, rehearsing how we are going to put it to Mr. Villa and company once we get our hands on them. Though it is pretty hard to give it your all when the only thing on the horizon are those cursed hoards of cactus, I think that every one of us who has fired the artillery pieces got a good sense of how real this can get.

Up to this point, however, the only thing we have had to shoot at are mirages. When we are not on maneuvers, we are either doing routine drills in camp or simply chewing the fat, which has got a bit dry over these last months. It's interesting to see the changes that have come over the boys. Even those who appeared to be the most gung-ho in the beginning have sobered a bit with camp life. I suspect most of the boys share the mixed feelings that have grown in me. Though these mobilizations may be important to our country, it would be nice to get on with life.

Grampy's return to civilian life was short and sweet. As the battle clouds began to gather on the European horizon and the drum beats grew louder, the deployment gave him a foretaste of what was to come—roll call, parting.

We settled back into our seats, as the conversation returned to civilian life and the everyday. I perked up a moment, as Dad asked about Grandma Jane—the searching, uncertain note in his voice was carried over in Grampy's response, brief and unclear. Memories of an evening waltz returned to mind. Then, as business and politics sifted into the conversation, our thoughts started to wander off to exploits of our own.

Fidgeting discreetly on the sofa, we tried to catch Mom's attention with an assortment of hand signals, coughs, and frowns, in order to make our bid for an exit.

Finally, after we had sat more or less quietly for what could be deemed a suitable period for grandchildren, we were excused. Giving Grampy a kiss, we ran off to shed our formal attire and, scooping up sandwiches from the kitchen counter, attend to heroics of our own. Grampy was a treat, but he was still an adult. They would get on fine without us. Not so with the neighborhood softball team. Nat, Bea, Brad, and I surrounded nearly the entire infield. Our services were needed. Duty called!

6

THE LAURENTIAN CLUB

*ASPARAGUS OMELETS....*Who ever heard of asparagus omelets? Apparently not Grampy, but that didn't seem to bother him. Putting down the menu, he ordered them just the same—for all of us! We stared beseechingly across the table at Dad, hoping he would intercede on our behalf with the Lord. But, Dad made it clear to us that this was Grampy's outing, and he was the boss. A poor consolation, but asparagus omelets it was. As our waiter brought in our meal, Nat and I disconsolately watched the party beside us dig into big, juicy Canadian steaks, while we ate eggs for lunch—less than an auspicious beginning for our autumn fishing expedition!

The meal over, Nat and I slipped out to the front of the hotel to wait for the taxi, which would escort us over the last leg of our journey into the Quebec wilderness. Below us, Shawinigan Falls stretched out around us—a peaceful Canadian town, built on a hill, with sidewalks that strolled up to the foot of stores and offices. Old apartments were etched with clotheslines, lazily flapping their colors in the afternoon breeze. Leaning up against a rail, my gaze followed the main street down to a park and group of mothers, gathered around a cluster of benches. In and between their conversation, they cast sideways glances at their children, busily engaged in rounding up the dappled leaves that lay strewn about the grass and flower beds. A quiet hung over the town, as if the pace of life had not yet quickened its precincts. A first, a second, a third autumn was upon us.

The taxi pulled up in front of the hotel, rousing us from our reflections and presenting the first obstacle of our trip. The driver was a tall, friendly, verbose Canadian, who spoke nothing but French. His hearty greeting was a reminder that we had crossed the border and were now guests in another's land. After repeated forays with the parlance—which succeeded in little more than eliciting an increasingly perplexed look on Henri's otherwise affable face—we paused to assess our situation and seek other means to close our communication gap. Our "Frenglais" had thoroughly drained the famed romance out of the French language.

Finally, having almost given up hope, Dad had an idea. Taking up a fishing rod, he waved it in the air, exclaiming "Feesh! Feesh!" The charade worked "parfaitement." Piling our equipment into the car, we bid adieu to Shawinigan Falls, our jumping-off point and, gathering up a head of steam, headed off for Lake Edward and the Laurentian Club.

As we drove out of town, we quickly realized why we had been advised to leave our own car at the hotel. We hadn't gone three miles before we left the hardtop behind us and made our way along a two-way dirt road, which, a couple of miles later, narrowed to one grassy lane and, finally, a series of potholes that set our pace for the next fifty miles into the wilderness. As Grampy said, this was "getting away from it"—all the comforts of civilization.

Dad and Grampy were familiar with the route and settled in with Henri, who, in the place of conversation, was favoring us with what we ventured to be a version of the Canadian national anthem. As for Nat and me, after we had been jostled about like dice in a shaker, we decided to make the best of the situation, entertaining ourselves by sticking our heads out the window and dodging the branches that hung over the road.

Our autumn fishing trips were a highlight of my youth. Not only were they an opportunity to slip away with Dad for a week, but with Dad's dad, Grampy, as well. In those years, when both Dad and Grampy (even in his retirement) were busy, and more, with life's affairs, the trips to the Laurentian Club were a kind of backwoods pilgrimage for Nat and me. We looked forward to the date weeks in advance, grateful that—among our many cousins—time, age, proximity, and gender all qualified us for these men's outings. As exciting as the fishing itself was, even more so, in a deeper and quieter way, was the opportunity to have our sires all to ourselves in the wilds for a good week.

"Are you enjoying yourselves, boys?" Braced by the fresh air and the prospect of a week of fishing, Grampy turned around in his seat to check up on us. The omelets had become well scrambled, and all we ventured was a happy nod.

As we bumped on into the wilderness, Nat and I took a break from our exertions and, pulling our heads back inside the windows, leaned against the front seats, while Grampy called to mind a tale about the Laurentian Club that had left an indelible mark in our memories.

Fish were not the only creatures that one was apt to catch in these wilds. On an earlier trip, legend had it, Grampy had come close to landing a bull moose. From the report, I wasn't sure who was more surprised, Grampy or the moose who, all but submerged under the water, lifted his sizeable snout full of weeds out of the lake, to find a barbed fly buzzing around his nose. Whatever the case, Grampy's guide backpaddled the canoe mighty quickly to the shore from whence they had just cast off, as extending out above and beyond the moose's snout was a hefty rack of antlers, which, in similar circumstances, had been known to cradle the bow of a canoe in its embrace, before neatly capsizing it, and all aboard, into the "drink."

As the tale came to an end, we settled back into our seats to catch our breath. Ahead of us, the woods thinned. Then, with a deft turn of the wheel, the car pivoted around a corner, and we were there—that is, at one end of a very large and full lake. We climbed out of the car, doing our best to account for all our spare parts and elated with the prospects of solid ground. Then, before we realized what was happening, our equipment was unloaded, and, with a parting flourish of the anthem, Henri headed back to civilization, to retrieve some more "crazy Americans."

* * * * *

So here we were, deposited in Mother Nature's lap. The late afternoon was rapidly approaching, as Nat and I glanced about. A poor facsimile of a road lay behind us, the Canadian wilderness all around us, and in front of us a vast body of virgin water stretched out, with the Laurentian Club not even a consoling speck at the far end. Nat and I were about to learn our first and most important lesson in serious fishing, to say nothing of life itself: patience. Gathering up rods, nets, and gear, we joined Dad and Grampy, who, retrieving their packs, headed for the dock in front of us to wait for the boat that (rumor had it) would collect us.

The land was as beautiful as it was undisturbed. At our feet, lily pads meandered out from the dock, gently breaking the water's surface with touches on green. Along the shoreline on either side of the dock, birch and pine trees leaned out over the lake, laden heavy with boughs that sagged until they disappeared into their watery reflections. Shedding our memories of the trip, Nat and I sat down beside Grampy, following his gaze as it traced the wooded shoreline, in and out of coves unbroken.

The lake settled into the stillness of the afternoon glow, its red-blue surface interrupted only by an occasional ripple, as a trout rose for a fly. Turning to Grampy, I asked if there were any big fish in the lake. My question elicited a smile, as Grampy proceeded to stretch his hands a good three feet apart, "Lake trout; you'll see a couple of trophies this evening in the lodge." Expressions of wonder mirrored themselves in Nat's and my faces, as Grampy reached into his fishing bag and drew out a small, rectangular, silver container. "Worms are not the fare of choice. This kind of fishing, boys, is an art." Grampy opened the container, revealing neat rows of flies, each one striking in its pattern and coloring.

Leaning forward, Grampy introduced us to the feathered bait: Parmachenee Belles, Gray Ghosts, Muddlers, Silver Doctors, Wolly Buggers, Yellow Drakes, Evening Dun, Spotted Caddis, and slender Nymphs. The names were as colorful as the flies.

"Do you know what they are made out of?" We shook our heads. "Have a good look." Grampy placed a small fly in Nat's and my hands.

"Feathers? . . ."

Grampy nodded, "Most of them are from the wood duck, along with herons and occasionally even eagles." We turned the flies in our hands.

"Is this some kind of hair?" I looked up at Grampy.

"From deer, which gives it the brown coloring of the flies themselves. Sometimes a little tinsel is even thrown in—a flash to catch the attention of the fish." Nat and I nodded.

Reaching into the container, Grampy picked up a large gallant fly, with a scarlet streak that had caught my eye, "Last time I was here, I caught that three-footer with this Royal Coachman, just off the opposite shore." I lifted my gaze out across the lake. "The fish took nearly all of my line, and a number of times I wasn't sure I was going to get it back. My rod was nearly bent double." Grampy shook his head, "I played that fish for a good half-an-hour, before I was able to draw it close enough to the boat for us to get her into the net. And, even then, we weren't sure it would hold her." Grampy set the Royal Coachman back into the container and packed up the host of flies. Tobacco, I noted—along with a club—was conspicuously absent from his supply of bait.

Afternoon was passing on into evening. The sun cast a parting glow off the trees on the near shore, before descending into the horizon. Leaning up against my knapsack, I turned my sights across the cove, as a trout broke the still surface for a fly. Ripples spread out over the lake, before settling once again into the depths. I breathed in the quiet of the evening.

Grampy lifted his glance to the surrounding woods, "Did you boys know that your Great Great Uncle, James Wingate Weeks, surveyed a good bit of the New England border between the United States and Canada?" Nat and I shook our heads. Leaning back against the dock post, Grampy filled in our picture of young James, of prior wolf fame. Apparently, like his younger brother, William, James had strayed from the beaten path in his day:

"During the years when Lancaster was being settled, boys, country life produced a class of men and women who not only acquired the variety of skills necessary to survival on the frontier, but who also had a strong sense of public service. These individuals readily offered their talents to their state and nation. James Weeks was an example. He had acquired a reputation as a surveyor, which was an important profession in the early days as our country was getting established. When the Commissioner and his surveying party arrived in Lancaster on their trip north, they sought out someone in the town who was familiar with that neck of the woods. Great Uncle James was recommended, and he agreed to join the party, as soon as he could arrange his business to be absent for a couple of months."

As the evening mist rose up around us, Grampy traced James' steps for us, on through the wilds of the Northern Kingdom—until the purr of a motor reached our ears, summoning us to the end of the dock. Out of the mist, the outline of an old, ten-foot outboard took shape and slowly glided toward us. As the bow of the boat neared the dock, its pilot extinguished the motor and, then, rose to greet us in broken English.

René knew Grampy from previous trips and, stepping onto the dock, welcomed him with a warm handshake, which Grampy passed on to Dad, Nat, and me. Short and stocky, with a quiet smile that peeked out from under his mustache, I liked René immediately. His old red-and-black checkered lumberman's jacket, thick wool trousers, and a flannel cap blended in with the simple backwoods setting. After exchanging a few words, René eyed our gear and, then, set about loading it into the boat. We lent a hand, until everything was safely stowed away under the prow.

Climbing on board, we pushed off, sliding through the water until the small motor picked up and carried us out of the reaches of the land. As the dock faded into the shoreline behind us, the rest of the lake opened up, deep blues settling into violets, into blacks. Four miles down at the far shore, lights peeked out at us dimly from a clearing in the woods—the Laurentian Club and the end of our trip.

The boat moved slowly through the water, its wake rippling out over the still surface of the lake. Grampy sat beside me in the bow, the collar of his coat turned up, his fishing hat pulled snugly down over his brow. One hand braced itself firmly on the side of the boat. His other rested gently on my shoulder. As my gaze followed Grampy's over the waters, a light evening breeze brushed our cheeks.

> *Whenever I need a psychiatrist, I go fly fishing, holding a boat superior to a couch any day of the week. A fly rod is good for whatever ails a man. Any curable infirmity to which the flesh is heir is sure to respond to its persuasive therapy. And it is especially recommended for ulcers, nervous breakdowns, and the rigors of wedlock.*

Words of a certain Havilah Babcock, that Grampy had shared with us during our drive up from Lancaster, returned to mind, while overhead stars glanced down at us from the clear heavens, adrift in seas of their own.

As the still reaches of the lake spread out around us, Grampy sat forward in his seat, lifting my eyes to the silhouette that the evening had cast gently about him. Looking at my grandfather, I found myself wondering what reflections awoke out of his depths in rare moments like these. Yes, Grampy's life had been a busy one. I recalled being struck, when, discussing another matter, Dad mentioned that throughout much of his own childhood Grampy was off at work seven days a week, *Those were busy years; your grandfather was building his career.* Dad noted this fact, as though it was that and nothing more.

And yet, I was not sure. Though I didn't speak up then, a question lingered with me: What was Grampy seeking that appeared to be so removed from hearth and home? Dad's words returned to mind about how Grampy's ambition was to follow the footsteps of his father: Alderman, Mayor, U.S. Congressman, Senator, Cabinet Secretary. And that Grampy did, almost to a "t". But, I hesitated, what about Grampy's own footsteps? Did they get sidetracked along the way? Grampy wasn't Great-Granddad. I recalled the verse that rested below John Wingate Weeks' portrait atop Mt. Prospect. *Whose life in low estate began. ...* Grampy's beginning benefited considerably from the hard work of his father. The foundation had been well prepared for him, leaving the question: Where were Grampy's own efforts, his "genius," called upon?

As my eyes rested on Grampy, his face gently lit by the waxing moon that rose over his shoulder into the night sky, I wondered what role a wife and partner played in Grampy's life, to say nothing of children, grandchildren? I wondered whether Grampy sensed the deep love I felt for him. These questions were difficult to put into words, as was the uncertainty that suddenly filled me: Amidst the successes that marked Grampy's life, was there a part of my grandfather that felt lonely, lonesome, alone? I reflected, as my thoughts returned to the Lord of Cat Bow, adrift on his island of roses. Now as then, I was unable to find the words to express the feelings that awoke within me. Nor did I understand why the gruffness that was a part of Grampy's nature had drawn me ever closer to him over the last years.

Our boat continued on into the night, its bow gently parting the waters. My glance followed Grampy's out across the lake, searching the twilight to discover what it was that drew his gaze. As the peace of the night settled around us, I slowly understood that these trips, neglected loves of Grampy's, were not simply outings. No. I sensed that such voyages helped him clear the passageways that led inward, reconnecting him with those deeper currents that ebbed and flowed in his depths.

A familiar melody stirred on Grampy's lips, ebbing on silently within me: *All night, all day....*

* * * * *

As we approached the shore, two figures, with swaying lanterns in their hands, walked down to the dock to greet us. Behind them, farther up on the bank, a row of lodges nestled into the night—plumes of smoke rising out of their chimneys. René turned off the motor, and we slowly glided into the arms of the guides who bid us "allo."

The boat was quickly unpacked and secured to the side of the dock. Then, gathering up our gear, we started up to the main lodge, leaving behind a row of sleepy canoes rolled over on their sides. Steps climbed up to the porch and entrance of the lodge. Opening the door, Grampy led us on in. Resting our gear in the hallway, Nat and I glanced about. To the right, a spacious living room opened up before us, decked with thickly woven rugs and gently lit by kerosene lanterns that hung from the beams. From wall to ceiling, nook to cranny, every part of the abode was wood—finely aged pine that was well warmed by the large stone fireplace at the far end.

Grampy took off his jacket, hanging it on a peg by the door. Glancing up, the eyes of the wilds were upon us. Along the walls of the living room, striking trophies of fish, fowl, and beast gazed down from on high. Overhead, a familiar moose with a towering rack of antlers held sway over the pack. On either side of the venerable old timer, deer, bear, and bobcat heads peered at us, while trout, bigger than Nat and I had ever seen, never mind imagined, rose for the fly among the rafters. As the adults continued across the living room to greet fellow members of the Laurentian Club, Nat and I lowered our sights to photos and pictures which told the story of the hunt. Hardy parties of men, rifles resting in their arms, stooped around felled moose and bear. Strings of trout—Lake, Brook, and Browns—spread out at the foot of canoes. And hunting parties, flushed with the chase, posed good-naturedly on the steps and porch of the lodge, their featured trophies in hand.

At the far end of the living room, a hulking sink-down sofa basked in the cordial warmth of the fireplace, framed at both ends by stacks of logs. Cards, cribbage boards, poker chips, and a backwoods array of books and magazines congregated on old maple tables that gathered around them hospitable companies of chairs.

Nat and I could have ended the trip at the fireside, but before we were able to settle in, Grampy and Dad pointed us toward our rooms, "We have a big day ahead of us; no sleeping late. A tired fly won't catch the eye of any fish." So it was. The miles we had covered that day, land and water, were catching up to us. Gathering up our gear, Nat and I followed our paternal guides upstairs, the lanterns casting their soft glow before us.

* * * * *

"Rise and shine!" The voice was clearly distinguishable, even in my sleep. I opened my eyes in time to see Grampy push aside the curtains in our room and hoist up the window, "Breakfast in fifteen minutes." Grampy smiled at us, bundled up in our covers, before heading back out into the hall.

The cool morning air filled our room. Hopping out of bed, Nat shut the window and pulled on his trousers in record speed. Bracing myself, I followed suit. We were dressed in a flourish. In the hallway, Dad was prodding water out of a hand pump. Neither electricity nor plumbing were a part of this fishing trip. Such deprivations, apparently, were part of the dues one paid for the privilege of going to the source. Reading our minds, Dad announced that the outhouse was out back, adding a gentle nudge to Grampy's exhortations, "Keep going; we've got a big day ahead of us."

Our morning ritual completed, Nat and I followed the path through a sunlit clearing to the dining hall, a simple wooden building atop the ridge that looked down over the lake, whose waters we parted the night before. Inside, we joined Grampy and Dad at a table. Coffee in hand, Grampy looked up to greet us, "Are you boys hungry?" We nodded unabashedly, as we sat down and unfolded our napkins onto our laps.

A young woman followed us to the table and asked if we were ready to order. We turned to our host, who glanced down at the menu, "Let's have some eggs—" My heart began to sink. Grampy's eyes continued across the menu, "—ham, bacon, hash-browns, toast, and cereal." Nat and I uttered a quiet grace. Dad glanced over at us, smiling, "You'd better store up, boys. The only lunch we are going to have is what you catch this morning."

The order in, Grampy pulled a book out of his canvas tackle bag, which he had slung over the back of his chair, "I found a passage this morning that I thought you boys would enjoy." Grampy opened to a page he had marked, "Listen well, this was the regular fare for many young men who cleared this neck of the woods. *PAUL BUNYAN'S COOK*," Grampy glanced at the title before he served up the passage:

The men (seated 13 at a table) started the day with oatmeal and top milk. The next course was cheese (1 pound per man) and molasses cookies, followed by pancakes, maple syrup, and large slabs of sow butter. (Some stuffed a few pancakes in their pockets for snacks). The men then dug into SEVERAL helpings of bacon and eggs, plus bread spread with butter and apple butter. The meal was topped with a bowl of baked apples, stewed prunes, lemons and raisins.

The noon meal at the camp consisted of stewed venison, baked beans and pork, boiled potatoes and creamed gravy, rutabagas, squash, bread and honey, hickory nuts, molasses cake and coffee with cream and sugar.

Supper included salmon loaf and crammed peas, fried potatoes, hard boiled eggs (6 for each man), bread and butter and jelly, pickles, cranberry strudel, blueberries and cream and tea laced with maple syrup.

Despite the amount of food put 'down the hatch,' the lumber-jacks never got fat. Dr. Colley remarked that if everyone ate as much as her maternal grandfather, the food supply in the world would be reduced by two-thirds. And, if everyone worked this hard—well, draw your own conclusions!

Dad nodded, as Grampy closed the book, "Those men burned a lot of calories." Nat and I were almost full by the time our plates arrived —a modest appetizer by the good doctor's account. Our work was cut out for us, and our appetite returned as we started in.

* * * * *

Our guides were waiting for us in the field behind the dining lodge. As we walked up, Maurice, the older of the two, stepped forward to greet us. Of medium height, his soft blue eyes were set off by a sturdy chin and thin crop of dark hair. Exchanging handshakes, Maurice introduced us to his partner, Jean. Grampy had fished the area thoroughly over the years, and he and Dad discussed the prospects with the guides before the itinerary was decided upon. We would fish six lakes that day, all separated by portages of approximately one mile, before ending up at another lodge on Lake Cinq that evening. I was a bit taken aback by the trek before us, but, before I was able to entertain any doubts, the guides had hoisted the canoes onto their shoulders, adjusted their head straps, and the procession was off.

The trail led through a wooded field, brightened by autumn wildflowers and ferns. The path was well traveled, and, before long, Nat and I, getting our second wind, stepped around the adults and, our fishing rods angling over the trail, forged on ahead. At the base of a small hill, a familiar patch of blue peeked out from between the trees. Lifting our fishing rods, we doubled our pace to the water's edge, in order to cast forth our lines.

By the time the rest of the expedition had arrived, Nat and I had landed a good dozen lily pads. Grampy eyed our catch with a smile, as the guides eased the canoes off their shoulders and into the water, "We won't fish this lake, boys. You've already discovered why it is called Hay." Grampy and Dad settled into the canoe with Maurice, while Nat and I, abandoning our catch, climbed aboard with Jean. The lake was small, and it wasn't five minutes before the guides' powerful strokes landed the canoes on the opposite shore, in a bed of reeds. "The next lake, feesh," Jean assured us as we disembarked and, spurred on by his words, set off once again.

Jean's words proved to be an understatement. Nat's fly barely graced the surface of Lake Clair before a trout struck. "I've got one!" Nat yelled; Jean laughed, and, my arms flailing, I excitedly cast my line out over the waters (to cousin Wade). The fish must have been waiting, because a moment later my fly was on the run.

Dad and Grampy cheered us on from the bank, before climbing into their canoe and heading out to join us. A moment later, all four lines were casting across the waters. Nat and I quickly discovered that the fish congregated in the shallows just off the shore. As Jean steadied the canoe, we directed our flies between the trunks of fallen trees and at the foot of boulders that rose up out of the lake. We had never seen such sport. The fish struck everything that hit the water. Before long Grampy and Dad had tied on a second fly and began to pull the trout in by the twos. Their hurrahs joined ours, as our rods, one and all, were straining with the action.

* * * * *

By lunchtime, we had an appetite—and the fare to go with it: twenty-five speckled trout, averaging a good pound each and as fresh as the cool lake water. Grampy settled back against a slender birch that brightened up the clearing along the shore, while Dad and Nat set about with Jean to gather wood for a fire. After unloading his pack, Maurice returned to the water's edge, to clean the fish. Following our guide, I sat down on the bow of the canoe that had been pulled up onto the bank. Taking out his knife, Maurice stooped down and lifted a still trout out of the back of the canoe.

Drops of blood muddied the clear blue water, as Maurice quickly slit open the soft, white underbelly of the trout. My eyes followed the motion of the knife, while Maurice went on to scrape the fish's guts, with the backside of his thumb, into the water. A second deft cut released the trout's gills, arching its head limply back. I watched silently as Maurice swirled the fish back and forth in the water, cleaning out the remaining blood and entrails, before placing the trout on the grass at my feet, its damp body glistening vacantly in the noonday sun. As Maurice reached for a second fish, I rose and went back to join the others.

Nat and Dad were stooping in front of the fire, kindling its blaze. Grampy, who had watched Maurice and me from his seat, handed me an apple from his knapsack. Nodding, I sat down beside him and turned my glance to the lick of flames that had begun to creep up on the wood.

The fire good and hot, our catch was laid out in two large, rustic frying pans; water was set to boil in an old pan that Jean pulled out of his pack; and tea, bread, and butter were spread out on a large flat rock beside the fire. Dad added some oranges, Grampy a handful of Hershey bars, and we started in.

We ate quietly for a few moments, our thoughts passing over the morning's fishing, before Grampy reached for a tea bag, "Last time I was here, your Grandma Jane and Aunt Virginia were with us."

Nat looked over at Grampy. "How was the fishing?" he asked gamely.

Grampy reflected, "The men did fine. But the ladies had trouble accustoming themselves to the bottom of the canoe—not to mention the swarm of flies that went whisking by their ears with our lines." Grampy smiled quietly, "They confessed that they were expecting something a bit more civilized than the fishing party that they found themselves in." Grampy's smile spread on my lips, as I imagined the two belles, bonnets pulled down over their eyes, stowed aboard our canoes in the midst of the Northern wilderness.

"Was that the celebrated trip that the Rices joined you on?" Dad turned to his father with a twinkle in his eye.

Grampy thought a moment before nodding, "Pret and Bertha, yes." Grampy sat forward, as the story returned wryly to mind, "Bertha was a delightful, but rather high-strung, lady, who had difficulty accustoming herself to the outhouse." Nat and I swapped glances. "Not only was she disenchanted with that particular establishment, she was equally reserved about the distance that the outhouse was set from the lodge— generally a good hundred yards down wind and off in the woods." The smile crept up on Dad's face. "One evening, as Bertha mustered up her resolve and headed out the back door, your 'Uncle Charlie Squibb,' who was actually quite devoted to Bertha, grabbed a bear skin rug from the floor and, winking at us, slipped out the front door. Apparently, he had a rendezvous in mind." The smiles broadened. "It wasn't two minutes later that a scream pierced the night, and, before we knew it, poor Bertha was back in our midst in a fit of hysterics. We had all we could do to contain ourselves, as she described the bear that came lumbering and woofing down the trail to greet her." Grampy glanced across at Dad, "I don't think Pret got Bertha within shouting distance of a fishing camp after that."

* * * * *

Dad eased a branch into the fire, while Grampy poured hot water into his cup. We joined him with some tea, as the conversation turned to more serious subjects—Great-Granddad's conservation efforts, a story that we had only caught snatches of over the years.

"There is an act, boys, that takes the name of your great-grandfather, which provided landmark legislation in the conservation field. Passed in 1911, the John Wingate 'Weeks Act' not only helped to preserve many of the forests in the states, but it has also been a model for other countries, including Canada." Grampy reflected, "The story of this act points out many of the qualities that made your great-grandfather a leader in his day."

We set our plates down by the fire, as Grampy settled back again against the birch, "In the early part of the century, the harvesting of timber had gone too far. Many of our most scenic parts of the country, including the White Mountains in New Hampshire, had become scarred by the clear-cutting methods that had developed." Grampy lifted the cup to his lips and blew on the tea, before drinking slowly. "Your great-grandfather, who grew up on the land, realized that a stop had to be put to these excesses, and he was aware that there wasn't a great deal of support for his conservation views—not only in the House Committee on Agriculture—where any bill was to make its first appearance—but among the leadership of both parties, whose influence was at its strongest at that time."

"Despite all this, it was a tribute not only to your Great-Grandfather, but to the Speaker of the House of Representatives, Joseph Cannon, that Cannon appointed his colleague, Weeks, to the Committee on Agriculture." Grampy reflected, "Before accepting the appointment, the two men had an important conversation, during which your great-grandfather advised his friend and colleague that he would serve if that was Mr. Cannon's wish, but that he wanted to make it clear that he didn't share the Speaker's views on all the matters relating to the business of the committee. Cannon responded that he was aware that this was the case, referring in particular to the Forestry Legislation, and added that he was not putting your great-grandfather on the committee because he wanted a spokesman for his views. Rather, Cannon stated clearly, he recognized that the Agriculture Committee was becoming more and more important, and he felt it was essential that there be, among its members, 'experienced businessmen.' "

Dad nodded quietly, as Grampy lifted the cup once again to his lips. I took a drink with him, before Grampy set his cup down between his legs, "The Speaker went on to say that, although he recognized that forestry legislation was coming, he felt it was still too early for the government to purchase private lands. However, Cannon did tell your great-grandfather that if he could frame a forestry bill, which, as a businessman, your great-grandfather himself was willing to support, then he would do what he could, as the Speaker of the House, to make sure the bill got a good hearing." Grampy looked at Nat and me, "And it did. Although, Cannon himself did not end up voting for the bill, the act passed, after much hard work, by ten votes."

Grampy continued, "The bill was a classic example not only of your great-grandfather's practical business sense, but of his ability to build support for an idea." Dad refilled our cups, as Grampy went on, "One of the first things John Wingate Weeks realized was that the only way such legislation could pass was if there was unified agreement among the North and the South. He devoted a good bit of time building this base. The next roadblock your great-grandfather tackled was businesses' opposition to the conservation measure, specifically the interest of the paper companies. Well aware of how businessmen looked at such matters, he searched for solid arguments that could be forwarded, which emphasized the *practical* merits of the bill." Grampy reached his cup out to Dad.

"Your great-grandfather found what he was looking for in a report that had come out on the influence of forestry on stream flow, the focus being on the White Mountain region. The conclusion of the report was that the soil erosion, and consequent runoff from the clearcutting, were degrading the quality of the water in the rivers. As was becoming increasingly recognized, this was creating problems for the operation of the mills. This aspect of the issue found expression in the title of the act: *An Act to enable any State to cooperate with any other State or States or with the United States for the protection of the watersheds of navigable streams and to appoint a commission for the acquisition of lands for the purpose of conserving the navigability of navigable rivers.*" This act was an important mile-stone in what has come to be known today as the environmental field."

Nat's glance passed across the lake, "Great-Granddad must have loved the land."

Grampy turned to Nat, "He did, but he wasn't romantic about it." Grampy reflected, "Your great-grandfather grew up on the land, and he realized that it wasn't simply a paradise. A lot of hard work was required if people were to make a living for themselves. It was clear to him that what would make America a leading nation would be our ability to transform the raw materials of the earth into products, so that the citizens at large, like himself and his family, could not only survive, but have access to the goods and services, which, in earlier times, had been reserved for the privileged few."

Nat and I listened with interest.

"Part of what made your great-grandfather one of the most widely consulted men of his day was his ability to look beyond his own political interests. He knew that, given our two-party system, the political process, by its very nature, involved what some people might call compromise." Grampy considered, "For him it was much simpler than that. Your great-grandfather recognized that his views were not sacrosanct, that he was not in possession of the God's truth. He was, therefore, willing to work with colleagues, representing differing views, in the trust that, if reasonableness was kept in mind, progress could be made. His first Post Office Appropriations Bill, not an insignificant issue by any measure, was a case in point. Framed by your great-grandfather, it was, at the time, the only bill in the history of our country which was passed by the Senate without a change of word."

Grampy paused, "Your great-grandfather was not only completely versed in the issues, but he made a point of understanding as fully as he could the concerns and objections of his fellow members, to which he gave due and thoughtful consideration. This fact was recognized by his colleagues, which was why he was trusted by both parties."

We finished our tea and gathered up the wares.

* * * * *

After lunch we split up. Nat and Dad continued on in one canoe, while Grampy and I joined Maurice in the other. Throughout the rest of the trip, Nat and I rotated, getting tips from the older folks. Grampy was an accomplished fisherman, and I was careful when I shared the canoe with him. I had heard about a slight mishap that had occurred a few years back, in which Grampy, this time, was the center of attention. He was fishing at the Dartmouth Grant with the college's president, John Dickey, and another friend of his, who went by the same last name, Edward Weeks, Editor of the "Atlantic Monthly" magazine.

As the story went, undoubtedly polished a bit over the years, the Weeks' canoe was sliding into a dock when Edward, the younger and, apparently, more agile of the two, anxious to get onto the next lake, jumped out without warning. This sudden shift of weight caught Grampy by surprise, who moments later found himself neatly deposited in the "drink." Not accustomed to such a dunking, Grampy picked himself up out of the water, wiped the reeds from his head, and, in a clear but slightly waterlogged voice, said, *God damn you, Weeks!*

The warmth of the afternoon sun sent the fish down to the cooler springs at the bottom of the lake, slowing down the action. Grampy took the silver fly box out of his fishing bag, "If we are going to catch any fish this afternoon, we will have to reach down to them."

As Grampy glanced over the wet flies, my thoughts went back to his description of his father, "Grampy, were you close to great-grandfather?"

Grampy looked up, as he handed me a familiar scarlet fly, "I had a great deal of admiration for him." Grampy paused, "He was probably the greatest influence in my life."

I held the fly in my hand, glancing from it back to Grampy, "What was great-grandfather like?"

Grampy drew a colorful Parmachenee Belle out of the host, before lifting his rod and reaching for the end of his line, "In many ways he was a simple man, a person who grew up here on the land and never lost his connection with it, even though for much of his life he lived in the metropolitan centers of Boston and Washington." Grampy snared his old fly. "At eight, he went to the district school in Lancaster, which was a good, two-mile-walk from his home. He used to tell us how, in the cooler months of the year, a big box stove, which was looked after by the boys in the class, heated the schoolroom. Your great-grandfather took his turn, carrying a bundle of kindling wood with him to the school in the morning to get the stove going for the day's lesson."

I listened, as Grampy bit the line free just above the old fly. "One of the things your great-grandfather often said later in his life was that he couldn't be thankful enough that he was born on a farm, where he was expected to pitch in and do chores as soon as he could toddle about. The hard work he did at home provided the foundation for all he was to accomplish in later life, because it gave him, as he put it, habits of industry and good physical health." Grampy reflected, "As the school year was a good bit shorter in your great-grandfather's day—due to the fact that the children were needed on the farms—John Wingate Weeks also learned quite early that when you have little education, you have to know how to use your head, think for yourself."

Our gazes met. I nodded, considered, "Why did great-grandfather leave Lancaster?"

Grampy threaded the fishing line through the eye of the fly before looking up at me again, "For the same reason that young men all over the country leave the places where they were born. He wanted to get to know the world and discover what he had to do in life."

I watched Grampy, as he wrapped the end of the line three times around itself, before drawing it through the loop he had formed, just above the eye of the fly, and pulling it tight. "Where did great-grandfather go when he left home?"

"Well, when he was sixteen years old, the Congregational minister in town asked him if he would be interested in seeking an appointment to the Navel Academy at Annapolis. The family considered it carefully and decided that the opportunity was an important one. Your great-granddad's only reservations were whether his father could spare him on the farm."

The guide steered the canoe into the shade of the cliffs that rose out of Lake Rond, casting its sheer granite shadow about the still watery surface around us. As Grampy continued, I listened with awakening interest to his description of a life that he, indeed, admired, "Though your great-grandfather, the largest student in class, was very popular with his classmates, and excelled in all activities that had to do with strength and endurance, he did not start off as a brilliant student. Rather, he was a steady, hard worker, who advanced higher each year and highest at his time of graduation, where he was chosen as the 'best balanced' man in the class."

The pause was a brief one, "It is interesting to note that this man, who was later to become the Secretary of War in two presidential Cabinets, was a real peacemaker at the academy. When trouble arose between his battalion, of which he was Sergeant-Major, and the town police, he was made chairman of the committee to adjust the matter, which he did to everyone's satisfaction."

Grampy closed up his fly box and tucked the silent swarm back into his fishing bag, "After graduation and a stint in the navy, including a cruise to China, your great-grandfather headed down with an ex-navy friend to Florida, where he did some surveying, before being offered the position of Land Commissioner for the Florida Southern Railroad. During that time, as he was fond of saying, he just missed making his fortune." Grampy tossed his line out of the boat.

"Your great-grandfather bought a tract of phosphate land for two dollars an acre and felt fortunate to sell it later for four dollars an acre—which he considered a handsome profit. A few years later, the same land, which turned out to be the richest in phosphate in the area, sold for many hundred dollars an acre. Not a gambler by nature, soon after, your great-granddad turned down the opportunity to buy a good plot of land on Biscayne Bay, which has come to be known as Miami."

Grampy chuckled, "Though your great-grandfather didn't excel in land speculation, he did acquire another treasure, a young lady from his neighboring town of Littleton, New Hampshire, who happened to be visiting in Florida at the time—Martha A. Sinclair. Their acquaintance grew; a courtship followed; and they were married in October of 1885. In due time, your Great Aunt Katherine and I arrived on the scene."

Raising his rod, Grampy slowly drew the line from his reel, as he glanced out over the rippling waters. Glimmers of light played in and among the shadows. Grampy continued, "Not long after, young John Wingate Weeks was working for one of the first banking and brokerage firms in the country, Hornblower & Page, which soon became Hornblower & Weeks. Your great-grandfather guided the growth of the firm over the next years, from two partners and three employees in one Boston office, to thirteen partners and six hundred and sixty-four employees with offices in New York, Chicago, Providence, Detroit, Portland, Maine, Cleveland, Ohio, and Pittsburgh, Pennsylvania."

Grampy lifted his gaze up to the cliff, before casting out his line. One, two, three, four times, . . . he drew it, back and forth, in ever-expanding casts, before the fly came to rest in a quiver of shadows near the base of the cliff. Grampy was silent, as his eyes settled on the fly. Drawing out my line, I followed Grampy's lead, sweeping the fly back and forth in shorter casts, before sending it on its way out over the waters. Gathering the loose line in our hands, we settled back with our featured bait into the sunlit shadows of the pond. The ripples spread out about us.

"Grampy?" I searched for words, as reflections rose up all around me, "What made Great-Granddad the way he was?"

Grampy gazed out at his line, lifting the tip of the rod to draw it taut, "At appropriate moments, Stuart, your great-grandfather used to share with me words by James M. Hughes. They meant a lot to him, as they have to me over the years: 'A plain bar of iron is worth $5. The same bar of iron, when made into horseshoes, is worth $10.50. If made into needles, it is worth $4,285. If turned into balance wheels for watches, it becomes worth $250,000.'"

Grampy looked at me, "The point of the story, of which your great-grandfather was a prime example, is that this is not only true of iron, our natural resources, but it is true of another kind of material: us, our human resources. Your value, as a person, is determined by what you make of yourself." Our gazes met before Grampy continued. "From business, it was a natural step for your great-grandfather into public service, beginning in the Congress and then the U.S. Senate."

I nodded at Grampy, before turning my attention back out to my line. We let our flies quietly settle to the bottom of the pond. I drew in the slack, "What was the most important bill that Great-Granddad worked on when he was in the Senate?"

Grampy reflected "The most important bill he worked on was probably the Federal Reserve Act."

"What was that?"

Grampy turned his attention from his line, "It was an act which
established a central bank in our country."

"Why was that important?"

Grampy smiled, "Finance is the language of business, Stuart. One
of the least understood and most important professions in our, and any
developed nation, is banking. A central bank determines its country's
monetary policy—that is the way money is supplied to and circulates
in an economy."

"What effect does that have?"

"Have you ever found yourself watering the garden when suddenly
the hose went off?"

I shook my head.

"If you were making your living as a gardener, you would not be
pleased. The same is the case, regardless of your profession. Money is
the lifeblood of an economy." Grampy considered, "The only way an
economy can grow is if the money supply grows. Our central bank has
been given the responsibility for determining the growth of the money
supply and, thus, the well-being of the citizens of our nation." Grampy
looked out across the water, "There is an expression that has been
attributed to one of Europe's great financiers: 'Give me the control of
the supply and the circulation of money, and I don't need politicians or
an army.' "

My eyes glanced off the cliff. Grampy's remark confused me. I
paused, searched for words, "How did Great-Granddad feel about the
bill?"

"It was not an easy vote for him. With his background in business
and banking, your great-grandfather was considered the most knowl-
edgeable Senator on monetary policy. Even the head of the opposite
party, President Wilson, sought his counsel. Your great-grandfather
worked hard on the bill and was responsible for over four hundred
amendments to the Federal Reserve Act. At the end, he said that he
wasn't sure a good bill could be drawn up, but that, at least, it would
bring about much needed improvements in the banking system. With

that in mind, he put aside partisan politics and voted against his party for the bill's passage."

Grampy reflected, "His main concern was that the citizens' understanding of monetary affairs keep pace with this major step of establishing a central bank. Such a balance, he felt, was critical to preserving our free democratic system, above all when dealing with matters of the purse.... I'm not sure your great-grandfather would be encouraged with the progress that citizens have made."

Grampy turned his eyes back out over the waters. I glanced down at my line silently, as reflections rose up all around me. The language of business; the business of America?...

Grampy's words about Great-Granddad rippled on within me, turning my thoughts to another family member, Doctor John Weeks, who had also made his way north and about whom I knew little, except that his interests in medicine, education, and theology distinguished him from the worldlier Weeks of my acquaintance. Dad had said little more about our early ancestor, than that when the American Revolution began, the gentleman moved to Halifax, Nova Scotia, where he later became the Bishop.

Sunlight glanced off the shadows of the trees that glimmered in the watery depths. I lifted my gaze and asked Grampy about our earlier forebear, "Why did Doctor Weeks leave the States?"

Grampy turned to me, "Doctor John Weeks? He was loyal to the crown and didn't agree with the Revolution."

I was puzzled, "I thought the Revolution was a good thing. Didn't it give us our freedom?"

Grampy nodded.

I looked at him, "Didn't Doctor Weeks want to be free?"

"I'm not sure the issue for him was freedom. He felt that the colonies belonged to England and that they had no right to press for their independence." Grampy pointed to my line. It twitched once, twice.... I turned my attention back to the rod, gripping the line between my fingers. It was still again, as the ripples settled back into the lake.

My puzzlement increased, "*Did* the colonies have the right to press for freedom?"

"His son, Captain John Weeks, who settled in Lancaster, thought so. He was an intense patriot, who served as an officer in the Revolutionary Army. After the war, Captain Weeks was chosen as a delegate to the Convention held in Exeter, New Hampshire, whose vote for ratification of the Constitution broke the tie among the remaining fledgling states and gave our country its governing document."

I was silent a moment, "What, then, was the issue for Doctor Weeks?"

"He was only the second generation in his family that was born in America. Like others in his day, he maintained his ties with England, where he finished his education before he went into medicine. I assume that he had established a good practice and was satisfied with life as it was."

I reflected on Grampy's words, "Was he afraid that if there were a revolution, things would change?"

Grampy smiled, as his eyes scanned the water, light touching shadows, touching glimmers of light that were cast out over the pond by the wisps of a breeze, "I think that's a safe guess."

"Why did the others want change?"

"The colonists had been used to pretty much deciding their own affairs since New England was settled, and when the Crown started to interfere, they weren't pleased."

My curiosity grew, drawing my attention away from my line, "Why did England interfere?"

Grampy drew out more line, lowering the tip of his rod till it touched its watery reflection, "They had a sizable debt they had to pay off from the wars they had been fighting in Europe and against the French in America, and they wanted the colonists to chip in, since they figured we had benefited from the defeat of the French, as well."

I lifted my rod gently, before resting it again on the side of the canoe. My glance turned from my line back to Grampy, "And we didn't want to pay?"

Grampy shook his head, "Have you ever heard of the expression, 'Taxation without representation is tyranny'?"

I nodded, this time positively.

"Well, that was the point for Captain John Weeks and the colonists who stayed to fight. If they were going to have to pay taxes for the wars, they wanted, at the very least, to be represented."

"They weren't?"

"No, in leaving England, they left behind their rights as Englishmen, which included representation."

My thoughts returned to the Loyalist, "Grampy, why didn't the question of representation bother Doctor John Weeks?"

"As I said, he felt secure the way things were."

"Was he already represented?"

"His interests were."

I reflected, as my gaze traced my line over the surface of the lake, "What would you have done if you were in his place?"

"In *his* place?" Grampy considered, his eyes glancing off the cliff, "One never knows, Stuart. There are two sides to every story—even when one doesn't hear much about the other side." Grampy paused, "An argument can be made for the fact that both the slaves and the Indians would have been better off if we had remained under British rule." The uncertainty grew in me; Grampy went on, "Not only was slavery banned in England in 1810, but, before the Revolution, the British had established the Quebec Line, which said that all land west of the Ohio Valley belonged to the Indians."

I thought about Grampy's words, "You mean if we hadn't fought for our freedom, the slaves and Indians would have had theirs?"

"If the British had held to their word; foreign policies change."

The twitch returned, drawing more slack out of the line. Grampy motioned for me to gently raise the tip of my rod. I did, waiting for the pull....The pond was still. Only light and shadows played across the surface, harboring fluid reflections of cliff and woods. Our conversation nibbled at me.

"Grampy, you always spoke of the Revolution as a great thing."

Grampy nodded, "It was; I'm not questioning that. The war had to come. Settlers like Captain Weeks, the doctor's son, who had left the security of the more established settlements on the coast and were on their own, appreciated this fact more than those who remained and prospered from their connection, and often dependence, on England. What those who set off on their own earned, they earned largely from the sweat of their own brow, and they weren't about to see it taken away from them by anyone."

"How about the slaves and Indians?" Grampy looked at me. I

searched for words, "How could we fight for our own freedom, only to take it away from others?"

Grampy's gaze passed over the waters. Ripples gathered and spread. "Sometimes what seems like a war is only a battle—one of many." Grampy's voice was quieter, "The revolution had to come, but whenever something is gained, something else is lost, not just for those peoples I mentioned, the slaves and Indians, but for the colonists as well. It was a long and costly engagement for our young country—and one, as Lincoln well understood, that didn't resolve all the issues."

Grampy's words settled into the reflections. I glanced back out to my line, dipping beneath the blue-brown surface of the water and journeying on down through the currents to probe the depths. Cliff, pond, woods, . . . all around me, nature cast her sylvan reflection, merging the heavens and earth in a dappled autumn tapestry. I lifted my rod, tightening the line and sending slight ripples out across the surface. Somewhere below, a fly stirred and, then, settled again into the depths.

A question lingered. I turned to Grampy, "Was Doctor John Weeks a Republican, Grampy?"

Grampy lifted his gaze from his line to me, "They didn't have Republicans then."

I reflected, "Would he have been?"

Grampy considered my question, "There are different factions in the Republican Party, as in every party—some are more conservative than others. Doctor John Weeks probably would have belonged to the more conservative branch of his party."

Grampy's answer, though clear, left me unsure, "Were some of our ancestors Democrats?"

"Some."

"Why?" My question was leading me to an uncertain conclusion.

"Everybody has their own views, Stuart. A number of your forebears, including your great-grandfather on my mother's side, were rather stubborn." Surprised, I looked at Grampy, until the earnest look on his face gave way to a smile. A donkey perked its ears up in my memory, as I mused on his words. Although I trusted that a crossbreed between an elephant and mule was *not* out of the question, it was beyond my powers at the moment to reconcile the two.

I gazed out over the lake, "Grampy, was Bea a Republican?"

The question surprised Grampy, who reflected for a moment, "Politics wasn't a great interest of your grandmother."

I looked at Grampy, "Why not?"

"She was more interested in who a person was, than what views they held. She felt that people are often better than their politics and philosophies." Grampy considered, "I suspect that's why she was so beloved by many."

My gaze rested on Grampy, who glanced at his watch, before nodding to Maurice. As the canoe turned out of the shadow of the cliff toward the far bank, we slowly drew our lines up out of the depths. Dad, Nat, and Jean followed us to shore. The fish had given us all a break.

* * * * *

Our portage to the next lake was a short one, which followed a stream for a few hundred yards till it flowed into a branch of Lake Dauphine. As the guides paddled, we fished the far shoreline, landing our flies in the amber-brown shadows that began to gather beneath the trees. Then, as the sun sank into the horizon, Grampy reeled in his line and, reaching for his fly, said, "Let's move on to the lodge. It's been a good day." Maurice's strokes lengthened. I picked up my paddle and joined him, the other canoe moving up beside us.

We paddled quietly for half an hour, up the branch of the lake, until we came to the main body of water, which spread out in a vast expanse of dark blues and purples all around us. My eyes followed the bow of the canoe to the far end of the lake and a small clearing a good six miles off. Other than the clearing, the shoreline rippled into the wilderness, flowing on for miles and miles in every direction.

As we left the inlet behind us and started across the lake, an evening breeze greeted us, brushing my cheeks crisply. The first chill of winter gripped the autumn air. Resting the paddle for a moment across my lap, I pulled up the collar of my coat. Above us, a waxing moon, that was to grow in fullness over the week to come, climbed on into the heavens. Shifting in my seat, my eyes returned to Grampy, his silhouette cast once again gently about him in the evening.

"Your grandmother was a real match for Grampy. She was one of the few people who could stand up to him when need be, and she did so out of a deep love." Dad's words, from one of the few occasions when he spoke of his mother, returned to mind. As the currents flowed back in, I took a deep breath.

The stillness was broken by the call of a loon. Gazing across the waters, the bird was nowhere to be seen—only gathering tides of purple. Then, as I dipped my paddle back into the water, the call rose up once more into the evening—singular, searching, forlorn....Grampy pointed to my left, our glances ranging out over the depths, until silence settled again over the lake, and we sat back into our seats.

Maurice's strokes picked up, strong and steady, moving the canoe on through the waters, which lapped quietly against the hull. Overhead, clouds, white with darkening patches of gray, scurried on before us toward the setting sun. I lifted my head to a melody that played on my lips: *Angels watching over me, my Lord....*

WINTER

The thermometer was down to around 25 below this morning. Got the furnace going early and stoked up the embers in the old fireplace. It looks like the Presidential peaks got a good dusting of snow last night. Things are pretty quiet around here. It will be nice when the family arrives for Christmas.

Sinclair Weeks, Diary, December 17, 1968

7

THE RIDE NORTH

"MOM, let's go!"

As we yelled from the car for Mom to hurry, we caught glimpses of her through the frosty window, bustling about in the kitchen. Her last-minute recollections were further complicated by the fact that this winter, in order to give Santa a shorter journey, we were bringing Christmas (along with all of its packages and trimmings) up to Grampy in the North Country—a little closer, we figured, to where it belonged. Finally, emerging from the house, her arms full of apples, cookies, and other tidbits that tided us over on our trips, Mom squeezed in among the mittens, scarves, skis, and holiday cheer.

"You sure you haven't forgotten anything, dear?" Dad folded the newspaper and turned toward Mom. Smiling sweetly, she gently shoved a carrot into his surprised mouth, before unloading the rest of them onto our laps in the back seat. We were off!

It was about five hours from Concord to Lancaster, door to door. That is, not counting those rest stops, which were both inevitable and, invariably, poorly timed, as I began to realize....With the rest stops, it was close to six hours—*if* we didn't pause for dinner, which was our mounting refrain as soon as we hit the New Hampshire border. Eleven, thirteen, fifteen, seventeen, our appetites were hearty.

Our route in the early years, before Interstate 93 cut a long straight swath through the Granite State, was a leisurely one that wound through many a Massachusetts and New Hampshire town, which, over the years, had taken on a pleasant familiarity to us. One of the last and most memorable towns we came to, before we hit the New Hampshire border, was Tyngsboro, Massachusetts. Tyngsboro was noted (to us at least) not only for its resonant name, but for its towering steel bridge— a vintage construction that defied any and all the laws of gravity that we were able to conjure up. Just outside of Tyngsboro, we shifted our sights (along with the load of the car) to the right, to catch a glimpse of a large and colorful rectangular sign, "Benson's Wild Animal Farm." That detour we had made a number of times over the years, during day outings with an enthusiastic pack of friends.

In New Hampshire, our route—like that of a Concordian of old, Henry David Thoreau—followed the Merrimack River north, through Nashua, Hudson, Litchfield, Merrimack, and Reeds Ferry. Many of these locales greeted us and our fellow travelers with a welcome sign at one end of the town and bid us a fond farewell with a second sign ("Come Back Soon") at the other end. Straddling Mom and Dad's seat, Bea and Brad ticked off the names of the towns, one after another, to mark our progress.

North of Reed's Ferry, the outskirts of Manchester came into view. At one time the textile center of the North, Manchester's mills—which, by our speedometer, followed the Merrimack upriver for an unbroken mile—never ceased to astound us. In earlier years, we would lean farther over Mom's and Dad's shoulders, and ply them with our ever-recurring queries: "How could a building have so many lights? (The poor person who had to change the bulbs!)"—"Did one hallway lead through the whole mill?"—"How many bricks do you think were used to build the mill?"— "How could one build such a big building?" As the mill flowed on with the river, our questions became weightier and weightier. "*How does the ground hold it up, anyway!*"

Apparently our fascination was shared by many a young man and woman of old, who, setting forth from their village farm and shop, flocked, along with civilization, to the Big City. The industrial age had humble beginnings. In the words of young Harriet Farley—

> *I arrived here safe and sound, after being well jolted over the rocks and hills of New Hampshire; and when (it was in the evening) a*

*gentleman in the stage first pointed out (the mill town) to me, with its
lights twinkling through the gloom, I could think of nothing but Pas-
sampscot swamp, when brilliantly illuminated by 'lightening bugs.'*

As Manchester's mills faded out of sight in our rear-view mirror, we
turned our glances ahead to Concord, the capital of New Hampshire.
From Manchester to Concord was a nineteen-mile stretch, both picturesque and, for the most part, uneventful. Hooksett, Suncook, Bow were
quiet New Hampshire towns, with their aspiring church steeples, town
halls, and a solid general store or two. New Hampshire held firm to life's
essentials.

The last notable landmark before we reached Concord announced
itself in a towering plume of smoke, which, a bend or two up the Merrimack, puffed out of a colossal structure on the bank of the river. Wires,
cables, fences, mountains of sand and black substance,... tracks and
trains surrounded what Dad matter-of-factly declared to be a coal-fired
power plant. Another bend of the river was upon us, before we knew
where to begin with our questions. As of yet, the wonders of electricity eluded us, and, settling back into our seats, we allowed the power
plant, coal and all, to disappear back up its towering stack and into blue
yonder.

Concord, with its gold-domed state house, marked the halfway
point of our journey—time to stretch our legs and fill up our respective
tanks. Leaning with Dad into the off-ramp turn, we cast our eyes up the
road for HoJo's—the ultimate, we fancied, in dining. In those days, the
finer inns and hotels on the route were by-passed, relegated to wait a
few years until hamburgers ceased to be the greatest thing between two
pieces of bread, and we discovered that sirloin came off the same cow.

So it was, HoJo's and hamburgers. And, as youngsters—not yet
privy to the unwritten codes of behavior—we made sure to acquaint
ourselves with everybody who graced that fine establishment. Edging
through the double glass doors, we would besiege the counter, count
the number of rotations we could make on the stools, pore over the
menus, and swap stories with any and every sympathetic soul within
earshot. By the time our hamburgers arrived—complete with catsup,
onions, pickles, relish, potato chips, and mustard—we had worked up
an appetite.

* * * * *

The second half of the trip was more relaxing. Before we left HoJo's, we took a moment to rearrange our north-bound "sleigh," so that Bea and Brad could hop in the back and stretch out. A good full stomach, coupled with the excitement of the day, sapped our remaining energy. As we passed the state house, a smile returned with a memory of another of our forebears, a certain Grandpa Sinclair, whom Dad had only cursorily sketched. A Littleton, New Hampshire Democrat, and vigorous leader in his party's affairs, the old gentleman had been an outspoken candidate for Governor and for the United States Senate, in the days when Republican pluralities were as solid as New Hampshire's granite.

Over the years, Grampy had filled in Dad's picture of our forebear, "During the winter of 1897–98, while the family's house was under construction, we were living at the Woodland Park Hotel—and Grandpa Sinclair came to pay a visit. Grandpa loved a good yarn and wasted nobody's time with brevity. He also had developed a very effective way to assure the attention of his listeners. Wherever he went, he carried a brass ear trumpet, which is the thing I remember best about him, because he aimed it at me like a gun when I spoke to him." Grampy had etched the image of the old gentleman indelibly in my mind.

"During Grandpa Sinclair's visit, the subject of E.S.P. (Extra Sensory Perception) came up. Apparently, Grandpa Sinclair had a close friend, H.M. Jones, a Representative from the town of Bath, who had a fit of it. When the House was in session," Grampy had noted, "it was H.M.'s custom to drive to Woodsville, stable his horse, and take the train to Concord. This he had done on the day in question, he told his friend, Sinclair."

"The train crowded, H.M. found himself seated beside a young woman, both pleasant and stylish. Conversation started and prospered—especially after it developed that they both were going to Concord and both aiming to put up at the Eagle Hotel."

"Arriving at the hotel desk, they found that the rooms reserved for them were at opposite ends of the same floor. Hers was No. 39. Pleasantly surprised, she invited H.M. to drop in. Caught off guard, H.M. made some excuse about 'errands' at the state house, across the street, to which the young lady gaily responded, 'Then perhaps after you have made your calls!'"

"'Didn't really have much to do,' H.M. told Grandpa. So he went back to the Eagle, collected his bag, went up to his room, and fixed himself up. After fidgeting a bit, H.M. decided that the young lady's invitation was innocent enough. So, he opened the door and started down that plush-carpeted corridor. The hallway was as quiet as a tomb as H.M. arrived at room No. 39. By this time he admitted to Grandpa Sinclair that he began to have second thoughts. Shaking them off, he started to raise fist to knock on the door, when he heard his wife's voice clear as a bell, '*Hiram!*'"

"'It was mighty disconcerting,' H.M. confessed. Quietly retracing his steps, he went back to his room. H.M. told Grandpa Sinclair that he tried to turn his attention to other matters, but without much luck. 'I got to thinkin', land sakes alive, H.M, you're a sane man. No matter how convincing you thought that voice was, it just *can't be*.' Well, H.M. started down the hall again, but before he could so much as touch a knuckle to that door, it happened again, '*Hiram Jones!*' The voice was louder and more emphatic."

The wry smile on Grampy's face returned to mind. "By this time, the poor man was pretty discomfited and said, 'Believe me, Sinclair, I *know that voice*—and I quit, right there.' Grandpa Sinclair listened sympathetically, as H.M. puzzled over the episode. Finally, at a loss for an explanation, the Representative from Bath sheepishly asked his friend what he would have done if he had been in his shoes?"

"'Well, H.M.' your great great-grandfather replied, tilting the ear trumpet toward his abashed colleague, Y'know, I'm so deaf; I don't know if I'd aheard her!'" The smile broke on my lips.

* * * * *

We left both the state capital and its gold dome behind us, its luster undimmed in the winter evening. As we continued north, Bea and Brad settled down, doing their best to share the pillows and blankets that we had brought along, while Nat pulled out his jackknife and plastic bag and started to whittle a Christmas ornament for the tree awaiting us. I turned my gaze out into the night. At last, Mom and Dad could enjoy a few precious moments of peace.

This was my favorite part of the trip. As we settled in, Dad would often recount episodes from earlier days when another family by the name of Weeks made their journey northward. The date was 1786, and the roads were not even trails. The blazing was done by Captain John Weeks, who was to represent the North Country in the state legislature.

Captain John Weeks was accompanied by his own six-year-old son, John Wingate, and elder daughter, Patty. Mother, and the two youngest Weeks, stayed in Greenland, New Hampshire, to tend to the home fires and to await news from the Northern Kingdom:

> We shall move into our log house this week. It will be a very comfortable one. The logs, all peeled, are smooth and clean. The house is eighteen feet wide and twenty feet long. We shall have one comfortable room and two bed rooms. Our family now consists, besides myself, of one hired man, one girl, one boy, one cow, one heifer, one hog, one sheep, one dog, one cat, and one chicken. . . .

Although a donkey was conspicuously absent from the roll, the Weeks did have a pair of geese, which they planned to take back home with them in the fall. Short and sweet, the letter (which, apart from the enduring fly, bore a striking resemblance to our summer cookout choral rendition) ended with the assurance that mother would be pleased to see the little family and proud of Patty's management of it. And so it was. The records indicated that Mrs. Weeks made the trip in the autumn of that year, following her husband on horseback through the White Mountain Notch, her seven-month-old daughter in her arms. Head on a pillow, I peered out into the darkening evening, as my thoughts went out to my young forebear, James, who rode along behind his mother on the same horse.

With the movement inland, trails began to etch the wilderness. At times, the passage north was halted on account of sickness, adversity, or inclement conditions. Shelters and log cabins were thrown up along the route and, depending upon the circumstances, remained, forming the rude beginnings of an outpost or settlement. As more pioneers passed through, the trail widened to accommodate a sturdy wagon, drawn by a team of horses or plodding oxen. The settlements grew into little vil-

lages, not only receiving pioneers on the way north, but sending back
news of fertile farm land in the Upper Connecticut Valley, teeming
with fish and game.

Years unfolded into decades. As the demand grew for wood to hoist
the masts of ships and to stimulate trade, rails began to reach north,
prodded on by an impatient steam engine and box cars. By this time,
the little log cabin belonging to the Weeks family had grown with a
view that looked out to neighbors and a village that was to take the
name of Lancaster, a reminder of a shire across the sea whence the first
settlers' journey began.

* * * * *

Over the years, other members of the Weeks family helped widen
the route both North and South. Great-Granddad, who had followed
young Harriet Farley south to the city lights, was at the helm of the
family's first automobile expedition to the North Country. This harrowing journey in a Pope-Toledo, two days in duration, was due not so
much to the car nor the weather, but rather to the roads, which threw
a constant veil of dust over the assortment of veils and goggles that led
the way.

As co-pilot, Grampy's earliest recollections of the trips to the *fabled
frontier town of my forebears, far up the valley of the Connecticut River and
north of the mountains* were vivid ones. On Uncle James' farm, out on the
North Road, Grampy had two older cousins, one of whom owned and
trained three yoke of steers. The three young Weeks used to practice
driving the steers, a yoke apiece, up and down the dusty roads, over the
course of the summer months. Come Labor Day of one year, the three
lads kicked up their heels and guided the teams right on down to the
Lancaster Fair grounds, where they slept with their beasts of burden,
so as to be up bright and early the next morning to groom them for the
exhibition. Great was Grampy's glee when his pair won a ribbon, and
he found himself parading his prize-winning yoke of steers around the
big ring before the bandstand crowd.

With the following years, Grampy picked up the pace. By the time
he himself had climbed into the driver's seat, the state of the roads had
improved considerably, and the trip from Boston to Lancaster had settled around 8 hours. During the fuel rationing that accompanied World
War II, these getaways to the country were dearly prized by Grampy,

who saved his gas coupons over the course of the week, in order to fill up his tank for the weekend. In later years, as Commerce head, Grampy was to have a hand himself at more improvements of the route, inaugurating the first hard-surfaced highway system, which, Dad recounted, reached its climax in the completion of the greatest engineering and construction project in the history of the world: the Continental U.S. Interstate and Defense Highway System. But that, too, was now a few bends behind us.

As we drove on north, my thoughts were gently interrupted by a song, a first followed by a second, that rose on Mom's lips, *Oh, Mister Moon, moon, bright and shiny moon, oh won't you please shine down on me. Oh, Mister Moon, moon, bright and shiny moon, hiding behind those trees....* Lifting my gaze to the heavens, I marveled, ever and again, at the moon's sure sense of direction. No matter how fast we went, or which way the car turned, the faithful old orb managed to keep up with us as we headed north.

A familiar Plymouth steeple passed in the night, ... a bright orange Jack-O-Lantern sign ... and, soon after, the fenced-in platforms of a slumbering trading post, its well-fed and seasoned bears in peaceful hibernation. Up, up, up the road led us, by the great Indian Head, its silent gaze searching the dark horizon, and on into Franconia Notch. Stars filled the heavens, raising my eyes to a great stone face, retiring into the shadows of the night.

> *Men hang out their signs indicative of*
> *Their respective trades.*
> *Shoemakers hang out a gigantic shoe;*
> *Jewelers, a monstrous watch;*
> *Even the dentist hangs out a gold tooth;*
> *But up in the Franconia Mountains,*
> *God Almighty has hung out a sign*
> *To show that in New England He makes men.*

Words of a native son, Daniel Webster, came quietly to mind, adding a flourish to the Almighty's hand and turning my thoughts to another account that, some felt, portrayed the great orator himself. Hawthorn's beloved story, "The Great Stone Face," had been passed down through the generations of my and many a New England family, revealing a truth about our culture to which I was slowly beginning to awaken. The industrialist of immeasurable wealth, the celebrated warrior, the revered statesmen, . . . in the end it was the poet who grasped the 'promise' of that simple, aspiring, and illumined soul, Ernest. We are the ones we've been waiting for? Can it be?

On through the Notch we drove. Dad's peaceful tenor voice joined Mom's, as the heavens rose up all around us:

> *Children sleep, the moon is high.*
> *Angels watchin' over me, my Lord.*
> *You're safe, and love is nigh.*
> *Angels watchin' over me.*
>
> *All night, all day, angels watchin' over me, my Lord.*
> *All night, all day, angels watchin' over me....*

* * * * *

"Wake up, we're here." Mom's voice stirred us from our dreams. I lifted my head from the back of the seat and glanced out the window, as the car rolled into the driveway on a soft carpet of snow. Rubbing their eyes, Bea and Brad sat up to take their bearings. All about us, snowflakes filled the night air, glistening in the lantern that shone over the front door. "Cat Bow!" Nat said with a yawn, as he reached for his boots. Excitement awoke in his voice.

As I climbed out of the car, the stillness of the night gathered me up in its chilling embrace. Glancing about, signs of winter were everywhere. A hefty pile of logs from the woodshed had been neatly stacked in the side entrance. Beside the garage, a toboggan stuck its head out of a snow bank, and icicles, long on the roof, hung down above the muffled outline of bushes that huddled up against the sides of the Big House.

Collecting our wits and gear, we started for the front door, as above us smoke rose lazily up out of the chimney, merging with the falling flakes. We knew that Grampy would be sitting up by the fire, waiting for us with a good book, bowl of popcorn, and his old friend "Jack Daniels." Pushing open the front door, sleigh bells announced our arrival.

In the entrance room, an owl glanced down at us from its shadowy perch atop the shelves. Kicking the snow off our boots, we deposited our bags in front of the fireplace. The excitement of arriving at the farm had chased away the last traces of sleep. Shedding our coats, we hurried on through the living room, warmly lit by the evening lamps, and down the hall, past the rows of closets, to the Pine Room. Sure enough, Grampy was up—or had been. We paused on the threshold to behold the master of the house, tucked into his old plaid bathrobe and reclining back on the sofa by the fire. Feet resting on the old hearth bench, the Lord of Cat Bow, was, as Dad was accustomed to saying, "the picture of comfort and relaxation."

"Hey Grampy, what do you say!" Coming up behind us, Dad gently pushed us into the room and stepped forward to greet his father. Opening his eyes, Grampy surveyed us with a sleepy smile and, then, held out his hands, "You made it." Nodding, Dad leaned over and hoisted Grampy up, yawns and all, into a big bear hug. Grampy winked at us, as we watched with delight. "Nuts!" Our smiles broke into laughs at his words.

"Are the cows in the barn?"—"Is there still hay in the loft?"—"If we're good, can we go on a sleigh ride?" We had a thousand questions, including some considerations regarding Christmas, which was only two days away. But, just as the fire was beginning to chase away the chills, the old grandfather clock sounded ten resonant chimes, and Grampy called a halt to the proceedings, "Time to go to bed, children. We will discuss it all in the morning."

We started to protest, but Mom and Dad turned us around and headed us toward the door. As we retrieved our bags and started upstairs, Grampy announced that we could have any room we wanted in the house—except, of course, his. Our footsteps quickened, Bea and Brad heading down the hall toward Dad's old room, Nat and I, our sights on the War Room. After running the toothbrush across my teeth and slapping cold water onto my face, I hopped into bed. Quite content and with ample food for dreams, I drifted off into my own winter wonderland.

8

THE BLESSED BARN

"WE BEAT 'UNCLE CHARLEY' down to breakfast and had done some preparing for him, knowing he not only relished a good bowl of porridge in the morning, but a good practical joke as well. . . ."

Dad held up his hand for Nat and me to be quiet as we entered the sun porch. Grampy glanced up at us from the table, before turning back to the others and continuing with his story, "Ned had gathered up some sawdust from the barn and poured it into Charley's bowl. The rest of us added fruit, berries, and syrup, topped off with fresh cream. Adele watched us getting things ready, but didn't seem convinced that her good husband was up for the serving we had dished out. Finally, as we heard Charley's footsteps coming down the stairs, we carefully set the bowl at his place," Grampy pointed to where Mom was sitting, "and bid him a hearty good morning."

A smile touched Grampy's lips, "Charley acknowledged our greeting, but didn't say much more. He was pretty hungry and, spying the bowl filled to the brim, sat down in front of it and dug right in." Dad broke out laughing. Nat and I were getting the drift. Grampy carried on, "Well, we all watched in amazement as the old boy took one bite after another of that damned sawdust. Finally, Adele, who was sitting right beside him, couldn't control herself anymore and blurted out, '*Charley, stop! For God's sake, stop!*'"

The room broke up in laughter —Grampy leaning his elbow on the table and wiping his eyes, Dad doing his best to catch a breath. Mom was the most restrained and, I suppose, sympathetic of the listeners, pointing to our places across the table. Nat and I were not quite sure what to make of the whole affair, as we quietly sat down.

When the laughter subsided, Dora stepped into the sunporch with glasses of orange juice on a small plate, for Nat and me, and traces of a smile on her kindly face. Though I doubt she would have served Uncle Charley that bowl of "porridge," I suspect this wasn't the first time she had heard the story.

Grampy took a big breath, "Those were wonderful days." Dad nodded. Yes, our father had been the subject of a number of equally colorful episodes that had become engraved in the family annals. To that subject, Dora was able to speak from firsthand experience.

The hell-raiser of the family, when Dad got a bit rambunctious, it was Dora's job (in Grampy's absence) to take things in hand—even if it meant, as on occasion it did, wrestling young Sinclair to the floor. These accounts delighted us and were self-righteously brought up to Dad (a justification for our antics) who, needless to say, denied it all—doing his best to camouflage a grin. The house, however, bore a number of mementos from his earlier years. The hole he cut in his bedroom door as a boy, in order to be able to discern who was seeking entrance, was but one testimony to his remarkable facility for getting into mischief. And, if Dad still insisted on his probity, we would go to the ultimate judge, "The Lord" himself.

Grampy was not one for sparing the details. To Dad's chagrin, he recounted how during one harrowing stretch of our father's childhood—previously eluded to—it wasn't unusual for Dad to find himself enroute to his room as many as two to three times a week, without dinner. It seemed that, among his other knacks, our father had the rather ingrained habit of insisting on getting his "two cents worth" in at the dinner table—whether his opinions were solicited or not.

Apparently, "young Sin" didn't understand that the expression, "children are to be seen and not heard," applied to him as well. To be truthful, I kind of admired Dad for his stubbornness (as I suspect did Grampy)—but two to three times a week! Be that as it may, I felt a special debt of thanks to Dad's kindhearted sister, Aunt Patty, who snuck him up provisions after the fact. If it hadn't been for her solicitude, our poor father-to-be might have wasted away.

Reflecting back over such accounts, I've often wondered if Dad's spunk might have had deeper and more mystical roots—roots that stretched back through the legendary ranks of the Knights Templar to Grampy's Scottish ancestry. Among the family files, I had come upon a portrait postcard of a stern and rather forbidding-looking gentleman clad in plaid, with a cloak slung across his shoulders, a sword poised at his waist, and a decided expression on his face. The painter, Henry Raeburn, had set Sir John Sinclair (St. Clair), 1st Bart of Ulbster, in a barren mountain setting. At Sir John's feet, boulders rose up, with the stump of an old tree, into a dark and beclouded sky that enwreathed the Bart's countenance like a brooding halo. Little would I have guessed that this stern looking forbear was not only known as "The Queen's Knight," but that his affections had been immortalized by the poet, Dunbar, in a verse that defied my aspiring grasp of the English language:

> *Sir John Sinclair begouth to dance,*
> *For he was new come out of France:*
> *For any thin that he do micht,*
> *The ane foot gaed aye unricht,*
> *And to the tother wald not gree.*
> *Quoth ane. Tak up the Queen's knicht:*
> *A merrier dance micht na man see.*

In musing over Sir John's portrait, I fancied that Dad's namesake had been afflicted by a delicate curse—for lack of a better name, the "Curse of the Sinclairs." It didn't seem entirely without reason. After all, every member of the Weeks family, who had inherited the name, Sinclair, had something of a primal and impetuous dash. It was not easy to put the trait into words, as it was more of an aura that emanated from the gentlemen.

The first of the clan on the shores of the new world—a colonist *who stood for Massachusetts, rather than the Crown*—was immortalized within the public record, for *swearing by God and calling John Hall of Greenland ould dog and ould slave, and that he would knock him in the head, fined ten shillings for swearing, and to have an admonition for his reviling and threatening speeches, and fees of court, three shillings.* In the ensuing year, the old-timer must have had something of an epiphany, for he was elected Selectmen of Portsmouth (NH), topped off by a stint as constable and sheriff.

Following in his forebears' footsteps, old Grandpa Sinclair, ear trumpet cocked, clearly had a good dose of the dash. From what we could make out, Grampy (propelled into life with a shot of strychnine) had been soundly smitten. Dad had gone to admirable, if considerable, pains to carry on the tradition, and the Sinclairs in my generation ("rub-a-dub-dub, thanks for the grub") suggested that the strain, such as it was, had lost little of its verve.

The only explanation I could come up with was that one dark and dreary night, the progenitor of the clan had happened upon some wily wizard amidst the Scottish moors, and, if his pluck resembled that of the Sinclair in the portrait, did not endear himself to the old conjurer. The rest of the story was history, in all the living color that we experienced—first- and second-hand, down through the generations.

As puzzling to me as the source of the spell, was the change that came over Dad with the years. It was hard to imagine how such a lively and rambunctious soul managed to accommodate himself to ways more straight and narrow. Though it never occurred to me at the time to inquire further. *Commit Thy Work to God* was the Sinclair Clan motto, emblazoned across the ancient coat of arms—a shield, bearing to all who confronted it a majestic black cross.

Eggs, bacon, and toast, accompanied by Cat Bow's choice raspberry jam, followed the orange juice, as we made plans for the day. First on the agenda was the barn. Nat and I wanted to confirm Grampy's annual census report. As the adults arose to confer on Holiday matters, Nat and I excused ourselves and headed out to the entrance room to bundle up.

* * * * *

It was a beautiful day, clear, crisp, and cool. The snowfall had been heavy the night before, and, except for the road that had been given a good plowing that morning, the farm was packed in for the winter.

Pausing in the driveway, my sights fell on the old elm that extended its snowy branches out into the morning, etching the blue winter sky. Farther up the driveway, the barn settled into the white hillside, its great sloping roof decked with a fresh blanket of snow. There was a distinct resemblance between the barn and the Big House. Aside from being the same color and sleeping roughly an equal number of inhabitants, both buildings, as noted, were almost identically constructed. In the center of the barn, rails connected the two wings, fencing in a paddock space that allowed Janie and her stall mates an opportunity to stretch their limbs in more favorable seasons. Exchanging snowballs and good-hearted jeers, Nat and I headed up the drive.

Our steps quickened as we approached the barn. Pausing in front of the large, sliding doors, Nat pulled from one side while I took a hold of the other. Together, we managed to budge the doors enough to slip through.

The inside of the barn was a good deal warmer than the outside. As our eyes grew accustomed to the darkness, we glanced about. It was a beautiful barn, we fancied, built on a solid foundation of oak floorboards. To our left, the near wing led down to the tool rooms, tractor stalls, and the quarters of Rob and Prince's, the two towering work horses, whom we looked up to with great fondness and admiration. In front of us, along the left side of the barn, large grain closets and sawdust bins peeked out onto the main floor, which continued down to two more sliding doors at the far end.

To the right of the far doors, a ladder climbed up through a universe of glistening spider webs to the hayloft. Their nimble weavers had been busily at work through the night, casting out delicate patterns, which gleamed in the sunlight that filtered in through the large, loft window. To the left of the sliding doors, the second wing led down to the tack rooms and riding stalls. Janie shared her quarters with two fillies, Punch and Judy, who, in respect to outings, were considerably more forthcoming. Just to our right, a long wooden ladder hung horizontally along the inside of the barn wall, beginning at one door into the cow parlor and ending at the far end of the barn at the second door.

Hearing the scraping of shovels, we slid open the smaller doors into the cow parlor and were greeted by a sight and smell that was a near-inspiration. The Cat Bow herd, thirty Holsteins strong, lifted their great dreamlike heads to greet us as we stepped into their parlor, pausing to pay our respects to their progenitor, the old bull, Benjamin, who lumbered about, chewing his cud in a solid steel-barred pen of his own. Jim Mosher and Bill Rines added their friendly greetings, glancing up from between the stanchions where they were scraping up the souvenirs the herd had deposited the night before. Always eager to mix it up, Nat grabbed a shovel, while I stepped forward to survey the assemblage.

Cows are truly remarkable creatures. Along with laying claim to four stomachs and a tongue that can circumnavigate their nose, they also have the uncanny ability of making one feel utterly conspicuous. As I walked down the center aisle of the parlor, I felt as though I were the guest speaker at some stately convention. I definitely had the floor, as all eyes were upon me.

Many a time, when I was quite alone, I took advantage of my captive audience to brush up my public speaking. Mounting a bail of hay, I would acknowledge the old chairman (Benjamin) in the corner and, then, proceed to address my distinguished gathering. It was quite a feeling, standing there in the prime of my youth surrounded by over thirty tons of vociferous beef. Often I fancied myself as an impassioned statesman and, rising up on my tiptoes, would deliver stirring orations, ranging from the vicissitudes of childhood to the future of the dairy industry. As was the custom in those days, I was wont to open my deliveries with a lighthearted story befitting the occasion:

Daniel Webster had been invited to speak in Boston's Faneuil Hall one July afternoon . . .

So I often began, casting my gaze across the herd:

It was a sultry day, and the young man, who was assigned to look after Mr. Webster's needs, remembered everything—except, to his dismay, a refreshing drink for the great orator. Aware of Webster's predilection for something strong to ignite his spirits, young master Broeksmit (my maternal great-grandfather) hurried about till he had ferreted up the remains of a bottle of whiskey and cool jug of cow milk.

I tipped my cap to the bovine assemblage.

*By the time the young man got back to the platform, Mr. Webster
had begun. Not wanting to distract the speaker, Broeksmit poured
the whiskey into the jug of cow's milk and set it down on the edge
of the platform.*

Other than an occasional shake of the head or swish of the tail, my
audience appeared disaffected. Undismayed, I carried on:

*About a half-hour into the speech, Webster was steaming. Casting
his eyes around, he spied the jug of milk. Though not exactly what
he had in mind, the orator took a breath and stepped to the side of
the platform. Lifting the jug, he proceeded to take a healthy draught,
then, wiping his lips, he paused for a moment... "My God, what
a cow!" young Mr. Broeksmit heard the orator exclaim under his
breath.*

Daisy swished her tail.

Pleasantries aside, politics was another issue that was apt to come
up, as I had thought long and hard on an anonymous text that I had
happened upon in one of the alcoves of the Big House. The subject was
the various "isms" of the day and the slant a pronounced one:

*SOCIALISM: 2 cows; give both to government; they give you the
milk.*

*COMMUNISM: 2 cows; give both to government; government
shoots you; keeps cows and milk.*

FASCISM: 2 cows; give milk to government.

NAZISM: Government takes cows; leaves you holding bag.

*NEW DEALISM: Shoot one cow; milk the other; pour milk down
the sink; apply for relief.*

*FAIR DEALISM: 2 cows; swap them for a political job in Wash-
ington and milk the public.*

As was the custom at Cat Bow in those days, our free enterprise
system had the last word.

CAPITALISM: Sell one cow and buy a bull.

So it was!

Waving my arms, I launched forth on matters of state, until my rapt audience would lose the thread and proceed to moo me off my make-shift platform. A brief digression to the oat bin succeeded in winning once again the ladies' good graces, and, walking up and down the aisles, I would dole out equal portions, while I inquired about their health and familial relations.

A number of the heifers, with whom I was on friendlier terms, allowed me to cozy up to them, after their appetizer, with a good neck rub. This barnyard ritual afforded another unique glimpse of these extraordinary creatures. In response to my ministrations, the gals would stretch their great necks out further and further, dilate their damp nostrils, and transfix me in their lugubrious stares. What universes I beheld in those bovine depths defied expression, but the symbiosis between man and beast was pretty near transcendental. Not infrequently, a good half-hour would be spent in such inclinations, me rubbing and Gertrude, Isabell, and Daisy rolling their lolling eyes.

At the far end of the cow parlor were the calves, my staunchest supporters. The calves kept the parlor lively, as there was a constant exchange between parents and children. As soon as I would approach their pens, the mothers would bellow forth, starting a chain reaction of moos that literally resounded through the rafters. I loved the calves, feeling a common bond, due to our age. But, the mothers would have nothing to do with my gestures of comradeship. Thanks to their protestations, it often took a good fifteen minutes of patient coaxing before the young ones' curiosity would get the best of them, and they would come close enough to nibble the sleeve of my jacket or lick the salt from my hand.

After cleaning up, Bill Rines would collect the milking equipment. A native son of Lancaster, Bill had joined Grampy in 1928, and he and his wife, Esther, had stayed on over the seasons, which took him from the summer hay fields and gardens, to the autumn orchard and wood-lot, and on into the Christmas tree plantation and Sugarbush—before the cycle of the seasons renewed itself with the help of a good dozen wagonloads of manure, "spring tidings," that Bill spread over the fields. Amidst all his labors, Bill always had time to catch us up on the goings-on around the farm, patiently answering our questions about bird and beast, flock and feather in his thoughtful manner.

Milking was the highlight of the morning. We would all huddle around the cows' flanks, avoiding the swishing tails, and watch Bill coax out the rich, warm milk that sang against the side of the pail. It didn't take long before every cat in the barn had joined us, taking it upon themselves to retrieve any misdirected drops. Milking took a good part of the morning, as the newfangled milking-machines hadn't yet found their way to Cat Bow. Bill worked his way slowly up and down the aisles, easing the cows into their positions in the stanchions, setting his stool down by their hindquarters, and, leaning his cheek up against their warm flanks, placing his bucket into range. By and large, the ladies didn't seem to mind Bill's quiet exertions and gave freely of their milk, while they lazily chewed and re-chewed their cuds.

The last chore was to pile the cows' troughs high with hay. Scrambling up into the hayloft, I made sure the decks were clear below, before tipping a half-dozen bales over the edge and onto the hard wooden floor. Between the flights, Nat would escort the bales on into the cow parlor, spacing them in front of the troughs from one end of the stanchions to the other. Then, loosening the twine, we each grabbed a pitch-fork and sent the hay sprawling into the troughs, with our best wishes for a hearty meal. The cows needed no further prompting. Tails and tongues aswishing, they dug into breakfast with much gusto.

Our chores concluded, Nat and I, joined now by Bea and Brad, who had arrived to help us dole out the hay, retraced our steps, up the ladder and into the hay-loft. In those years, sky-diving was a prime pastime on the farm. While one of us mounted a stack of bails to its teetering peak, the others would arrange the loose hay in a great pile below. Then, fists clenched, we whispered a quick prayer, took a deep breath, closed our eyes, and sallied forth....Our first landing was in the soft cushion of hay. From there our momentum carried us up, on, through the barn doors and down the hill to the Big House, where lunch was awaiting us, along with a surprise: Grampy had planned a sleigh ride that evening, Christmas Eve!

* * * * *

"When your dad was a child, your grandmother and I used to take the children for winter outings in our old family sleigh." Grampy slipped one foot snugly into his boot, before sitting back on the wooden bench in front of the blazing fire in the entrance-room hearth. Behind him, the old owl glanced down at its Lord from its cranny atop the bookshelf. Pulling on our sweaters, we settled around Grampy on the two broad-backed love seats.

"We would hitch up the sleigh to the pacer, the fastest horse in the stable, and we would 'pick up a few friendly brushes'—as the expression went in those days—with other drivers along a nearby stretch in town that was a favorite rendezvous for such weekend winter pastimes." I smiled as I imagined Grampy holding Grandmother Bea in a warm bearskin hug, as he urged the horses on. Champing at the bit, we helped Grampy pull on his other boot. Then, as he rose to don his sweater, we zipped up our coats and, all bundled up, headed outside for our own winter's 'brush.'

Above us, a full moon suspended in a universe of stars bathed the sleepy countryside in a swath of light. Spurred by the excitement and chill that nipped at our cheeks, we turned our steps quickly up to the barn.

Bill was draping the reins over Punch and Judy as we arrived. Crowding around the sleigh, we gently patted the horses' sleek, brown bodies. The fillies responded to our touch with spirited whinnies and, stamping their hooves impatiently on the snowy road, appeared to be as excited as we were to set off into the night. Stepping up to the horses, Grampy lent Bill a hand, running the reins through their hitches, down along the lady's flanks. Working quietly alongside Bill, Grampy seemed to enjoy the prospect of the outing as much as we did. Finally, the harnesses in place, Bill carefully backed Punch and Judy up to the sleigh—an old black rig with wicker seats that had been eased out of its hibernation. The last straps secured, Bill held the horses by their bridles, while Grampy gave us a hand. Eager to keep the old bear-skin rug company, we piled in to the sleigh.

Climbing aboard, Grampy gathered up the reins, before turning around to inspect the troops, "Everybody bundled up?"

"Yup, Nat answered as Bea and Brad huddled up close to us, stretching the old black rug to its limits. Smiling, Grampy turned back to the horses and nodded at Bill, who glanced one last time over the rig and, then, let the bridle go. "Come on girls!" Not a word more was needed. We caught only a parting glimpse of Bill, who stepped back under the eaves of the barn, before the sleigh was swept away.

At the bottom of the drive, we flew by the Big House, aglow with lights, and on by the grove of pines at the bend in the road, and, then, the fields themselves, submerged under a still blanket of snow. Spurred on by the evening breeze, Punch and Judy strained at the harness, causing the bells to ring out, as they pulled us up the hill and under the archway of boughs laden heavy with winter's white foliage. Exhilarated, we tossed cheers into the night, while the forest huddled up around the banks of snow on both sides of the road.

Glancing up from the folds of the bearskin rug, I watched Grampy sitting up straight in the seat, his crop lightly playing about Punch and Judy's flanks. Above him, stars peeked through the bare tree tops, distant glimmers of light that traveled on before us. The sleigh was drawn on through the woods. And then the heavens, deep and full, opened up again, as the Baker Farm approached, cast in the pale light of the moon. The old barns, silhouetted in the open field, passed on our left—the farmhouse on the right—before the road once again plunged into the shadow of the woods. On we rode, through the wind and snow and night.

As we neared the end of the road, Grampy drew in the horses' reins and, in a gentle voice, slowed Punch and Judy to a trot and, then, a walk, "Easy, girls. Easy. . . ." As the sleigh came to a stop, we sat up in our seats, almost as winded as the fillies, whose heavy breaths sent plumes of air into the cool night. Turning around, Grampy rubbed his wool mittens over Bea's flushed cheeks. "What do you say, boys and girls!" Our teeth were achatterin', but our hearts were aglow.

After the horses had rested a moment and began to tug once again on the reins, Grampy turned the sleigh back toward the farm. We could have ridden forever, but the night was moving on, and a warm fire awaited us at the Big House. Prodding Punch and Judy into an easy trot, the sleigh returned down the road, breaking new tracks through the gathering snow. The wind at our backs, Nat and I raised our heads and opened our mouths, straining to catch the wayward snowflakes that began to drift down all around us, out of the night sky. And then, before we knew it, the sleigh emerged from the woods, and Cat Bow opened up once again all around us.

Grampy pulled up the horses around the snow-decked circle in front of the Big House. As the runners came to a halt, we shed our furry rug and, thanking him exuberantly, climbed quickly down from the sleigh. Out of the bear's warm embrace, we were eager to get inside. Mom and Dad promised that a cup of hot chocolate would be waiting, along with a winter's tale. *'Twas the night before Christmas....*

9

CHRISTMAS AT CAT BOW

A KNOCK ON THE DOOR ushered Nat and me out of our dreams, as Bea and Brad poked their heads into our room and whispered loudly, "It's Christmas; wake up!"—before continuing down the hall to carry their tidings to Ma and Pa, who, up to that moment, were enjoying a sound sleep. Turning his head on his pillow, Dad quieted their appeals, "Get dressed children and wait in your room until your mother and I come. It's still early."

As I lay in bed, wisps of a dream dispersed, leaving a trace of sadness: Alone, Grampy drove the sleigh on into the night, lifting his searching gaze to the wreath of stars that brightened the heavens.

After what seemed a time interminable, Mom and Dad stepped out of their room and motioned to Bea and Brad at the far end of the hall, before collecting Nat and me from the War Room to head down stairs. By that time we had shed our enveloping quilts and contracted our younger siblings' Christmas cheer.

Hearing footsteps, Grampy rose from his desk in the Pine Room. A bright shine on their faces, he and the old grandfather clock greeted us at the foot of the stairs with a hearty tone, before the Lord of Cat Bow followed the procession on into the living room. Grampy had been long awake and, we were to discover, had conferred extensively with Santa earlier that morning.

The living room breathed bounteously the Christmas spirit. A small, old-fashioned, children's sleigh, with a brightly painted wooden seat, held open the door. Dangling from the windowpanes, delicately cut lace snowflakes offered a twinkling reflection of the winter land-scape that spread out behind them into the day. Atop the windows, colorful quilted comforters warmed the room.

The Christmas tree filled the near corner of the living room, her-alded on high by an adoring angel that gazed down beneficently upon us. A handsome spruce that Bill had taken from the property, the branches of the tree sagged under the weight of colorful bulbs, sparkling tinsel, a host of glittering ornaments, and popcorn and cranberry strings that slipped in and out of its evergreen embrace. Our gazes, however, didn't rest long on the tree. Rather, it was the bright boxes and packages, of every conceivable size, shape, and disposition, laid out at our feet, that captured our attention. Breakfast could wait on this fine morning.

When Mom and Dad gave the word, we searched for names and doled the gifts out accordingly. Grampy sat back in his chair, rocking behind his smile. The master of the house, to him the first tributes were brought. Stationing herself beside Grampy, Mom copied down the names of the presents and their generous benefactors, while Dad gathered up the boxes and wrappings, which he presented to the trash can with his season's greetings.

Praise God from whom all blessings flow, and I wonder if the ineffable Nelson now realizes that there are things that money can't buy. Grampy put down the note and lifted up a sparkling bottle of water, bearing the alluring label, "Martin Meadow Pond Elixir." "Ketchum!" Grampy laughed. "Now I know why he lugged that bucket of water up from the lake at the end of his last visit." Grampy eyed the sparkle with a suspi-cious grin, "It's been treated!"

The Lord of Cat Bow had both a devoted and a colorful circle of friends from all over the country. Each year, gifts began arriving shortly after Thanksgiving and continued to straggle in well into January. Grampy enjoyed Christmas as much as the rest of us and, taking the presents we handed him, set them on his lap, adjusted his glasses, and read the tender and often humorous notes attached.

Anything and pretty well everything emerged from the wrappings: books, china, pictures, plants, exotic drinks, elaborate odds and ends for a purposely designated cranny of Cat Bow, and a colorful assortment of apparel—from outlandish ties to a bulging pair of suspenders—for his wardrobe. Food, however, was Grampy's favorite, and about halfway through the proceedings he was wont to call a halt to the festivities, while he sampled a box of chocolates that had arrived on his lap. The sweets came from his oldest and dearest friends, who knew that there was no better calling card at Cat Bow than a fresh box of fudge.

By the time we had finished opening the last of the presents—a strapping toboggan that had been tucked away behind the sofa—we came to the unanimous conclusion that Santa had done an admirable job—particularly given the smoldering chimney that he had had to contend with the night before. Quite content, we gathered up the gifts and headed upstairs to get dressed up for Christmas lunch. The rest of the family would be arriving within the hour.

* * * * *

Laying our Sunday School clothes on our beds, Nat and I proceeded to don our holiday attire. This was *not* our favorite part of Christmas. Even at our advanced ages, we deemed wool suits, button-up shirts, and ties an infringement upon youth. But there was nothing to be done. Despite the mounting ranks of grandchildren, a benevolent monarchy still held sway over Cat Bow. This was the one day of the year when all were expected to look their best.

Pretty much dressed, except for our new Christmas bow ties, whose abbreviated ends managed to elude us, Nat and I followed Bea and Brad down the hall to Mom and Dad's room for inspection. It was their job to apply the inevitable finishing touches. Belts had to be tucked into their loops, top buttons tussled with, and our respective heads of hair given a good brushing.

After a seemingly endless amount of patting, tucking, and rearranging, Dad steered us in front of the mirror to pull together our bow ties. This was the most disconcerting part of the whole affair, as we confronted our vis-à-vis with a mixture of skepticism and dismay. Finally, satisfied that we were as presentable as could be expected, Mom rummaged through her suitcase, producing two red Christmas vests, with bright silver buttons. Ignoring our moans and groans, she cheerfully slipped them over our shirts. Finished! Bea and Brad were next in line.

Our loose ends all accounted for, Dad slipped into his jacket, Mom patted a curl, and we marched on downstairs—the parents in tow—to join the rest of the family in the Pine Room. The festivities had just begun. Leaning up against the crackling fireplace, Grampy, book in hand and dressed (we were pleased to discover) in a bright red vest of his own, had the floor:

> *... When all through the house,*
> *Not a creature was stirring, not even a ...*

Grampy glanced down over his glasses at young cousin Charley Weeks, who, perched on a stool at the Lord's feet, eyes bulging, returned Grampy's animated gaze. ...Mouse! All eyes upon him, Grampy read on:

> *The stockings were hung from the chimneys with care,*
> *In hopes that Saint Nicholas soon would be there.*
>
> *The children were nestled all snug in their beds,*
> *While visions of sugar plums danced in their heads.*
> *And Mamma in her kerchief and I in my cap*
> *Had just settled down for a long winter's nap*
>
> *When out on the lawn there arose such a clatter,*

Uncle Bish gave a wastebasket a quick drumming, to which Grampy nodded his approval:

> *I sprang from my bed to see what was the matter.*
> *Away to the window I flew like a flash,*
> *Tore open the shutters and threw up the sash.*
>
> *The moon on the breast of the new fallen snow*
> *Gave a luster of midday to objects below.*
> *When, what to my wondering eye should appear,*
> *But a miniature sleigh and eight tiny reindeer;*
>
> *With a little old driver, so lively and quick,*
> *I knew in a moment it must be Saint Nick.*
> *More rapid than eagles, his coursers they came.*
> *And he whistled, and shouted, and called them by name:*
>
> *Now, Dasher! Now, Dancer! Now, Prancer! and Vixen.*

Lifting his hands, Grampy summoned the chorus. The adults joined in full force for a line, "On, Comet! On, Cupid! On Donner and Blitzen!" before Grampy gathered up the reins:

> *To the top of the porch, to the top of the wall!*
> *Now, dash away, dash away, dash away all!*

Lowering his voice, Grampy took a breath for us all:

> *As dry leaves that before the wild hurricane fly*
> *When they meet an obstacle, mount to the sky,*
> *So up to the housetop, the coursers they flew*
> *With a sleigh full of toys, and Saint Nicholas too.*
>
> *And then in a twinkle, I heard on the roof*
> *The prancing and pawing of each little hoof.*
> *As I drew in my head,*

While Grampy cast an eye over his shoulder at the fireplace, Dad quickly eased out of his seat, carefully pulling a bright-red Santa Claus hat from his jacket pocket.

> *and was turning around,...*

We nodded...held our breath, as Dad crept around the couch. Then, before Grampy knew what was happening, Dad stepped over the bench and pulled the hat snugly down over Grampy's eyes. *DOWN THE CHIMNEY SAINT NICHOLAS CAME WITH A BOUND!* And stole his father's line.

As the laughter subsided, Grampy found his place in the book and, making sure everybody was in their seat, threw the tassel of the hat over his shoulder, and read on:

> *He was dressed all in fur, from his head to his foot,*
> *And his clothes were all tarnished with ashes and soot;*
> *A bundle of toys he had flung on his back,*
> *And he looked like a peddler opening his pack.*
> *His eyes how they twinkled! His dimples how merry!*
> *His cheeks were like roses, his nose like a cherry.*
> *His droll little mouth was drawn up like a bow,*
> *And the beard on his chin was as white as the snow.*

The stump of a pipe he held tight in his teeth,
And the smoke, it encircled his head like a wreath.
He had a broad little face and a round little belly
That shook when he laughed, like a bowl full of jelly.

We children added cheers to the jovial chorus:

He was chubby and plump, a right jolly old elf.
And I laughed when I saw him, in spite of myself.
A wink of his eye, and a twist of his head,
Soon gave me to know I had nothing to dread.

He spoke not a word, but went straight to his work,
And filled all the stockings; then turned with a jerk,
And laying his finger aside of his nose,
And giving a nod, up the chimney he rose.

He sprang to his sleigh, to his team gave a whistle,
And away they all flew like the down of a thistle.
But I heard him exclaim as he drove out of sight,

We all breathed out. Grampy opened his arms, his sparkling red vest topped off by his new hat:

MERRY CHRISTMAS TO ALL . . .

The finale was drowned out by our applause.

Yes, Grampy had conferred extensively with Santa the night before, and the Pine Room was all decked out for the occasion. Sprigs of mistletoe hung in the doorway, a discreet red blush on their berries. A buxom wreath reposed in the south window, and an embrace of green ivy twined itself around the old musket, which stood guard over the fireplace. At the far end of the Pine Room, a gallery of Christmas cards, depicting a festive tableau of the Holiday Season, lined the broad windowsill. And in and among the cards, small crystalline globes enveloped enchanting winter scenes, which disappeared in a gentle flurry of flakes when we tilted their small universes upside down.

Below the windowsill, the cocktail tray, anointed by its water pitcher, (a great, colorful, porcelain fish) was bubbling. All around us on tables and benches, the Christmas cheer had been generously bestowed. Macaroons, ribbon candy, taffy, lace cookies, topped off by the annual shipment of peanut-brittle from Cousin Margaret in distant Seattle, filled bowls to the brim—alongside the old standbys, popcorn and nuts, which had been spruced up with a layer of caramel and a distinct cashew taste. Spacious and warmed with the family cheer, the Pine Room emanated the joy of the season.

As the adults settled in by the fire, I joined the cousins who had congregated across the room, around the old cobbler's bench, adorned with cubbies and alcoves, brimming with dominos, cards, poker chips, a cribbage board, backgammon, and assorted knickknacks to keep us grandchildren pleasantly distracted. Hands were dealt and dominos lined up, as we happily caught up with our contemporaries who had arrived earlier in the day.

Amid the festivities, a photo album was discovered, around which we gathered on the sofa. A gift from 'Uncle Charlie Squibb,' the pictures, vintage shots from Grampy's earlier years, complete with captions, added a youthful flair to Cat Bow's distinguished rogues gallery, helping to put our grandfather into perspective. Glancing through the photos, I searched Grampy's more youthful expressions for familiar traces of the Lord of Cat Bow.

WHERE DO WE GO FROM HERE? Dressed in boyhood tights, a striped sailor's shirt, and prim laced boots, Grampy gazed out innocently at the world from his perch atop the great stone balcony that encircled great-granddad's mountain home. The clear, azure horizon provided a fitting backdrop for the young lad's childhood dreams.

The neighboring picture added four years and a good six inches to the story. Grampy had jumped down from the stone balcony, descended from the mountain top, and landed erect on his own two feet. Arms folded staunchly across his stomach, the tights, sailor's shirt, and tender glance were replaced by a pair of knickerbockers, coat, tie—and another, more worldly expression on his face—*READY, yes, TO FACE THE CRUEL WORLD.*

And off Grampy was in the next photo, apace in a rowboat and headed for the opposite shore. The sober look on Grampy's youthful face was overshadowed by that of the stooped and aged oarsman. *FIRST INDICATION OF EXECUTIVE ABILITY* read the subscript. Neither party appeared particularly taken by the arrangements, as Grampy's sights were directed straight ahead.

The scenes shifted with the seasons to a snowy winter panorama. Bundled up in a baggy winter parka and an enveloping scarf, our grandfather gathered his ski poles into a precipitous tuck on the summit of the Mt. Prospect Skiway. At the tip of his skis, two long, straight tracks, iced over the night before, raced down the hillside, before ending abruptly in a good-sized mound of snow. From what we garnered, in Grampy's younger years, the foot gear of the day, vintage Barker Boots, allowed little if any lateral movement. Once one pushed off, it was *BOMBS AWAY!*

Judging by the awnings, arches, and architecture of the following picture, the next stop was "Gay Paris." Adorned in his stylish suit and bowler hat, Grampy found himself besieged, in one of the cities famed squares, by a flock of pigeons—one on each hand and a third astride his bowler hat. *DOWN ON THE FARM*, the caption read, eliciting a demur laugh from the petite Madame who looked on in the picture.

From Paris, the montage returned to more familiar climes. *TWO SECRETARIES*, Grampy was clearly coming into his own, as, hands tucked into the vest pockets of his three-piece suit, the young man struck a commanding pose in front of the old Pope-Toledo car. In the background, his father, cigar in hand, gazed steadily over his son's shoulder.

As my cousins turned the pages of the album, I glanced over at Grampy, sitting back beside the fire. Glimpses of the grown lad gently lit his face.

* * * * *

When the last of the family had gathered and found a seat on sofa, bench, chair, lap, or floor, Cousin Kim asked Grampy for a story. Her motion received a hearty second, and, turning our attention to Grampy, we all sat back to listen.

"A story. . . ." Grampy gathered up a handful of nuts, as he cast his eye over the grandchildren, "Well, late one fall in the forties, after your parents had grown up and left home, I was up here on the farm with some friends, including a couple of old Battery Boys, when I got a call from the stationmaster, who was a bit beside himself. 'Mr. Weeks,' he exclaimed, 'we have just received a carload of longhorn steers, which appear to be an early Christmas gift to you from some admirer in Texas. They've been cooped up for the last two thousand-five hundred miles and are getting pretty ornery....'" Grampy nodded, "I was almost as surprised as the stationmaster and, knowing something of the temperament of Texas cattle, appreciated the fact that the gentleman was anxious to have the cargo unloaded."

"Well, I told him to hang on; we'd be down as soon as we could. Then, conferring with my battery-mates, we decided that the only way to handle the situation was to have a North Country round-up." An exclamation rippled through the Pine Room. "In those days, we had a good stable of horses on the farm, and, grabbing our hats, the six of us saddled up and headed off. We didn't arrive at the station a moment too early. The longhorns, who by this time had traveled across nearly the entire continental United States, were almost as edgy as the stationmaster.

'What now?' was his question. Your 'Uncle Ned' and I looked from the stationmaster to the cows, to each other. I don't remember who gave the word, but a moment later the doors were flung open, and Battery B, those in attendance, were off after the steers, who fortunately had a good sense of direction and headed out of town the way we had come."

Grampy shuffled the nuts into his mouth, before sitting forward and wiping his palms between his legs, "Though the cattle didn't take awfully well to our hooting, hollering, and horses, they did appreciate the grass that lined the road back up the hill toward the farm. We managed to ease them along,... until, at the top of the hill, one of the boys, figuring that the worst was behind us, succeeded in prodding the lead longhorn into a trot, which, with the steepening incline, turned into a run and, soon thereafter—the rest of the herd hot in pursuit—a stampede."

The younger grandchildren who had a seat hung onto it. "Well, somehow a couple of us managed to get our horses out in front of the herd and turn them down the road toward the farm. From there, none of us stopped until Cat Bow came into sight."

Dora arrived just in time for the grand finale and, allowing Grampy to round up the last of the steers, announced that lunch was ready. We needed no further prompting, as we had savored the smells filtering from the kitchen all morning. Out we went, Grampy finishing up his drink and storing some popcorn in his pockets for later, as this time he brought up the rear.

* * * * *

What a feast! We grandchildren had never seen such a meal in all our lives. The whole farm had made a contribution, led by the Christmas goose plucked up on the platter before Grampy at the head of the table. The main dish was flanked by jelly, stuffing, gravy, and pitchers of cider, while smaller bowls full of peas, carrots, potatoes, onions, squash, and bread decorated the sideboard. The adults took their seats at the dining room table—Aunt Frannie filling the empty seat across from Grampy at the far end of the festive board—while the rest of us secured a place at the card tables that had been set up around its flanks. Our talk tapered off as we started into the meal.

The Lord of Cat Bow presented quite a picture. Sitting forward at the head of the table, his sleeves rolled up and his legs spread apart, Grampy dug into the goose with much gusto. We watched him approach her from all angles, poking the old lady with his fork and ruffling her feathers. Finally, when he was sure that all eyes were upon him, he popped a tasty morsel in his mouth (how an "oyster" ended up in a goose, we could not fathom) and winked at us as he licked his lips.

After most of us had gone through two good helpings and a number of us were debating a third, Grampy came over to *"make sure we were getting enough."* His napkin peeking out of his shirt, he put his hands on the back of Bea's and Barbara Sherrill's chairs, and, with a playful note of concern in his voice, asked if we had room for dessert. Taking a deep breath, they nodded their heads. Ice cream and pie were still to come.

As the plates were finally cleared, Grampy rose, rapped his spoon on his glass, and called for our attention. Dad and Uncle Bill ribbed him good-naturedly, until he told them to 'hush up.' Then, placing his knuckles on the table, Grampy announced that he had a few thoughts to share, appropriate to the season. The considerate note in his voice rippled over the family. Setting down our forks and knives, we sat back quietly to listen.

"How many of you children know what that picture is about?" Grampy pointed behind him to a painting on the mantel above the fireplace. Turning in our seats, we recognized a familiar battle scene spanned by the famed bridge. "'By the rude bridge that arched the flood, their flag to April's breeze unfurled, here once the embattled farmers stood, and fired the shot heard 'round the world.'" Grampy glanced about the room at us younger members of the clan.

"That print by Amos Doolittle depicts the Battle at the Old North Bridge in Concord—the first time that the colonists made a deliberate armed resistance against the British." Grampy's eyes rested for a moment on the scene.

"'One if by land and two if by sea.' As Longfellow described in his famous poem, the British had marched out from Boston to seize the Patriots' arms and provisions that had been stored in Concord, the seat of the Provincial Congress. What the British weren't expecting was that the provincials were a step ahead of them. The evening before, word had gotten out that General Gage was preparing a search-and-destroy mission, and the bulk of the weapons and provisions were quickly moved to the outskirts of Concord and neighboring towns."

"When the British arrived in the center of Concord, they were not pleased." Grampy glanced down at us, "The Minutemen, considerably outnumbered in the beginning, had mustered on the hillside above the old North Bridge to wait for the reinforcements that began to arrive with the dawn. All was quiet, until one of the men, Joseph Hosmer, noticed a plume of smoke rising up into the April morning. Turning to Major Butrick, his commander, Hosmer called out, *Will you let them burn the town down?* His words roused his fellow Minutemen. *I have not a man who's afraid to die!* echoed the response. Their ranks swelling with Minutemen companies from Acton, Lincoln, Bedford, Littleton, and many a town across the state, and as far north as New Hampshire, the Provincials quickly fell into their columns and advanced on the British who held the bridge." My eyes moved from Grampy back to the print. Flames sparked the fireplace.

Grampy lifted a glass of water to his lips before continuing. "Isaac Davis, Captain of the Acton Company, and his young fifer, Abner Hosmer, lead the column. Clear instructions were given not to fire unless fired upon. The colonists were facing fellow Englishmen." Grampy paused, "And so it was. In the face of the advancing Provincials, the British companies retreated to the far end of the bridge. As the Minutemen drew near, warning shots were followed by a direct volley, which broke the strains of the fife. The Hosmer boy fell dead, a bullet through his heart. Moments later, a second bullet struck down Captain Davis. '*Fire, fellow soldiers, for God's sake, fire!*' Major Buttrick called to his men, as he leapt forward. A volley rang out, killing three British soldiers and wounding nearly a dozen more." Grampy's pause lengthened, "The American Revolution had begun."

My eyes rested on the print of the still spring landscape, elevated "by the rude bridge that arched the flood," as Grampy carried the story on—a running battle back to Boston, the ensuing blockade of the city, the Battle at Bunker Hill, and five long, dark, and trying years in which the young colonies struggled to band together to fight a war of independence against the most powerful nation in the world.

"On Christmas eve, our country was at a crisis point. After the alarming victory at the North Bridge in Concord, the British had rallied and landed on our shores one of the mightiest armies of the day. In response, George Washington, who had been chosen to head up the Continental Army, was able to muster only 19,000 troops." An earnest note touched Grampy's voice.

"It was hard times for the cause of liberty. Congress and the states faced the overwhelming task—in a country whose sympathies were clearly split between the old order and the new—of supplying, equipping, and paying the costs of the war. Not a few American farmers and merchants preferred to do business with the British, who were able to pay in gold or silver coin, than to supply the goods that were desperately needed by Washington's troops, in exchange for the paper money that had been printed."

Grampy's gaze returned to us grandchildren, "As the winter of 1776 settled over the colonies, the British had pushed the Continental troops off Long Island, over the plains of New Jersey, and on across the Delaware River into Pennsylvania. With the approach of Christmas, the weary and battered Continental Army huddled in their frozen camps, doing their best to preserve the remains of their rations. While the British, confident that the war would soon be over, turned their thoughts to the Holiday Season, Washington and his officers drew up a plan. On Christmas eve, the Continental Army would gather up every boat it could, recross the river, and attack the Hessian forces in Trenton."

Grampy paused, "No one knew what the outcome of the attack

would be, but Washington and his officers were clear of one thing: unless there was a major turn of events, the battle for independence would *not* go on. If the British forces didn't destroy the remains of the Continental Army, the severe winter and declining morale would."

Grampy's eyes returned to the print, "The crossing was made in the middle of the night, and the Hessians were taken completely by surprise. Trenton fell to Washington's troops, and soon after Princeton followed. A flame had been kindled in the darkening winter nights. In the new year, it grew brighter and spread across the colonies, as the citizens of this land renewed their struggle for the precious rights that they had first stood up for at the old North Bridge in Concord."

Grampy's eyes rested on the print, mine on his. As he settled into his seat, reflections from Grampy and my conversation during our fishing trip arose, casting my thoughts to the inscription on the powder horn, belonging to a Jedidiah Weeks, that hung, alongside its Revolutionary War musket, over the fireplace in the Pine Room:

> *What I have within shall freely go.*
> *To bring a haughty tyrant spirit low.*

The flames died down. Lunch concluded, and my cousins and I turned our sights to our new toboggan and to the run that was awaiting us, down to the lake—our chance, Barker Boots aside, to give the youthful Sinclair a run for his money. Bundling up, we set off on the immortal trail of the Ski & Tumble Klub.

* * * * *

As the clock struck ten that evening, an escort of young cousins hurried to the Pine Room to fetch Grampy. It was time for the Jackie Gleason Christmas Special. Seldom did Grampy watch television, but, when he did, it was Jackie he tuned into. Old Jackie had no more loyal a fan than Grampy. Taking Grampy by the hand, they led him back down the hall to the living room, where they placed him in his rocking chair in the middle of the floor. The rest of us pulled up benches or sprawled out around him on the rug, as Jackie extended us his Season's greetings. He and Crazy Googenheim were in rare spirits.

Grampy watched with pleasure, until his laughs broadened into yawns. Slowly but surely, as an active day, warm fireplace, and hearty meal upstaged Jackie, Grampy's head settled back against the cushion of the rocking chair. The quintessence of relaxation, as Grampy's snores mounted, we glanced around gleefully at each other, doing our best to keep from laughing. But, as Grampy reached his crescendo, we were no longer able to contain ourselves. Hearing our laughter, Uncle Bill followed Grampy's trail of popcorn down the hall. At the door, a smile lit Uncle Bill's face, before he walked over to his father and shook him gently on the shoulder, "Hey, Grampy, what do you say?"

Grampy opened his eyes and looked around at the rest of us, who were doing our best to suppress our laughter. Then, acting as if nothing were amiss, he leaned forward, rubbed his hands over his eyes, and said, "Well, you youngsters can stay up all night if you want, but I'm going to bed." With that, he saluted Jackie, hoisted himself out of the chair and, patting Uncle Bill on the back, headed upstairs.

We rose to our feet and passed his tidings on. It was getting late, and Grampy's yawns had become contagious. As we bid the last of our cousins good night and switched off the lights, the old grandfather clock announced the end of another Christmas, with twelve long chimes. ... *AND TO ALL A GOOD NIGHT.*

SPRING

A cold, windy, March day. Some sunshine, but clouding in toward the end of the afternoon. Routine, except for a trip to the Sugarbush with the ladies after luncheon. Bill came out with the horse and wagon, and we all rode in style. The first sugar operation ever witnessed by "mes dames" Bradford and Bourne. They appeared to get on fine with Mother Nature.

Sinclair Weeks, Diary, March 24, 1970

10

SUGARIN' OFF

SPRING CAME—a first, followed by a second. And the sap was running! Opening the old wooden door of the sugarhouse, Nat's and my gazes rested on the Lord of Cat Bow, stripped down to his flannel undershirt and engulfed in a majestic halo of steam that rose out of the boiling vats of sap. As the sun drew the sap up from its roots to the crowns of the trees in the sugarbush, Bill Rines stoked the stove, and Grampy stirred the brew. The maple grove was overflowing, at our sire's service.

Kicking the wet snow off our feet, Nat and I walked across the wooden floor to the steaming vats. In bubbling eddies, the liquid flowed down through a long metal pipe from the holding tank, perched on the rafters outside the sugarhouse. Cool and dark, the sap was directed along a series of channels, its consistency thickening with each turn, until all the excess water had been boiled away, and it was drawn off as syrup.

Casting a careful eye over the vat, Grampy reached down and picked up an old ladle from the stool beside him. Then, dipping it into the syrup, he raised it to his lips, gave it a couple of good blows, and passed it to me. Taking it from his hand, I opened my mouth to sample the finished product, Grade-A Cat Bow Farm Maple Syrup. Nat leaned forward, as Grampy dipped the ladle back into the foaming brew and brought forth more of the elixir. The taste on our lips was all we needed. Pulling on our gloves, we headed out to tap the source.

The sugarbush of rock-maple trees spread out over a white blanket of snow around the sugarhouse, the main section rising up through a tapestry of open trails into a bright and well-thinned grove before us. Apart from the trees, the incline was the most important part of our backwoods operation. Everything was set up so that the flow was down, gravity standing in for pumps that otherwise would have been needed to move the sap from the holding tank on the knolled rise in front of us down into the vats themselves. Other than the sugarhouse and holding tanks, the rest of the operation was in Mother Nature's hands. Cold nights to keep the sap fresh and sunny days to draw it up from the trees' roots were an integral part of the recipe—and the farmer's earnest prayer. Tap holes bored carefully into the trees, diverted the upward flow of the sap through the spouts and, thence, into the buckets that were suspended from hooks on the trees. All that was left for us to do was to gratefully collect the precious liquid and start it on its way toward the sugarhouse.

Nat and I followed Rob and Prince's hoof marks through the snow, straight up the trail. Overhead, the sun rose into the bounteous heavens, brightening the forest and lifting our spirits. A breeze led us on into the grove, imparting the invigorating smell of thawing earth. The farther into the sugarbush our steps carried us, the greater were the number of buckets that congregated around the maple trees. As the sap dripped off the spouts and into the buckets, it sang out against the metal, setting off a sylvan symphony all around us. Wading through the snow, we stopped now and again by a near-lying maple, to catch our breath and draw back the lid of the bucket, in order to make sure its contents had been collected and that we were on the right trail. With the passing of the seasons, we had come to know the sugaring operation well and were glad, as we grew older, to be able to lend a helpful hand.

Arriving at the top of the sugarbush, Nat and I spied Jim at the east end of the grove. Just behind him on the trail, Rob and Prince were hitched to the old sled that carried the large, metal collecting tank. Quickening our steps, we angled over toward them. Jim was making his way around the maple stand, emptying the buckets from a good sized rock maple as we arrived.

Working slowly and carefully, Jim poured the cool sap into his pails, which he had set in the snow at the foot of the tree. Stepping up behind him, Nat picked up one of the pails and started for the collecting tank, while I retrieved an extra pail from the sled, gave Rob and Prince a good rub, and set forth expectantly through the snow for a neighboring tree.

The collecting of the sap was nearly as enjoyable as its sampling. The constant singing of the drops against the bucket lifted our steps as we moved from one tree to the next—front, back, side; high taps and low. The uncovering of each bucket was a revelation. Tapping the side of the bucket with our hand, we would make a quick mental estimate of its fullness. Then, setting our pails down, we carefully slid the arched lids back, catching a glimpse of the reservoir of fluid that had been stored in the roots of the tree. Sometimes it took two or even three buckets of sap to fill our collecting pails. Other times, one flowed to the mark.

On occasion, when a large tree hosted four or even five buckets, a tap would come up dry, and we would continue around the trunk to try our luck with another spout. More often, as we eased back the lid, we were delighted to discover that we had arrived just in time to stem the flood. The sap was poised at the bucket's brim. Depending on our pluck, we would either secure an extra pair of hands, to steady the pail, or gather the bucket in a gentle bear hug, lift it as tenderly as we could off the tap, and, holding our breath, navigate its sloshing contents over into one pail . . . and on into a second that had been called to the scene.

Breathing out, Nat and I waded back through the snow to the sled, where we hoisted the bucket of sap up, over, and into the collecting tank, watching with pure delight as our harvest flowed forth. Yes, Grampy had put the taste on the tip of our tongues, and we knew that our work was cut out for us. Forty gallons of sap were required to make one precious gallon of syrup. A lot of evaporated sweetness hung in the air around the sugarbush.

On we went, following the sled through the grove, until the collecting tank itself was filled to the brim, and Rob and Prince turned their mighty steps back down the trail to the sugarhouse. The rising sun had set the sap aflowing in our own bodies, and, climbing aboard the damp vessel, we loosened our scarves and coats and sat back to enjoy the ride. Nat and I had come to know the sugarbush well over the seasons, pointing out the more bounteous trees in the grove. Some of the most stalwart of the maples, old gnarled giants, with crowns that spread out across the heavens, seemed to have a direct line to the center of creation. Yes, we felt serenely at home in the sugarbush's melting midst.

* * * * *

Arriving back at the sugarhouse, Jim eased Rob and Prince to a halt beside the main holding tank. Then, climbing down from his seat, he walked around to the back of the sled and, unhooking the pipe, lowered it over the tank till the sap flowed out in a tide of foam. As the main tank filled, our eyes followed the pipe on down to the second tank, set up in the rafters outside the sugar house. The smell of syrup rose with the steam, and, hopping off the sled, we followed Jim down to the sugarhouse for the lunch break.

The steam had cleared as we opened the door, and the old walls of the sugar house were sweetly gleaming. Dad had arrived while we were out in the bush and was helping Grampy and Bill drain off the syrup into the large, metal Cat Bow containers. Hanging up my coat by the door, I paused to glance at a cartoon that had been tacked up to the wall. This time it was not Grampy who was the noted subject, but rather his father. *"What Y' studyin' Johnny, Geog'phy er 'Rithmatic?"* called a farmer, standing by his horse-drawn sled in the woods. The farmer's gaze rested on a young man with a yoke over his shoulders, from which were suspended two pails. Book in hand, the studious lad was heading off into the sugarbush to gather sap that was dropping into the legion of buckets. Time management par excellence! The cartoon was titled, "At the Bottom of the Ladder." The adjoining text read, *"John W. Weeks, Secretary of War, as a farmer's boy in New Hampshire was adept at gathering maple sap."* So the story went. We were glad to follow in Great-Granddad's bountiful footsteps.

Securing a couple of logs from the woodshed off the far end of the sugarhouse, Nat and I tilted them on their ends and sat down by the vat, pulling out our lunch. The sugarhouse was a simple, rustic structure, made of boards, beams, and a well chosen brace or two. Nearly as old as the woods in which it dwelt, the abode displayed many a sign of its trade. Axes, large and small, single and double-headed, leaned against the wall. Above them, a broad cross-cut saw spanned a good four feet of the rafters, and a pair of snowshoes hung from the far beam, bringing back a flurry of memories from the spring of 1914, when the snowfall was so deep that their webbed steps were the only thing that allowed the crew to make their way to the overflowing spouts on the trees. Off to the side of the vat, a row of buckets, worn and weathered, retired into the seasons, hosting nests of mice, chipmunks, and other furry friends that had been gently uprooted by our annual spring pilgrimage—the crumbs from our sandwiches our humble recompense.

Dad, Grampy, and Bill topped off the last containers of syrup, before joining us. Jim completed the party, collecting his old lunchbox from the shelf and pulling up a stool. Hungry from our labors, we all ate quietly for a few minutes, until Grampy pulled out a piece of paper and asked for our thoughts on a little poem he'd been composing to accompany the maple syrup crop that would soon be shipped out to kith and kin across the land. Jim perked up as Grampy started in:

> *Of all the good foods that are known to man,*
> *The high-flyin' turkey and the low-lyin' clam,*
> *There's none so good or ever can be*
> *As the boiled down sap of the Sugar Maple Tree.*
>
> *Suckling pig complete with apple,*
> *Chile con carne, Philadelphia scrapple.*
> *A three-decker sandwich with ham and cheese,*
> *Oysters Rockefeller, salmon and peas.*
>
> *Popover, crumpet, hot-cross bun,*
> *Cream puff, cruller or Sally Lunn.*
> *Some are good and some dandee,*
> *But none like the syrup from the Sugar Maple Tree.*

Nat and I swapped sympathetic glances.

> *Sukiyaki from old Japan,*
> *Peach ice cream or butter pecan.*
> *America, Africa, Asia, or Europe,*
> *There's nothing quite as good as our sweet maple syrup.*

The prairie oyster and the prairie hen,
Pan-fried trout for fishermen.
Roquefort cheese, ripe cantaloupe,
Terrapin stew or bird's-nest soup.

Liver of chicken, liver of goose,
Cream-cheese pie, or charlotte russe.
There's none so good, or ever can be,
As the boiled-down sap of the old maple tree.

Grampy took a breath. I looked at my soggy sandwich.

And if you don't think all this is true
Try the maple syrup we're sending to you.
A springtime greeting that you'll agree
Is as fresh as the woods of the North Countree.
And the only thing that could be any sweeter . . .

Grampy leaned the text toward Dad and Bill, who chimed in at the conclusion:

IS FOR US TO TELL YOU ALL THIS IN RAGTIME METER!

Nat's and my appetites were whetted. Jim was still digesting. As for Bill and Dad, they had apparently just finished helping Grampy add the finishing touches to the meter and menu.

* * * * *

Finishing our meal, Nat and I collected pieces of kindling from the woodshed and set to work carving wooden spoons, so that we could sample the syrup on our own. Lunch break in the woods was a time when the adults swapped a good story or two that they had heard over the intervening months—the tip of the cap going to Jim, the Old Vermont Farmer, and inveterate representative of the great republican virtues. Many of the stories, I had come to discover, had a pronounced partisan overtone. The meter still alive, Dad picked up the tune:

There was this old Vermonta who was invited to visit his friend in Texas. The evening after he arrived, he was taken by his host to the local Democrat meeting. Seated in the front row, they looked up as the chairman called the meeting to order in a strong, southern drawl, "Will awl da Democrats in da room please stand up!"

Jim lifted his head and smiled, as Grampy and Dad exchanged a wink.

Well, everybody stood up but the old Vermonta, who was seated directly in front of the chairman. Noticing the guest, the chairman leaned over his lectern and, a note of suspicion in his voice, asked the Vermonta if he was a Republican.

"Eh yup," was the response. Expecting a fuller explanation, the chairman continued, "And why you's a Republican?"— "Well," said the Vermonta, rubbing his chin, "My father was a Republican, and his father 'fore him was a Republican, and I reckon his father 'fore him was a Republican too...." Still not satisfied, the chairman retorted, "That's not a very good answer. What would happen, by God, if your Pappy was a horse thief!" Not missing a measure, the Vermonta responded, "WELL, IN THAT CASE, I GUESS I'D BE A DEMOCRAT."

Jim sat up, his soft blue eyes twinkling and laughed heartily with the others. Then, shaking his head and pushing his old cap up on his brow, he said, "Yup, that's a good one." The laughter continued, until Nat asked Grampy to tell the story about the Texan, who found his way back East. Bill nodded a smile, as Grampy gathered his thoughts:

Well, the Texan your Dad referred to decided one day to come East to pay his friend a visit. Seems he was interested in looking over the Vermonta's farm. Arriving in front of the house, the Texan asked his friend, who was sitting back in his rocking chair on the porch, how big his 'spread' was. The old timer took a long puff on his pipe and, gazing out across the fields, said, "Well, one border runs down by that old stream in the distance." The Texan turned and followed the direction in which his friend was pointing, continuing as the Vermonta motioned to the west along a row of trees, and then traced the line back to the porch, before leaning back in his chair.

"Huh," said the Texan, "that ain't veree big. Down at my spread you can get in a car and drive all day in a straight line, and you won't come to the end of my property." The Vermonta kept on rocking in his chair, "Eh yup, I once had a car like that, and I got rid of it."

Head down, Jim reflected for a moment, while we held our breath. Then, raising his head slowly, a smile awoke on his face, before breaking into a laugh, "Yes sir," he said dryly, "that must have been quite a spread!"

My carving finished, I rose and walked over to the vats to try a little dessert. The fire had cooled down a bit, and the dark amber syrup clung lightly to the spoon. Putting it to my lips, I continued on toward the open door, while the others packed up their lunches. My gaze lingered on the cartoon for a moment, before rising with my thoughts up into the sugarbush. Words Grampy had shared on our fishing trip returned to mind—recollections of his father's early years on the farm and the foundation his chores and hard work had provided him for the life that was to come. My eyes rested on Rob and Prince. Heads bowed, their forelegs gracefully bent, they waited patiently by the holding tank.

* * * * *

The rest of the afternoon was spent working the west corner of the sugarbush. Dad joined us, and we fell into step behind Rob, Prince, and Jim, easing the loads of the old maples, until the sun began to set, and the cool of the day turned our sled once again back to the sugarhouse.

As Bill shut down the wood stove, and the other adults pulled on their coats, Nat and I dipped our spoons one last time into the steaming vat. It had been a long day, and the syrup would give a welcome boost to our steps home. Waving good-bye to Bill and Jim, who closed up the shop, Nat, Dad, Grampy, and I followed the old lumber trail around the lake to the farm, retracing our broken footsteps through the snow. 'Uncle Bobby' Cutler and 'Aunt Eleanor' and 'Uncle Ned' Monroe were due to arrive at the Big House within the hour—fellow pilgrims after the holy elixir.

Shadows cast themselves about the forest, which had been drenched all day in sunlight. As I walked along beside Dad and Grampy, skirting thawing streams and fallen trees, I realized that my pace had slowed down over the last couple of years. No longer so bent on the inclinations of youth, I found myself turning a more attentive ear to the adult world and particularly to Grampy's life. Gradually, I realized, my grandfather was becoming a real person to me. Not that he wasn't before. It was just that, up to that time, he had been my grandfather and I his grandson, kind of like one of those immutable laws of nature, easily taken for granted; we had inherited each other. So it had been.

My gaze searched through the woods. But, things were changing. I wasn't sure whether the change reflected itself in Grampy's stride, which had slackened a bit over the last year, or if the shift was more inward. Though Grampy, as always, had a hearty greeting and lively tale at hand, I found that they didn't speak to me now as they had done before. Rather, the other, more tender, . . . susceptible side of his nature, which I had caught but brief glimpses of in earlier years, had begun to impress itself upon me.

As we continued on through the evening wood, Dad's and Grampy's reflections turned from the maple syrup crop to the farm itself. Grampy was quieter, as Dad asked him how he was finding country life now that Jane was completely bedridden, "It's not easy making the transition. Jane and I had looked forward to our retirement together, after the busy years in Washington."

Stepping around a stump, I glanced over at Grampy. The undertone that I had first detected during his surprise visit to our camp nearly six years ago rose once again to the surface. The evening shadows had spread, dimming Grampy's countenance and rousing in me the brooding image of his distant Scottish ancestor. Grampy paused, searched for words, "I never suspected it would be spent this way. . . ."

As Grampy's words rumored within me, I appreciated for the first time something I had long known without really understanding. Enthroned here in his Northern Kingdom with his enchanting, his enchanted lady, there was a part of Grampy—the Lord of Cat Bow— that was lonely, deeply lonely. The recognition brought with it a sudden uneasiness, uncertainty. The world that I was growing into, the world of "the fathers," was more real than I had imagined. I sensed that times would be changing, though as of yet I was unsure of what exactly that meant.

Our footsteps led us on. Dad glanced over at his father. "Why don't you take a trip, get a fresh wind, as the doctors have been recommending?" Grampy's thoughts were distant. Dad held back a low-lying branch for his father, before he went on, "There is nothing more you can do about Jane."

"We'll see. . . ." Grampy's response was terse. He turned his gaze down the lumber trail, bending right with the faint outline of the lake through a grove of still aspen.

I waited for Dad to speak up, but, after considering a moment, he was silent. His former youthful proclivity to get in his two cents worth had waned with the years—despite Dad having recounted to us earlier that Grampy had told Bea that he actually appreciated "young Sin's spunk." I followed quietly in their footsteps. So much was left unsaid.

As we continued on through the woods, the quiet of the evening settled around us, interrupted only by the sound of our boots breaking through the snow and the wind in the trees overhead.

The trail came out at the west end of the pasture, above the dock and boathouse. A layer of thin ice stilled the tides. Glancing up the field, the lights of Cat Bow greeted us from the hillside. Evening had settled into night. Above the Big House, stars skirted the ridge of Mt. Orne. As I lifted my eyes to the expanding heavens, the old melody returned to my lips, awakening memories of earlier years and cookouts in summer seasons:

All night, all day, angels watchin' over me, my Lord. . . .

* * * * *

"That syrup ain't bad." 'Uncle Ned' Monroe finished his last spoonful of vanilla ice cream, à la (Cat Bow) mode, and cast us a sidelong wink, under his bushy eyebrow, as he turned to his host at the head of the dining room table, "Where did you say you *bought* it, Sinclair?"

The austere portrait of John Paul Jones glanced down soberly over 'Uncle Ned's' shoulder.

The Lord of Cat Bow sat back in his seat and wiped his mouth with his napkin, as 'Aunt Eleanor' shook her head and 'Uncle Bobby,' his silk maroon tie tucked into his white shirt, glanced up over his spoon, wrinkling his gentle brow, "That's why I keep coming back here, Monroe."

Grampy placed his napkin on the table, "If you'd arrived a little sooner, Ned, I would have given you a guided tour; at least you might have earned your keep like you did in the olden days." 'Uncle Ned' raised his glass approvingly. I put my spoon down on the dessert plate and dipped my hands in my finger bowl. Reflections rose, returned to mind.

That evening, after a good warm dinner of red-flannel hash, Nat and I lingered at the dining room table with the notables—less obscure with the years. An inviting blaze was burning in the fireplace behind Grampy, who asked Dora to set the coffee tray down on the table. She did so with a quiet nod, then stepped over to light the bevy of candles in the corner of the room, before wishing us good night.

'Uncle Ned' secured an ashtray from the old hutch—collections, recollections filling its universe of drawers. My gaze rested on the colorful, old, ceramic hen, brooding away on the centerboard. Leaning forward, Grampy poured the cups of coffee, peering up over his glasses to take a count. One, two, three, four.... Nat and I stuck with the hot chocolate that accompanied supper. When all were served, Grampy took a capsule of pills from the tray, tossed two in his mouth, and chased them down with a drink, frown, and shake of his head.

Settling back in his seat, 'Uncle Ned' turned to us, "I heard a pretty good story the other day that you gentlemen might appreciate." The frown subsided on Grampy's face. Nat and I perked up with the others, as 'Uncle Ned' wiped his mouth with his napkin: "During Lincoln's candidacy for Congress, he attended a religious meeting where his opponent, Cartwright, was holding forth." I glanced over at Grampy, whose gaze was fixed on his old friend. "As Lincoln walked in and took a seat," 'Uncle Ned' continued, "Cartwright looked up and announced, 'Will all who desire to give their hearts to God and to go to heaven, please stand.' A smattering of men, women, and children stood up. Gazing about the hall impatiently, Cartwright boomed forth, 'All those who do *not* wish to go to hell, will stand.'"

'Uncle Ned' paused and glanced about, "All stood except 'Honest

Abe.' Glaring down at his opponent, Cartwright announced in his grav-
est voice, 'I observe that many responded to the first invitation to give
their hearts to God and to go to heaven. And I further observed that all
of you save one indicated that you did not desire to go to hell. The sole
exception is Mr. Lincoln, who did not respond to either invitation.'" The
pause lengthened, "Mr. Cartwright placed his two hands on the podium
and lowered his gaze to Abe, 'May I inquire of you, Mr. Lincoln, where
you are planning to go?'"

'Uncle Ned' drew a breath, "Lincoln rose slowly, 'I came here a
respectful listener. I did not know that I was to be singled out by
Brother Cartwright. I believe in treating religious matters with due
solemnity. I admit that the questions propounded by Brother Cartwright are of great importance. I did not feel called upon to answer as
the rest did. Brother Cartwright asks me directly where I am planning
to go. I desire to reply with equal directness, *I'm going to Congress.*'"

Laughing heartily, 'Uncle Bobby' sat forward and, placing his coffee
cup on the saucer, addressed Grampy, "Do you remember the U.S. Senate race in thirty-six, Sinclair, when we took on James Michael Curley,
the Purple Shamrock?"

Grampy glanced over at 'Uncle Bobby,' as he pushed his chair out
from the table and leaned back into the warmth of the fireplace, "That
was a run for our money if there ever was one."

'Uncle Ned' pulled a pipe and pouch of tobacco out of the pocket of
his brown wool sweater—before glancing across at Grampy and 'Uncle
Bobby.' "Weren't you gentlemen on opposite sides of the fence in the
primary?"

Grampy shook his head, "Yes, they let me climb into the ring, roll
up my sleeves, double up my gloves, and go a few rounds with the old
Champ, before", he glanced across at 'Uncle Bobby,' "you pushed Lodge
in on top of me."

"That's politics for you. You can't trust your own friends." A beguil-
ing glint lit 'Uncle Ned's' kindly face.

'Uncle Bobby' shifted an amused glance to 'Uncle Ned,' before
turning back to Grampy, "I don't know. After the primary was over,
we teamed up again and took on Curley together. I'm not sure the old
'Hizzoner' knew what hit him." I looked from 'Uncle Bobby' to Grampy.
Years had passed. The "Young Turks" themselves had grown older.

"What prompted you to go after Curley?" Dad glanced over at Grampy.

Grampy considered, "Like many of my generation, I had a strong dislike for Curley's brand of politics, which was glossed over by his dubious Oxford accent and glib promises. His ten-dollar wastebasket for his executive office, penchant for one-block taxi rides, and general squandermania had made Massachusetts the laughing stock of the nation." Grampy looked at Dad, "My campaign for Senator was based on the conviction that recovery and prosperity could be brought about only by a restoration of confidence in government. I announced that if I were nominated Senator, I would have as an opponent one whose record was probably the worst of any official in the history of Massachusetts. Well, Cabot felt the same way, and soon after he announced that he was also going to seek the Republican nomination."

Grampy glanced over at 'Uncle Bobby,' "Thanks to Lodge's fund-raiser, most of the heavy hitters lined up on Cabot's side."

'Uncle Bobby' raised his hand in mock protest, "Actually, I'm not sure I raised a penny. Pretty much all the expenses were paid by Cabot's in-laws."

'Uncle Ned' rubbed a grin off his face, "My understanding was that the telling blow was the roses that you all presented to the delegates' wives at the convention."

'Uncle Bobby' nodded, "Their exclamations drowned out Sinny's hundred-piece band. In the end, Lodge squeaked by and won the nomination by thirty-seven votes out of approximately seven-hundred delegates." 'Uncle Bobby's glance returned to Grampy, "You immediately moved to make the nomination unanimous, which increased the esteem in which you were held."

"Yes, and then took off up here to make up for lost sleep and clear my lungs of the smoke-filled rooms with some good mountain air, or try. I hadn't more than walked in the door, before the phone rang, and you all were on the line, asking me to take on the chairmanship of the Republican State Committee and run Cabot's campaign."

"We wanted to get you before you unpacked your bags." 'Uncle Bobby' smiled affectionately at Grampy.

"You did." Grampy stirred his coffee, as his thoughts were drawn back over the years to a lobster bake story he had shared with us of another Weeks–Lodge team.

"The campaign heated up quickly. Raymond Clapper, the syndicated columnist, called it 'the best provincial political drama of the year—a drama of flesh and blue blood.'" Grampy reflected, "Curley at first sneered at Lodge, calling him 'Little Boy Blue,' but held his hottest fire until later in the race. Not so with Charlie McGlue, the Democratic State Chairman. He took after me immediately, calling my campaigning 'ruthless political banditry' and warning that he had the names of 20,000 persons who had been illegally registered by the Republicans."

I glanced at Grampy, as 'Uncle Bobby' set aside his cup and picked up the thread, "Yes, Curley was overconfident at first, but the situation changed pretty quickly. You had us working day and night, Sin, to bring all the guns of the Republican organization into the battle."

Grampy leaned back in his seat, resting his elbow on the table, "As the race headed down the final stretch, it suddenly dawned on the smug Curley that he was in danger. 'Don't send a boy to do a man's job,' he growled. 'When my youthful rival was still wearing diapers, I was serving the Commonwealth of Massachusetts in the hall of Congress.... I'm going to give that Little Lord Fauntleroy the worse licking a man ever got.'" Bemused, 'Uncle Ned' unwrapped his bag of tobacco, as he glanced over at his host.

'Uncle Bobby' dipped a spoonful of sugar into his coffee, "Curley reverted to his old bull-necked sweater and brass-knuckle campaign tactics. He did everything he could to crush Lodge—even raking over the coals the reputation of Cabot's dead grandfather, Henry Cabot Lodge, Senior. But, Cabot didn't blink at anything Curley hit him with."

'Uncle Bobby' shook his head, "I still remember the huge rally we organized at the Boston Garden in the closing hours. The high patrician scorn of the young 'David' for 'Governor Goliath' shook the rafters. I'll never forget Cabot's words about how he had conducted the campaign calmly and sanely, with dignity befitting the office: 'I have indulged in no abuse and no political trickery—and I never will. I have always fought to help my fellow man—and I always will....'"

Grampy rubbed his leg, warmed by the fire, and shifted his seat, "Before the evening was over, Roosevelt had swept Massachusetts, and the Democrats took the Governor's and Lieutenant Governor's offices. Grampy shook his head, "Republican lights were blinking out, one by one, all over America, in what was to be our all time low. Only our candidate came through, beating the pants off His Excellency and becoming the lone Republican in the nation to win and replace a Democrat in the Senate."

Memories returned to the minds gathered. I watched as 'Uncle Ned' gently pressed the tobacco into his pipe with his forefingers. The dining room was quiet but for the crackling of the flames.

Grampy arose and, placing his napkin on the table, stepped over to the hearth to ease another log onto the fire. Striking a match, 'Uncle Ned' glanced up at him, as he drew on his pipe, "In your earlier years, Sin, you were something of a maverick yourself, what with getting young people and minorities involved in the party affairs."

Grampy straightened up and, wiping his hands, turned back to us, "After Truman's upset of Dewey in 1948 turned the tables on our party, that was the only way we were going to keep the Republican cause alive. The party needed new methods, new direction, and a new spirit to tackle the problems of our modern age. In the past, we'd run too many blue-blood tickets against the Democrats' Irish green. It was clear, to anybody who thought about it, that if we Republicans wanted to bolster our ranks, we had to offer greater political opportunity to citizens of varied ancestry, at all levels of Republican activity—from precinct work to highest constitutional nomination. Many people were shocked when I disclosed that in modern times not a single person with an Italian, French, Portuguese, Lithuanian, Greek or Jewish name had ever been elected to constitutional office in the state."

'Uncle Bobby' sat back in his seat, smiling, "You didn't exactly endear yourself to the party regulars with your notorious 'Republican Shake-Up Plan.'"

Grampy rested his arm on the mantel, gently twisting a toothpick in his mouth, "No, nor was that my purpose. I was ready to step on some toes, if, by so doing, it meant coalescing a strong Republican Party worthy of public support." He dropped the tooth pick into the fire. "And it did. The plan helped regain the Governor's chair, mobilize a full Republican force for the Eisenhower crusade, and served as a model for other states." Grampy warmed himself, before returning to his seat again.

"Yes, they were good years, but we don't seem to be able to hold on to them."

'Uncle Bobby' glanced over at Grampy, "What do you make of the growing unrest that is shutting down the college campuses across the nation?" My gaze settled with Grampy into his seat. He dipped his fingers in the finger bowl, cleaning off the ashes. Governor Reagan's recent words to the California legislature, asking them to drive "criminal anarchists and latter-day Fascists off the campuses" still echoed in my mind.

"I don't like it; I think Reagan is right when he says that higher education in our country is not just a right but a privilege." Grampy reflected, "The tensions have their root in this 'Great Society Program' that Johnson has foisted on the people. Too many Americans live within a system that they do not understand. Our economy is unique in the world. It is free and private, as opposed to being government-controlled, or one in which government is a party to cartels, price agreements, and the division of markets—so often the case in Old World Capitalism. When you find civil unrest, you often find a struggling economy that has lost sight of these principles that underlie a free enterprise system."

'Uncle Bobby' leaned forward, "There is an old expression, which could use a little more currency in our time: 'The reason why a dollar won't do as much for people as it once did, is because people won't do as much for a dollar as they once did.'"

'Uncle Ned' drew on his pipe thoughtfully, "You don't think that government has a role to play in making sure that small chicken farmers like myself don't get squeezed out of business by some brawny monopoly?"

Grampy glanced over at 'Uncle Ned,' "I'd be more worried about regulators snooping around dressed in white." 'Uncle Ned' smiled. The joke was apparently a private one. Grampy went on, "The point is that one can't always have one's cake and eat it, too, not even in this country. Our government has gotten too big. We have been spending beyond our means and creating large and growing deficits. The Keynesians, as they refer to themselves, haven't grasped the full picture that Keynes presented. They've picked up on his notion of 'Deficit Financing,' insisting that the government needs to help finance the economy in down cycles, when business is slow and people are needy. What they've forgotten, however, is that Keynes went on to emphasize that when the economy was up again, you have to pay the money back into the treasury, so that the debt can be paid off with the surpluses that have been created." Refrains from Congressmen Crockett returned to mind. Grampy reflected, "People don't like to pull in their belts. Too many of them would rather have the government take care of them, than to roll up their sleeves and work for their living."

My eyes lowered to the finger bowl; its ripples spread. Grampy set down his coffee cup, "The generations to come are going to inherit the excesses of the last years, and there are going to be some very serious consequences unless we wake up."

'Uncle Ned' lit up his pipe again, "I don't know much about politics." Blowing out the match, he turned to us, "But I'm interested in what you boys think. You're the next generation."

Nat reflected. I paused, turned from 'Uncle Ned' to Grampy, "I think the students are concerned about something more than our economy, the 'bottom line.'" The adults were quiet. 'Uncle Ned's glance rested on me. I considered, lifting my eyes to the picture of the old North Bridge above the fireplace, "I sense there is a growing feeling among my generation that the words, 'liberty and justice for all,' do not apply equally to everybody in this land."

Grampy sat forward, "There are a lot of myths that have grown up around these concerns." A firmness returned to his voice, "However, nobody in this country has a right to assume a position they didn't earn. America has always been a fluid society, where the person on top, at one moment, could find himself on the bottom, the next. Any man, regardless of his birth, could better his position and, if he applied himself, make something of his life."

"How about the women," 'Uncle Ned' glanced about the table, ". . . who seem to have abandoned us?"

Grampy looked over at 'Uncle Ned,' "The women may have had more opportunities than many realized or took advantage of."

"And the black people?" The words broke unexpectedly from my lips.

Grampy turned to me. Our gazes met. "We fought a Civil War over that issue, Stuart, and were the *first* country to do so."

I looked at Grampy intently. The truth I could recognize in his words. And yet for the first time I found myself questioning whether it was the whole truth.

Grampy leaned back into the flames, "Today these are often considered 'conservative' views." He paused, "That may be, but critics easily forget that conservatism also has its place in life. It bespeaks a philosophy that is not merely caught up in change, but is interested in change *when* that change also signifies progress. Continuity and steadiness on the course are no less important. When changes are made, they should be made with a full sense of accountability to the labors of those who went before and the expectation of those to come." I looked at my grandfather; his words were distant, "In this regard, conservatism takes a longer view than people often give it credit for." Grampy glanced across at 'Uncle Ned.' "John Sloan Dickey, president of Dartmouth College, used to say, 'Everything of any consequence is fastened at one end to the past and at the other to the future.'"

Dad rested his arm over the back of my chair, "There is an expression, boys, that has been around for quite a while now: 'In our youth, we are liberals. In our middle years, we become more moderate. In our old age, we take on the conservative mantle.'" I nodded. The expression I was familiar with. And yet, as I thought about it, I realized that, though I understood its meaning, I wasn't sure I understood the point. An assumption, unspoken, seemed to underlie the words.

Grampy returned to the main thread; the theme had grown with the years. "The strength of America lies in our free enterprise system. Prosperity is dependent upon the continuous and unlimited growth of our economy."

I listened, as the undertone arose once again in Grampy's voice, awakening an uneasiness within me. Growth—"continuous," "unlimited." The terms Grampy was using were being used, I realized, by more and more people to describe cancer—our consuming/consumer ethic. I breathed out.

As Grampy, 'Uncle Bobby,' and Dad went on to speak of our free enterprise system, the undertone grew—along with a sadness that welled up within me. Yes, my relationship with Grampy was changing in ways that I did not fully understand and yet that I knew were significant. Nat listened to the adults. 'Uncle Ned' set down his pipe on his saucer and leaned back in his seat. My gaze settled in the flames—yellow, orange, streaks of blue. . . .

* * * * *

". . . Your generation has a lot of challenges before you." The streaks of blue settled into yellow, into white. I drew my gaze out of the flames and lifted it to Grampy. Chimes from the old grandfather clock gently interceded into the conversation, . . . eight, nine, ten. Patting a yawn, Grampy placed his napkin on the table, "I'm turning in; it's been a long day." The Lord of Cat Bow rose with 'Uncle Bobby' and Nat. 'Uncle Ned' tapped his pipe against the ash tray, dislodging the ashes, before glancing across at me. Pausing, Dad rested his arm on my shoulder, "Don't stay up too long." I nodded, as he and 'Uncle Ned' pushed out their chairs and followed the others upstairs.

The dining room was quiet. My eyes passed across the table. Empty coffee cups, cloth napkins, a bowl of sugar, pitcher of cream, and a scattering of finger bowls lingered from the meal, harboring gathering reflections. My sights returned to the old cherry hutch, laden with its gilded treasures. An uncertainty filled me. Amidst the outer comforts and abundance of life, I realized that a certain longing, dis-ease lurked within my grandfather, the "lord" himself. My eyes searched the portraits that lined the walls—passing glances in the night—before resting once again on the battle scene above the fireplace. I looked at it long and then lowered my gaze beneath the span of its rude bridge, down into the still embers of the hearth. Words broke to the surface; I breathed in deeply: *The failures of success? A person cannot know his or her own value, even greatness, Grampy, unless we have a higher standard up against which we can measure ourselves.*

Sleep eluded me that night, as a dream, no longer young and innocent, awoke out of my depths—*America is great, yes, because America is good. And if America ever ceases to be good. . .*

II

THE SIXTIES

To set the course above renown,
To love the game beyond the prize,
To honor while you strike him down,
The foe that comes with fearless eyes.

Quoted in the Journal of Sinclair Weeks

* * * * *

Oct. 25, 1967

Rev. Dana McLean Greeley
President, Unitarian-Universalist Ass.
25 Beacon Street
Boston, Mass

Dear Dana:

I have on my desk a memorandum indicating that I owe you a letter in response to your request that I back your hand in the Unitarian-Universalist business.

While still thinking about it, I picked up the paper the other day and with some dismay noted the draft card destruction proceedings at the Arlington Street Church. Additionally, I noted your pronouncement with even greater dismay.

This letter is not to introduce the subject for discussion of any sort—but simply to say to you that I'm afraid you and I are too far apart to ever hope for a reconciliation of our views.

I do not quarrel with people who disagree with me, but in a matter of this character, where, in my judgment, the security of our country is at stake, I guess I can't participate with the present head of the Unitarian-Universalist Association in any project.

For a man in your position to counsel young men to break the law is one too many for me.

Sincerely Yours,
Sinclair Weeks

I nodded, handed Grampy back the letter.

"*Stuart...*" The undertone broke through the surface. I took a deep breath, looked at my grandfather. The hearth in the entrance room of the Big House was mute; flames sparked the Lord of Cat Bow's eyes, "...'*Democracy?*'...That's *pure* nonsense!" Our glances met. 1969. Sixteen, almost seventeen years old, I had come of age. The time had arrived for the Lord of Cat Bow and me to take up the issue.

Grampy's jaw tightened, "I'm sick and tired of hearing all this criticism of the system, people trying to tear down what took many of us a lifetime to build up!" Our glances parted. Grampy turned from me, took his coat and hat from the vestibule hook, and opened the front door. I breathed out and followed my grandfather out into the dawning spring afternoon. Above in the paddock, an aging donkey perked up her ears.

* * * * *

In the sixties, my universe split open. The political arena took on a tragic face, as a president was shot, followed by the assassination of his brother, who had picked up the torch, and by the murder of the civil rights leader, who raised the call for non-violence—John Fitzgerald Kennedy, Robert Kennedy, Dr. Martin Luther King Jr., One, two, three.

The internal bloodshed spread. Not long after Kennedy's death, the country was at war. Against the advice of our former president and Supreme Allied Commander, Eisenhower, we set forth once again to make the world "safe for democracy"—fighting a Vietnamese people, who themselves had fought over the years for their independence against Communist China. Communism/Capitalism; Cows/bulls?... The finer points were never made clear to the American public. And so, the People, We, sent the flower of our youth away to a war in a distant land that was to claim the lives of thousands upon thousands of young Americans, who believed in a country that no longer seemed to believe in them. I was entering into the flush of my teenage years, and the growing pains were becoming acute.

My gaze rested on Mt. Orne, cast against a brisk unsettled sky, before lowering to the farmhouse and barn. Along its gently sloping roof, the last patches of snow relinquished their chilled grip on the passing season. In their place, buds began to sprout on the branches of the sister elms that framed the paddock. April, 1969. Somehow the "Day of the Lord" had fallen to the wayside over the passage of the years. A first, a second, . . . a third spring was once again upon us. The embers kindled and flamed.

It was a time for deep reflection, a time for evaluating who I was and how the shrinking universe of an old New England family fitted into the picture of a turbulent and rapidly changing modern land. The questions, the challenges were both many and directed, above all, to those who stood for the older order. I glanced over at Grampy. He paused in the circle in the middle of the driveway to greet Penny, Wildcat's spirited successor—a retriever with a distinct golden hue. Jumping up on Grampy, Penny was eager to head off on her afternoon walk with her lord and master.

Grampy zipped up his jacket and turned toward the road. Our steps kept pace out of the driveway, our conversation falling behind. Spring—tentative, incipient—was in the air. The rays of sunshine loosed the fledgling song of the swallows that perched in the fluttering branches of the old elm. A sadness bloomed within me.

The great-grandfathers study war, so the grandfathers can study politics, so the fathers can study business, so the sons? . . . As the seasons carried us on through the sixties, President John Adams' words took on for me an intensely personal tone. *The sons?* I had grown up and into life, finding myself something of a *gray* sheep in our family. Try as I might, I had trouble seeing the world in the black-and-white contrasts that the civil unrest had brought out in Dad, Grampy, and, it appeared, many others.

The critics of "the Establishment" were viewed as radical—without, I sensed, a real consideration of what that word actually meant. *Power to the People! We Shall Overcome! Kill your Parents!* Words, a song broke on the lips of many of my generation, rising at times into a choral dirge, . . . retreating once again beneath our breath: *For it's one, two, three, what are we fighting for? Don't ask me I don't give a damn. Next stop is Vietnam. For it's five, six, seven, eight, open up those pearly gates. I ain't got time to wonder why. WHOOPEE, I'M GOING TO DIE!* Vietnam, Cambodia, Kent State. Three, two, one. . . . The fathers struck first, the sins being visited upon *their* sons. The critics of the Establishment? Were they not groping to get, finally, finally, to the *radicalis*, the *root* of the problem?

Yes–no. The shades of gray cast themselves upon me. I realized that it wasn't that simple. The spring before, I had stepped out of line, the lines of protest and revolt. Like many other schools, Milton Academy had become embroiled in the sixties. The youthful energy that had previously gone into classes, sports, parties, and other extracurricular activities, went now into demonstrations. Warren Hall, Whig Hall had emptied. The students gathered, along with the more vocal teachers, in a long line in front of the school and headed for the cemetery to stage their protest. I, along with the others who were around, was drawn into the current. At the traffic light, we stopped. When it turned green again, and the current swept on, I found myself stepping out of line—watching my friends, classmates, schoolmates, and teachers march by, one after another, after another. . . .

Why? What had happened? My thoughts turned to my parents. I was more fortunate than many of my classmates. I was a day student in a boarding school and had a family and home to return to each afternoon—a grandfather to visit on weekends and holidays throughout the year. They/he provided a staid, if increasingly precarious, balance to my own pained protestations—a blessing mixed and made more acute by the love that I struggled to keep alive for my father and grandfather during those years. Sinclair, Sinclair Jr., the sins of the fathers, . . . the sons?

* * * * *

Together–apart, Grampy and I walked on into a spring afternoon. My eyes followed the fence along the road. Buds gathered on flowers and bushes that rose out of the damp, quickening earth, releasing a fragrance, faint, into the air. Grampy's thoughts were distant; mine pressing—memories of a business breakfast meeting that Dad had encouraged me to accompany him to a few weeks earlier—an opportunity for me, the next in line, to whet my appetite for the political process. Unexpectedly, painfully for both of us, it was the beginning of a rift that would grow with the months ahead.

The speaker was a young Congressman from New York named Kemp, who, last I knew, had made a name for himself on the football field. Surrounded by Boston's business leaders, I listened, as once again the problems of our economy and society were laid out before us, followed, again—once again—by a neat set of solutions by the young, aspiring candidate. I found myself listening with an increasing discomfort, before finally raising my hand.

The speaker turned to me, "Yes?"

I took a breath, as a sudden tide of feelings rose up within me, "Congressman. . . ." Dad's foot pressed down on mine under the table. The room grew quiet. I looked from Dad back to the speaker. My heart beat loudly in my ears. I paused. They were waiting. I spoke, "Congressman, once upon a time, when our country was torn in a civil war, a president got down on his knees on the floor of the White House and prayed to a living God."

I stopped. Beside me, Bill McCrellish mumbled under his breath. His words were inaudible; all I could make out was the tone of incredulousness.

The silence deepened. I groped for the unraveling thread and took a breath, "As we find ourselves in the middle of a civil rights uprising and war in Southeast Asia, and demonstrations on our campuses, can you say something, Congressman, about Truth, about Beauty and Goodness, 'brotherhood from sea to shining sea'—and how these notions relate to the problems you've outlined?" The former quarterback paused, took the ball, faked left, right. . . .

"Stuart!" I turned in the lobby. The voice was clearer, "I don't believe you said that." Bill came up to me, standing off alone out of bounds on the side.

I looked at him, "I thought at least you'd understand what I was trying to say."

He shook his head, "I do. But Truth, Beauty, Goodness, good lord, man, you're not in Athens. You don't ask that kind of question in a gathering like this."

"Brotherhood?...Why?"

He paused, "You don't. The room was full of businessmen, politicians, and..."

"*Human beings*." Our gazes met, "I know, Bill. But how can you sit through such gatherings year after year after year with all the promises and pep-talk about new solutions to our problems?"

"You don't believe there are any solutions?"

"That's not the issue for me." I searched for words, "Congressman Kemp and many politicians today may know a lot, have plenty of position papers and programs, 'solutions.' But, how many have a feel, *a real feeling* for what the problems are that the people on the street, the majority of citizens in our country, are facing—the real issues? The main problem that seems to preoccupy many of our representatives is their reelection."

Bill took a breath. I looked at him, "I realize I made a fool of myself. But, as our country settles into a slumber, isn't anybody going to speak up about the real issues—the 'top line?' "

"Stuart, the business of America is *business*."

I took a deep breath, "I'm aware of that; I was raised on that phrase—along with the old fare of meat, potatoes, and vegetables. Business was what we talked about for years around the dinner table." I looked at Bill, "But, no one ever told me what the business of business is."

"It's making a buck."

"I don't believe it." A tone of anger stirred in my words. I glanced across the lobby at the group of business leaders, gathered around the Congressman, "That view is a lie that's in danger of becoming true."

Dad joined us. He looked at me silently. My foot was still sore. I breathed out, "Dad, I told you that you shouldn't take me to these meetings. I'm not a businessman or politician...."

"Stuart, did you hear the Congressman's response to your question?" I reflected. Dad spoke up, "He was honest. He said *he* isn't a philosopher or poet." Our gazes met. "Most of us aren't. We're too busy making a living."

"And how about living?" I paused, looked at my father. "I don't know if you can understand it, Dad, but I'm not just a *Weeks* anymore. I don't listen to the facts, figures, and position papers alone, the 'letter of the word'; I can't. I listen, try to listen, for a sense of truth—the 'spirit of the word.'"

"It's not that simple, Stuart."

I turned to Bill, nodded, "I realize that. But, we can also make it more complicated than it is—some people can, I guess. I can't." A heaviness settled over me. My glance returned to the Congressman, who started toward the door, "You all have been talking about how the speaker is 'aggressive, ambitious and intelligent'; 'He votes the way I do'; 'Maybe he's the man to call the plays for the nation. We need somebody to do it!'"

"That's real life, Stuart." An impatience gripped Dad's voice.

Words surged on the tides of feeling that rose within me, "Maybe it is.... Maybe Kemp is the person to call the plays. All the more power to him. I don't know. But, one thing I *do* know is that those qualities you all have referred to—aggressiveness, ambition, even intelligence—they are not the essential qualities you emphasized when you referred to a Lincoln or Washington. You mentioned other traits, traits not so different from those I sputtered out earlier: courage, integrity, compassion, sacrifice, even love."

I searched the faces of my father and older friend, "What's happening to our country? Why aren't those qualities mentioned anymore when we speak of who we want for our leaders? Why don't those words fall first from our lips? Aggressiveness, ambition—these other attributes that we give such ample voice to, where are they leading us? Wars, riots, burning cities, uprisings..." I paused, caught my breath. Our glances met, "I asked the Congressman about Truth, Beauty, Goodness—brother and sisterhood. What I was trying to ask in my halting way was whether anyone still hears the words of the old prophet: 'Without a vision, the people perish.'"

* * * * *

I breathed out. Grampy's steps, slower, more deliberate, led us on down the drive, alongside the fence, and by a sign in a sprouting grove of pines. Yes, much had changed over the last year in America, in our family, in my own unfolding life. *Brotherhood from sea to shining sea*—what had all those verses, anthems, pledges, that we had learned by heart, meant? Sunlight glanced through the shadows that stretched out before us into the afternoon. My thoughts returned to the conversation with Dad on the way home in the car from the breakfast meeting.

Philosophy?…"We fancy we hate poets, but we are all poets and mystics"—*human beings*. Words from Emerson rose up inside me, as I glanced over at Dad once again at the helm behind the wheel. Was I looking for another Athens here in the middle of America? My gaze continued on out the window of the car. High tech firms passed on the right, their portals reflected in the currents of the Charles River. The modern mystery centers?'Slow and stop,' Dad followed the flow of commuter traffic along Storrow Drive, outbound, the city of Boston fading away in the rearview mirror.

Ahead of us, the bend of the Charles River flowed into our vision, passing under a stately brick and granite bridge with three arches and a set of spires at each end. "Great-Granddad's Bridge," we called it in our early years. The path led over the water, across a neat swath of grass, and on up to another arch—smaller and simpler in design, "The Sinclair Weeks Foot Bridge." We approached with the currents and passed under its span, my gaze focusing on a blatant line of graffiti that had been scratched across its concrete surface:

> *STOP KILLING YOUR CHILDREN!*
> *GET THE HELL OUT OF VIETNAM!*

The bridges faded away, with the city, in the gathering stream of cars—flowing on, flowing on. *Great-Granddad*, U.S. Congressman, Senator, Secretary of War in two Cabinets and Republican Candidate for president. *Grampy*, U.S. Senator, Republican Party Finance Chairman, Secretary of Commerce with Eisenhower. *Dad?* 1945, the path was a straight and narrowing one from there, down the steps of the footbridge, across the lawn, and into the "Business School"—carried on in the momentum of the postwar years. Time, once again, to tend to business, make a living, and raise a family. The *sons?*...The currents flowed on—Boston, Concord, Lancaster.

* * * * *

Overhead, the clear, blue sky arched above Cat Bow, mottled by billowy clouds that gently shifted the heavens. Our steps carried us on into the afternoon. Grampy turned his gaze down over the greening fields to the lake. The anger had waned from his voice, "Stuart, did I ever tell you the story about Davy Crockett and his address to Congress?"

Coonskin cap, moccasins, rifle—a *dream* returned to mind, "I've thought of it often over the years, . . ." My glance passed from Grampy to another sign nailed to the fence, one of a growing number that, over the years, had also sprouted along our route out to the main road: *No Hunting and Trespassing.* ". . . Along with other words, Grampy, that you've shared about America, not its greatness alone, but its even more essential *goodness.*"

Grampy reflected a moment, before pursuing his thread, "Our native son, Daniel Webster, expressed Crockett's point in other words: 'Nothing can ruin the country if the people themselves will undertake its safety, and nothing can save it, if they leave that safety in any hands but their own.'" Sun broke through the clouds, clouds through the sun.

"Grampy?" I looked at my grandfather, "What you say is true. That's, in fact, what the students and radicals—echoing Lincoln's words of government of, by, and for the people—mean by 'Power to the People.'" I paused, "But, I wonder if it is that simple. What I was trying to say in the entrance room is that the forces opposed to the people undertaking their sovereignty, a 'participatory democracy,' are tremendous."

Grampy turned to me, "What are you referring to?"

"In the beginning of our country, only white male land owners had the right to vote. Black people, minorities, women, even white males who didn't own land were disenfranchised." I looked at Grampy, "It's taken centuries for these people to be considered full citizens, and, even today, minorities are still struggling for a voice."

"That's the way it has always been throughout history, Stuart."

"Why?"

Grampy paused, considered, "Perhaps because the people you're referring to, 'minorities,' have more power—real power—than even they themselves are aware of."

I nodded, as the words "Power to the People" passed through my mind, "That's why things are changing, Grampy."

"I can't go along with the lawlessness that is accompanying so much of what we are seeing these days."

The abruptness in Grampy's voice broke through in mine, "Their 'lawlessness,' Grampy, in many cases is an expression of their commitment to the *higher* laws of this land."

"I don't know what you are talking about."

I turned to Grampy, "I'm talking about what I, you, would do if we were in their place. I'm talking about the Declaration of Independence, the Bill of Rights, and New Hampshire's own Constitution. Each of these fundamental documents affirms this higher law." I paused. "They were written by individuals, our 'Founding Fathers,' Washington, Adams, Jefferson, Madison, Monroe, who had been sentenced to jail by King George III for tax evasion and protest."

Grampy's expression tightened. "You can't compare the situations."

I looked at him, "The newspapers reported yesterday that over thirty-three thousand American soldiers, the majority of them young men, *boys*, have been killed in Vietnam since January of '61—killed like outlaws in this undeclared, this illegal war we are in." I breathed out, "Grampy, you may not be able to compare the situations, but others can and do—young people, 'critics,' who don't want to be thrust into arenas of their fathers' making, who don't want to become human sacrifices in a half-hearted war in Southeast Asia—blacks and other minorities, who, having fought in our wars, built up our nation with their blood, sweat, and tears, want to see the fruits of their labors, laws that don't make a mockery of our ideals of 'liberty and justice *for all.*'" I looked at my grandfather. "Don't you realize, Grampy, that we are experiencing a *revolt?*" Grampy's gaze was distant.

Our steps carried us past the pastures, up the hill, and into the woods—the fence stumbling into an old stonewall that accompanied us on alongside the road through the tangled undergrowth. Puddles widened the distance that over the last year had arisen between Grampy and me. My glance passed into the forest, resting in the patches of snow that lingered in the shade of the gullies and at the foot of the large pines. Memories of a winter's season, two years ago, and of a brisk sleigh ride through the night, swept through my mind.

* * * * *

...The students, the faculty marched on toward the cemetery, bending left with the road. I bent right and then left again, seeking, struggling to find the balance. I left school—such as it was—with the mixed blessings of my father, and boarded a plane to join my cousins in France and, I was soon to discover, bump into more lines of protest, demonstrations, full scale riots on Paris' left bank, in its famed Place St. Michel, Saint Michael, ...followed by a sudden interlude in its retiring garden, the Tuilleries. As I settled into my seat in the plane, a melody from a musical show, "Up with People," that Ma had slipped into the schedule on the day of my departure, provided a searching backdrop to my thoughts:

> *Here we go, running after peace all day;*
> *Here we go, fighting along the way.*
> *Silly fools we'd be,*
> *Chasing after peace that way.*
> *You've got to walk with it, MY FRIEND.*
> *You've got to talk with it, MY FRIEND.*
> *You've got to sleep with it, MY FRIEND.*
> *You've got to be with it, MY FRIEND.*
> *PEACE RIGHT NOW; CARRY IT WITH YOU.*

* * * * *

Grampy and I walked on silently into the burgeoning spring season. Beams of sunlight stirred the shadows around us. I took a deep breath, as my thoughts turned back to earlier years. Often Grampy spiced a family meal with the words of President Calvin Coolidge, *The business of America is business.* A truism, I realized that I had taken Grampy's words on faith. There was no reason not to. The fruits of business were abundant in our family's life. With the change of the sixties, however, and my expanding view of the universe, a question had begun to pose itself more insistently: *And the business of business?*

The warmth of the afternoon took the edge off the chill; the puddles drew us closer together again. I turned to my grandfather, searching for the frayed thread of our conversation. "What drew you into business, Grampy?"

Grampy reflected a moment, "A very simple statement that I heard as a little boy growing up, 'only the productive can be strong, and only the strong can be free.'" I nodded, paused. He looked at me, "A classmate of mine had gone to work for Harris Forbes. I went in to see his boss about a job and got it. It was agreed that I should report for work on the day after Labor Day. It was not to be, however. In August 1914, Kaiser Wilhelm invaded France—and for a while nobody was doing any hiring or much of anything else, except waiting and watching."

"What did you do?"

"I looked around for other positions and got a job as a messenger for the First National Bank of Boston at the salary of six dollars per week." Grampy's voice was matter-of-fact, as his thoughts journeyed back over the years, "Feeling pretty secure, soon after I proposed to your grand-mother, Beatrice Dowse, which gave me an added incentive to work my way 'up through the cages' at the bank—until April 6, 1917, a day that every man of my generation recalls distinctly. I remember picking up the paper that morning. The headlines from coast to coast proclaimed that America was at war. Along with many other young Americans, I was headed overseas."

"The business of war?..." My glance passed down the drive that dropped off to the right, winding through the woods to the Balch's, Davidge's, Vashaw's, and Magoon's cabins on the pond—wagon wheels and windward wings. The breeze picked up, gently frisking the leaves that added touches of green to the forest of pines and spruce, on either side of the road.

Grampy continued, "It was more than two years before I got back to the bank again, finding myself docketed as assistant cashier and loaning officer and, then, later as the assistant to the head of foreign operations. I remained with the bank until 1923, when I resigned to enter the manu-facturing field, due to the insistence of one person to whom it was hard to say no, Bea's father, Mr. William Dowse. In 1923, your great-grandfa-ther was operating two companies, the Reed & Barton Corporation of Taunton, Massachusetts, at that time the leading manufacturer of ster-ling silverware in the country, and the United Carr Fastener Company in South Boston. Unable to find suitable successors in the companies, he decided to put them under my supervision. At the age of thirty, I came face to face with the daily problems of executive management in the fields of manufacture and marketing."

Penny came back to retrieve her master. Grampy gave her a pat, before shooshing her on. "When I took over Reed & Barton in 1923, I found a corporate picture that required some work. The company's debt was too high; important assets were overvalued, and there was a loose-end appendage, which I quickly decided to cut away."

I glanced over at Grampy, "How did the companies do?" Words.... My thoughts were distant.

"The hours in Taunton were long and the work hard. We had to scrutinize both sides of the decimal mark, from one day to the next, and carefully monitor the ebb and flow of dollars. But, before the year was out, things began to look up."

Grampy stepped around a puddle. A lightness lifted his voice, "One of the claims I am proud to make is that, under the motherly compulsion of necessity, I originated the 'cash-flow' theory of handling a business, before anybody else gave a name to it. Though an imposing sounding word, the invention was pretty straightforward. 'Cash-flow' simply meant that you had to have enough cash flowing in to take care of your requirements flowing out.

"During that period, I learned a number of important lessons, which served me well in the years to follow—first and foremost the fact that if one *has* to save money, you can. One morning, I asked how many telephone heads we had in the factory and offices. The answer came back: 'About one hundred and fifty.' I responded that 'Tomorrow we will have seventy-five.'"

"And?" I looked at Grampy, as he sent an errant rock scurrying off the road with his foot.

"It was done. Nothing was too small not to add up. If anyone had a pencil that was running out, they had to turn in the stub, in order to get it replaced."

"How did the others in the company respond?"

Grampy reflected, "At first, many of the employees were surprised. However, they quickly came to realize that these regulations not only helped us save money, but they set certain standards about the use of resources that soon became a matter of course in the shop—to the benefit of the entire operation. I think they also appreciated how the business was run. I had established a simple unwritten rule among the three of us who headed up the company. Kimbell, Upham, and I all had to agree on whatever was to be done. If one of us was firmly opposed to a particular proposition, we would not go ahead with it. The approach worked well; both companies began to pick up steam."

Grampy turned to me, "I learned more, Stuart, concerning the management of men, money, corporate production, and distribution from my war experience and later from the Great Depression than from any other phases of my schooling. *And* I was able to bring this experience into the other major field that our family has been involved in for the last six generations, politics. Starting in 1930, I began and ended my work days in the two companies as the mayor of Newton."

So it was. From the accounts we heard, while on quarter-deck at city hall, Grampy "steered a tight ship" through some of the roughest of waters. The Great Depression caught the "Boy Mayor" as he was entering into office—and rode right along with him through nearly his entire administration. Grampy kept the city afloat during the crisis by drawing on the fullness of his Puritan inheritance: frugality. The pennies were watched carefully. The result was that the administration not only managed to help those citizens who they determined were in real need, but it reduced the Newton tax rate during each of the six years Mayor Weeks was in office, *and* it built a new city hall and war-memorial building—"right smack in the middle of the Depression." Along with providing desperately needed jobs, the building project ended up costing the town a fraction of what it otherwise would have cost in more prosperous times.

* * * * *

The Baker Farm approached as the woods thinned into fields, offering a blustery view of the Presidential Peaks, which filled the horizon. Grampy went on, touching on the "Roosevelt Era"—more of a raw deal than a "New Deal," in his terse estimation—and, finally, his six years as the leading spokesperson for American business, as Secretary of Commerce under Eisenhower, trying to get the government out of the "not-raising-hogs-business."

An earnestness stirred Grampy's tone, "I was a champion of private business, Stuart, because all over America our free enterprise system was thinking new ideas, raising capital, manufacturing products, earning profits, meeting payrolls, and every year developing and improving inventions that created valuable goods and services, along with thousands of new jobs for the youth. This conviction was what turned my sights to Washington. I believed that we needed a Senate majority in the Capitol to curb wild-eyed radicals and promote a strong, healthy economic system which would spread affluence, while at the same time building a formidable base for national security."

Grampy paused in the road, "I was for business to have the means to support free enterprise, for I knew something that we easily forget today: If the 'bough' of free enterprise ever is broken by its critics, down would go labor, management, and all." A thought stirred in Grampy's mind. He looked at me. "Remind me, Stuart, to show you a book when we get back to the house."

I nodded. We continued on, Grampy turning his gaze to the Baker Farm which approached on our left, "Those who settled this land and made it what it is, expressed their views in simple words, 'Work hard; keep your nose clean; and earn your own living.'"

Stopping in front of the barn, a memory awoke a smile on Grampy's face. Pushing his hat up on his head, Grampy rested his hand on the fence beside the road, "During that period, Stuart, I also ran a chicken business on the weekends with Ned Monroe. As far as I can remember, Ned and I had the first chicken batteries in New England. The operation was so successful that Cat Bow not only sold eggs, along with their brooding mistresses, to the fashionable establishments across the North Country, but we attracted a good number of visitors, curious about our innovation."

Grampy patted Penny, who lingered at his side. "Your 'Uncle Ned' took charge of the housekeeping." The smile snuck up on Grampy's face, as he looked over at the barn, "One day my brother-in-law, Jack Davidge, a personable gentleman, with a flair for white-flannel trousers, came to call. He was curious about what we were up to and thought he would poke around a bit. Ned had just finished loading a wagon with chicken manure. It was pretty ripe, and he was anxious to ease it out-of-doors."

Grampy's smile broadened, as he leaned a hand on the fence post, "The wagon was heavy, and, as a result, Ned had developed the habit of getting a running start. This he did. Having gotten up a good head of steam, Ned started down the old runway for the back door at *exactly* the moment that Jack was coming round the corner. The timing was uncanny. Seeing those white-flannel trousers appearing out of nowhere, Ned jammed on the brakes, sending the entire load slopping over the front of the wagon and into Jack's lap." Grampy's smile broke into a laugh, prodding mine, as missing pieces of Grampy's and 'Uncle Ned's' dinner table tête-à-tête—on the subject of "chicken farmers" and "brawny monopolies"—the spring before fell delicately into place. Grampy turned to me, "From that day on, your Great Uncle Jack was a little more careful where he poked around." The smile passed over to my face, before settling into reflections.

* * * * *

Things had quieted down around the Baker Farm, as sleighs and farm machinery had taken over the roost. Pushing off the fence, our steps carried us out toward the end of the road. At the edge of the field, the stone wall accompanied us through the woods. Overhead, sunlight broke through the branches of the trees, quickening our shadows. Grampy lingered with his thoughts; I with mine—*Only the productive can be strong, and only the strong can be free.*

We walked on, my sights tracing streams of spring water that flowed down the banks beside the road, before disappearing in rude culverts beneath our feet. More signs—hunting, trespassing—tacked up to trees and posts, secured our way. As the fork in the road approached, my gaze rose up with Mt. Prospect into the heavens. Ranging clouds stole patches of blue from the sky, darkening the rays of sunshine that filled the afternoon. Grampy and I paused at the end of the road, lingering a few moments until Penny, who had trotted on ahead, glanced over her shoulder and, hesitating a moment, started back to us.

I turned my sights from the summit of Mt. Prospect and its fire tower to my grandfather, as an earlier conversation tugged gently on my memory, "Grampy, what would you say was the basis of the success that great-grandfather achieved in his life?"

Grampy's glance met mine, "Your great-grandfather, Stuart, was above all a practical man. He wasn't particularly responsive to what are referred to as the 'progressive' elements in politics and society, nor did he look upon political issues with the sense of altruism that many young people today are speaking about. Political issues, he felt, should be viewed from the angle of politics and business." Memories, distant, of a passage from an old newspaper article that Grampy had shared with us years past at a lobster bake etched my mind.

"Why business as well?" Curiosity mingled with the impatience that moved below the surface within me.

"Because business is integrally tied in with politics in this country."

"Any less so than philosophy or religion, the 'top line'—'one nation, under God, indivisible, with liberty and justice for all?...'"

"Your great-grandfather wasn't a stranger to any of these ideals. His focus, though, was on relating such ideals to the very real challenges of everyday life. He refused to compromise on an issue he believed in, and a number of times he sacrificed a good deal for the stands he took."

I looked at Grampy, "When?"

"The issue of the women's vote was one example."

"How did he stand on it?"

"He was against it. *But*," Grampy paused, "he wasn't a fanatic. He said simply and clearly that he didn't believe women wanted the vote and added that he would be glad, if desired, to pay for a poll of the women in the state to prove him wrong. Until then, however, he made it very clear that he would rather accept defeat than to compromise his position."

"What happened?"

"He lost his seat in the Senate." Grampy looked at me, "Defeated, as Francis Peabody indignantly put it, by 'long-haired men and short-haired women.'"

I reflected, "Was that being practical, Grampy?"

Grampy's glance followed a chipmunk that scurried across the top of the stonewall, before lightly leaping onto the trunk of a pine tree, where it proceeded to chide us energetically.

Grampy turned back to me, "As I said, by holding true to his principles, your great-grandfather roused the ire of certain individuals, who flooded the state with literature against him. Whether his defeat was primarily a result of a real understanding of the issue—which was your great-grandfather's concern, in the first place—or whether it was the inflammatory literature that turned the voters against him, we don't know. In any case, the defeat was only temporary. There was a large number of individuals, including his colleague, Senator Henry Cabot Lodge and President Theodore Roosevelt, whose estimation grew for John Wingate Weeks, because he was not only prepared to be proven wrong, but to accept defeat rather than compromise his principles. The fact that he was the only candidate who called off all his political gatherings, because the flu was epidemic at the time, also contributed to the loss of his Senate seat. It was these qualities which led, after your great-grandfather's defeat, to his being offered the post of Secretary of War in Harding's and later Coolidge's Cabinets."

Grampy leaned over to pat Penny, "Do you know the letter from your great-grandfather, which hangs above my desk in the Pine Room?"

I nodded, reflected, "Yes."

"That letter, Stuart, had a considerable amount of influence in its day. When I was serving in the Senate, one afternoon my colleague Gene Milikin, from Colorado, dropped in at my office. In the course of conversation, I showed him your great-grandfather's letter. Apparently, it touched a chord in him, because he asked for a copy, had it framed, and it stood on his mantelpiece as long as he remained in Washington." Grampy paused, "Six years later, he wrote to me to say that all the new Republican Senators elected at the fifties elections had visited him recently, and to the group he had read my father's letter—the point of his note being that every one of the Senators, in turn, had asked for a copy."

Dear Sinclair, there are two or three things I want to impress upon you.... A question lingered with me, "How did you feel at the time, Grampy, with respect to the position Great-Grandfather took on the women's' vote?"

"It wasn't an easy position." Grampy reflected, "Your great-grandfather questioned whether the majority of women wanted to vote."

"Why couldn't he have let the women decide for themselves?"

"He was prepared to, which was why he offered to pay for a poll soliciting their views."

"And?"

"He wasn't taken up on it, so he drew his conclusion from his own experience, which was that women were neither interested in voting, nor qualified to decide on the issues in a clear and intelligible manner."

I shook my head, "No wonder he lost."

Grampy turned to me, "You miss the point, Stuart. Your great-grandfather questioned whether the majority of women in his day had a real *interest* in, and thus understanding of, business and politics—and, therefore, whether their vote would be meaningful and contribute to the process."

"Is that how a democracy works—one group decides whether another is fit to vote? I assume most women have an interest in life. Is politics not related to life?"

A firmness gripped Grampy's voice, "Your great-grandfather was a practical man, Stuart. He wasn't interested in a democracy alone, but in an *enlightened* democracy. He would have said that voting wasn't simply a right, but a responsibility, and that the system wouldn't work unless the voters educated themselves—as he himself did."

The impatience stirred in me, "And what if only a minority of women had an interest in, and understanding of, the issues—such as women laboring under improper working conditions or questioning whether their sons should be sent off to wars in foreign lands? Should they be denied the vote—and, thus, the possibility of having their interests represented—because not *all* women may be 'educated' in the way that men deem suitable?" I looked at Grampy, "Are we men the only ones bestowed with wisdom?"

"No, but those who are in a position to speak up, can—and, hopefully, will—speak up for the truth *as they see it* and accept the consequences of their stand. Your great-grandfather did that. He didn't say he was right. He simply said what he felt, and he didn't maintain that women should never have the right to vote. Rather, that an educated vote required an appropriate education, and many women *in his day* were neither particularly interested nor educated in matters relating to the running of our country."

"As men saw fit."

"As reality dictated."

"Dictates?..." I looked at my grandfather, "Is that, Grampy, how reality works?"

"Often, yes,"

I reflected on Grampy's words, "And Great-Granddad lost."

Grampy considered, "Interestingly enough, he was beaten by a male vote—the last all-male vote in our nation."

My glance turned for a moment to the chipmunk, busily chewing on his own nut. Grampy's words prodded further thoughts, questions. "How would Great-Grandma have voted?"

"My mother?"

"Yes. Did Great-Granddad feel that his wife was capable of voting responsibly?"

"He knew she wasn't interested in voting."

"She was content to live with the consequences of her husband's and of other men's actions?"

"She trusted, Stuart, that the breadth of views would find adequate representation among the male voters, and she was not unaware of the fact that she and other women had an influence on their husbands' views."

"Indirect."

"Perhaps, but no less real."

I paused, looked at Grampy, "And Bea?" Grampy turned to me. I spoke up, "How did she feel about the women's vote?"

Grampy considered a moment, "She was able to appreciate both sides."

"How would she have voted if the poll had been held?"

"She was very active during her lifetime in many social causes. I suspect she felt that the time was coming for women to have the vote."

Penny pawed at her master impatiently. Grampy leaned over and scratched her ears, before straightening up and turning to me, "Stuart, your great-grandfather recognized that change was part of life—inevitable. That was not the issue. His concern, and that of others who may appear conservative, was, and is, that *change isn't always for the better.* Discretion is needed, along with some sober thinking, if change is to signify progress. Your great-grandfather saw that his task was to provide something of an anchor for our rapidly changing times." Grampy paused, "Do you understand that?"

"I'm not sure." I looked at Grampy, "It appears to me that the forces for preserving the status quo are pretty entrenched as it is."

"They may be, but your great-grandfather wasn't interested in the status quo alone. He wasn't born with a silver spoon in his mouth. Rather, he had to work hard for everything he got. And, during his time in government, he himself was responsible for many changes in the system. His concern, though, was that the forces for change did not always understand the foundation they were building upon and, thus, were content to throw it out entirely."

I reflected, "Grampy, how do you feel about the system?"

Our glances met, "My views are the same."

I paused, "Even with all the changes our country has gone through?"

"A person looks at the changes you are referring to from a different perspective when he has gone through a couple of world wars and is closer to the end of his life, Stuart, than to the beginning. I'm not sure that something as fundamental as human nature changes much."

I looked at my grandfather searchingly, "What, then, is the basis for progress, hope?"

"Hope...." Grampy's thoughts were distant. His sights continued on up the road—his route in earlier, more energetic years, when his walks often took him another three miles into Lancaster, to fetch the Sunday paper, attend to some business, or to visit a friend.

As we turned back with Penny toward Cat Bow, I lifted my sights up to the summit of Mt. Prospect, seeking to recall the verse that rested below Great-Grandfather's portrait, *Whose life in low estate began....* The afternoon sun slowly started its descent. Grampy's steps were slower, measured.

The chipmunk scurried up the trunk of the pine, as Penny trotted on ahead once again. We followed her tracks, our shadows trailing behind us into the afternoon. As we retraced our steps around the puddles, our reflections caught up to us.

Thanks to the famed Yankee industriousness about which Grampy had spoken, the growth of business had brought with it the accumulation of capital and the "Almighty Dollar." Over the last year, I found myself increasingly struggling with the blunt fact of American life that making money was held up to Grampy, and many in his generation, as a worthy cause. I thought back uneasily to a comment I had made during a discussion earlier in the year about how I assumed people went into business to make a particular *product*, develop a particular *resource*—what we referred to as 'goods' and 'services.'

My question didn't appear to speak to the point. Instead, Grampy asked me if I had ever heard the name, Russell Conwell—a Boston lawyer, he went on to say, who was so devoted to the worthiness of making money that he became a preacher and traveled across the country, giving a celebrated lecture entitled "Acres of Diamonds." Everyone, everywhere, Conwell exhorted, had a chance to get ahead, if they only looked nearby and discovered their "unseen diamonds." From what Grampy related, Conwell's words not only inspired thousands of youth to look around and make something of their lives, but the money that was raised from the admission to his lectures was used to found Temple University in Philadelphia, the purpose of which was to help finance the education of worthy young people, including many future businessmen.

Grampy's words had lodged themselves in my mind: "All through New England, it had been a point of honor for the rich to leave in their wills substantial fortunes for hospitals, libraries, parks, schools, churches, children's camps, and other benefactions. Scholarships and grants available for these causes would otherwise never have existed had not some inventor, capitalist, manufacturer, or salesman sweated for years to accumulate the funds that benefited his successors."

I was silent. I didn't doubt the truth of what Grampy was saying, but I wondered, once again, whether it was the *whole* truth or, even, the *main* truth. Simply expressed: Was benefitting others the central reason the old New England families made their fortunes—all too often in crowded mills with working conditions that degraded the "beneficiaries?" If not, why was so much made of the charity? Tokens of what?... Grampy's gaze followed Penny down the road. It was not an easy issue to address. *Bostonians don't have ethics*, the expression went, *as much as they have customs. And some don't even have that; they have habits.*

I thought back uneasily to a passage from John Kenneth Galbraith's writings. The subject of the story, an aspiring Harvard graduate student, in his bouts with his conscience ... *received some measure of reassurance,* the author affirmed, *from the local scene. He passed the graceful Weeks Bridge, worthy of the Seine and honoring a family prominent in national life and politics who, over several generations, had made no departure from the economic and social principles avowed by Herbert Spencer and Herbert Hoover....These were the survival of the fittest and the belief in wealth as a source of prestige and power, that wealth being the benign endowment of a discriminating Creator. Such views had enjoyed no slight measure of acclaim and were here commemorated. Were they not a lesson for his generation?*

I wondered. I wondered about the "point of honor" that Grampy had mentioned—the fact that New Englanders gave substantial amounts of *their* capital, *their* wealth to worthy causes....So we were told.

The more the assurance was given over the years, the more uneasy I had grown with the assumptions behind it. "Capital?" The word, I had discovered, came from the Latin, *caput*, meaning head. Indeed, mention was frequently made of the fact that every successful business starts as an idea. I reflected. The contrasting ways in which people spoke of this truth often struck me: "I *have* an idea!"–"An idea *came to me.*" The distinction, I increasingly felt, was as significant as it was overlooked. In the former case, it was a quick and natural step to move from *my* idea, the idea I "*have,*" to the firm conviction that the proceeds from the idea—as they realize, manifest themselves in large amounts of capital or wealth—are similarly *my* possession.

Who would question such an assumption in our Land of Free Enterprise? And "*an idea came to me?*" In the latter case, the route was not so direct or ingratiating. Instead, one ended up confronting the question: *Where* did the idea come from and for what purpose? A verse from our national song returned often to mind, with its quietly haunting melody, *America, America, God shed His grace on thee. And crown thy good with brotherhood from sea to shining sea.* I had been moved, but somehow not surprised, to discover that Ben Franklin never filed a single patent for "his" many and profitable inventions.

Our steps carried us back down the road and into the woods, Mt. Prospect and the encircling heavens receding back behind a dappled, spring patchwork of buds, leaves, and branches. I turned to my grandfather, as a question arose out of my ruminations, "Grampy, you've often said over the years that the business of America is business."

"Those are Calvin Coolidge's words, yes."

I nodded, "And what is the business of business?"

Grampy's sights rose with the trunks of the massive pine up into the afternoon, "It's creating wealth, making money."

I looked at him, "Is it?" The impatience gnawed at me, "If people want to *make* money, why don't they go to work for the Bureau of Printing and Engraving?"

"Stuart, a business can't provide jobs for others, never mind stay in operation, unless it makes a profit and grows."

Growth, 'Continuous,' 'unlimited', . . . *cancer?* I breathed in, looked at Grampy. The dis-ease stirred within me, "I am aware of that. Though, I wonder how many of the things that are produced are things that we really need."

"No one is *forced* to buy anything in this country." The firmness returned to Grampy's voice.

Our gazes met. I paused, spoke up, "Grampy, have you ever heard the term 'subliminal seduction?'" Grampy reflected. I looked at him, "It's a fancy word for mind control."

"And?"

"It's practiced daily by large corporations in our country, including the tobacco companies. As we speak—*this very moment*—there are hundreds of high-powered professionals, backed up by legions of lawyers and financiers, who are plotting how to target, *actually target*, young people, us, your grandchildren—many of whom do not understand the consequences of our actions—for addictions that will take thousands of lives." I paused. "That goes on all the time in this 'free enterprise' system you are defending." Our gazes met, "It's sick, inhuman—business as usual."

"If companies are so interested in letting citizens decide what they 'need,' why do they spend millions and millions of dollars a year on advertising—including draping half naked women over their cars and products?"

"That's what a free market economy is about. It's a competitive marketplace."

"Is that what competition breeds, decadence?"

"You're being extreme, Stuart."

"Am I?" Pain, sadness, anger coiled within me, "Are the companies selling women, human beings—to go along with the 'hands' and 'head counts' that produce their products?" I took a deep breath, "Grampy, do you realize that after all these years the cigarette companies are finally agreeing to give us consumers the story about the 'goods' they produce, bombarding us with advertising all the while to meet our 'needs.' *Smoking causes lung cancer, heart disease, emphysema, and may complicate pregnancy.—Quitting smoking now greatly reduces serious risks to your health....* The list is getting longer and longer. It's sick."

"So, what do you want to do about it—close down all the cigarette companies, put the thousands of people who are employed out of work, along with the farmers who grow the tobacco and the network of distributors?" Grampy looked at me sternly, "What are you saying, Stuart?"

"What am I saying?" I searched for words, "What I am saying, Grampy, is that we have built up thriving industries in this 'free enterprise system' of ours—cigarettes, alcohol—which are based not on health but on sickness, addictions. Thousands upon thousands of citizens are dying from tobacco related illnesses." I breathed out. "This isn't what our country, America, is about—sister and brotherhood."

"Nobody is saying that there is not room for improvements. Neither our system nor any other system is perfect. But, in this country citizens *can* get together, as they did during Prohibition, and make their views known on such matters, get legislation passed."

"Against considerable odds."

Grampy reflected, "Often, yes. It is not always easy. But, such challenges test whether people are really committed to the concerns they champion or whether they are simply interested in criticizing the system that provides for them."

"Is it that simple?"

"That's always been the way change has come about. Concessions have to be won from the status quo. Many people forget that earlier in history business, itself, had to struggle hard and undergo considerable trials before it succeeded in gaining a foothold in the earlier societies, which were often dominated by the inquisitions and intolerances of the church and state." Grampy considered, "Was it Plato who placed the businessman in the lowest caste, because he supposedly dirtied his hands with matters of the earth?"

A puddle drifted us apart. Grampy continued, "Nothing in life, Stuart, is perfect. But one thing you can be sure about, even if one doesn't like it, is that there is a reason why things are the way they are."

"What is the reason in the case of addictions such as smoking?"

Grampy paused, resting his foot on a limb that lay on the side of the road. He looked over at me, "Smoking's been a way of life in this land all the way back to the Indians. You can't expect people to change their habits overnight. It's only recently that concerns have arisen about the effects of tobacco, and they're not yet definitive."

"Grampy, smoking is an addiction."

"Addictions, Stuart, are part of life."

I looked at my grandfather, "What do you mean?"

"We're not angels. This world around us isn't heaven. You have to deal with human nature the way it is, even though it's not as perfect as you may like it to be."

I broke in, "How *is* human nature, Grampy?"

Grampy's sights followed the stone wall along the edge of the woods, branches and limbs softening its rough surface, "It's not always pretty. Those who have been in war recognize that." Grampy's gaze was distant, "Everybody carries their own wound through life. We can't push off our responsibility for this fact onto others—even big business."

I paused, glanced over at Grampy, "I don't understand what you are saying. Does that mean that businesses should be allowed to exploit our wounds, with all the advertising and hype that's out there?"

Grampy looked at me, "It's easy to criticize business for the problems you're speaking about. It's always easy to criticize the hand that feeds us." Grampy considered, "What one hears less often are people who ask the question, 'If business is destroying life, *why* is it doing it?'" Grampy looked at me. "Have you ever asked yourself that question?" Our gazes met. "Have you ever asked yourself what a business even is?" I looked at Grampy uncertainly. He shifted his weight on the limb, "You keep speaking about business. Who makes up a business?"

I glanced off and then back at him, "The management, directors. . . ."

"And *their* bosses—the hundreds, often thousands, of citizens who own shares in the company, along with the employees, vendors, distributors, consumers, you and me, who buy the products—to say nothing of the community, large and small, in which the enterprise operates and which chooses to sanction or not sanction its affairs." Grampy stepped back into the road, picking up the pace. My eyes followed a blue jay as it swooped between branches, before perching among the evergreen boughs of an old hemlock.

"Business is life, Stuart. If you're concerned about marketing these 'addictions' you've been speaking about, we're *all* implicated in the affair." An earnestness filled Grampy's voice, "People have to be responsible for their own actions."

"And the companies, the advertisers," I turned to him intently, *"what about their actions, their responsibility?* They are excused because many of them are in the business of making a profit—goods that are bad, services that are, in truth, a disservice? Grampy, the dictionary speaks of a consumer as 'a model U.S. citizen.'" Our gazes met, "Do you know what *'consume'* means?" Grampy squinted his eyes. I spoke up, "It means, 'To use up; to destroy; to waste.'"

"When it's excessive."

I took a breath, "Grampy, as a nation we comprise six percent of the world's population. We consume forty percent of its resources."

"And we produce *over* forty percent of the world's goods." Grampy's patience was strained, "We are an industrialized nation, Stuart. You can't compare apples and oranges."

"How long, Grampy, can this kind of consumption go on? There is not room for many other apples in the basket.

Grampy glanced off. I bit into my lip, "This consumer ethic of ours is cancerous; it's consuming, killing us." I took a breath, "It's crazy; it doesn't even make good business sense. The cigarette companies are providing the very fuse that is knocking off their *own* customers, and all they do is crank up their advertising even more and aim it at my generation, younger kids, to make sure that there are enough new customers to fill the depleting ranks—to make sure we're able to meet our 'needs.'" The pain, sadness, rose up in me, "Just because we call it a consumer ethic, it doesn't mean there is anything ethical about the way not just the tobacco industry, but other businesses are operating today." My breath flowed out. Our steps carried us through an abrupt puddle, churning our reflections.

My glance turned from Grampy into and through the woods—trees and gullies and a tangle of spring undergrowth, struggling to lift itself toward the light. "The first thing we should do is to be honest with ourselves—as you say, 'call a spade a spade.'"

I paused, went on, "Everybody talks about 'meeting needs.' Why can't we admit that the *primary, the overwhelming need* that is being met is the need of the heads of the companies to increase their profits at virtually all costs."

"Why do you focus on the negative side?"

I stopped in the road, our shadows lingering in the light, lingering in the shade, "Grampy, I'm not you. I'm me—a young person, student...." I searched for words, "We're embroiled in an undeclared war in Southeast Asia; our cities are burning down; our campuses erupting. What else do we see today when we open a newspaper, magazine, turn on the radio or TV?" Our eyes met, "Environmental pollution, violations of health and safety standards, . . . rape, murder, larceny, sickness, thousands upon thousands of people starving and in misery!" I stared at Grampy. "What other focus *is* there in this great land of ours?"

Grampy looked off, his glance searching through the darkening forest.

"Grampy," I turned to him, "I'm not looking for perfection. I'm talking about something much more basic, more human: care, consideration, goodness." I paused, searched his face, as memories of the business breakfast meeting returned disconcertingly to mind. "We pledge our allegiances to our flag, recite our emblazoned scripts, sing our national anthem, glorifying violence, war, and, it seems, do everything we can to keep from confronting our shadow as a nation—until it rises up to enlighten us, in the civil rights and related unrest that we are embroiled in now."

My voice was quieter, "How will anything change, Grampy, if people ignore these realities? How will things change if people don't devote their energies to waking up—even if it means taking a radical step like that of our forbears, one that gets to the root of the issue?" Grandfathers . . . sons. Our gazes met, parted.

Grampy turned his eyes down the road to Penny. We continued on. The sunlight filtered through the branches of the trees overhead, mixing with the afternoon shadows that followed on our weary heels. Words gave way to silence, gave way to words—searching, broken, pained.

"Things *aren't* perfect, Stuart. What do you want to put in the place of our free-enterprise system, socialism?"

I shook my head, "No...." Our steps carried us past the Baker Farm, retiring into the day, on down the road, and into the woods again.

* * * * *

Socialism. I reflected. The word evoked antipathy, disdain—fear in others, in me, a part of my self, fallen, that was my father's son, my grandfather's grandson. And yet, I was coming to realize that there was also another voice in me—the Stuart part of the Weeks—a voice that was struggling to come to expression, to speak out not just what I was told, but what I experienced: a growing disease in the faces of friends, neighbors, family, my grandfather—caught up as we were in our consumer/consuming ethic. The puddles broadened; the road, the current journeyed on.

Memories returned, only a few months old—Paris, student riots, and, between it all, a sudden interval, aside, a recognition—parting the ebbing backdrop of silence. I lifted my head, paused on the great stone steps that led down into the Tuilleries Gardens. The sword, the pen ... great-grandfathers and sons? Gazing over the gardens, recollections of earlier years, fishing rod in hand, line probing the depths, rose up within me—as, suddenly conscious, I resisted the gentle tug that had so often drawn me, pen and paper in hand, into Paris's alleys and passages. Fish/poem? Poised on the step, I resisted the tug a moment and instead allowed the invisible line to gently stir in my depths, awaken my consciousness....

Afternoon passed on into evening. Cries reached my ears from across the river Seine, as the demonstrations continued on into spring months. And then, in that moment, I realized something. I realized that what those hundreds, thousands of students, who thronged the Place, St. Michel, were looking, searching, fighting for was the experience—even if it were something as seemingly slight, fleeting as a tug—OF SOMETHING THAT WAS INVISIBLE AND YET, NONE-THE-LESS, REAL.

It was not easily found. They, we, hundreds, thousands of students, who filled the square week in and week out, were so full of our anger, sadness, pain that there was no room to breathe, to experience that which resided within the spaces and intervals of life—some thing, no, that was NOT a thing ... and yet, I realized, that could not quite be put into words. We no longer had the language to express the deep longing that stirred within.

My steps led me back to America, Boston, Concord, an all too memo-

rable business breakfast meeting, and on up again to Cat Bow Farm and its Lord—struggling, as I was, to kindle a love that meant more to me than I understood.

* * * * *

"No." Rays of the descending sun glanced over the road. I picked up the thread of the conversation as Grampy and I walked on, my glance tracing the stone wall on through the woods. "No, Grampy. I'm not talking about *socialism* or any other 'ism' or 'ology.'" I turned to him, "I'm talking about how we can become more *social*, more aware of the needs of our fellow citizens, and not just leave their welfare to 'Big Business' or an impersonalized system."

"What are you suggesting?"

I sought for words, "I'm not sure....I haven't had the experience you have." I reflected, "But, my thoughts keep returning to the words I referred to earlier, *America is great, because America is good. And if America ever ceases to be good, she will cease to be great.*" Grampy listened. The recollection was clearer. My eyes searched his, "What *do* those words of De Tocqueville mean to you, Grampy?"

"They are ideals, important ideals, Stuart. But, as I said, they have to be related to reality."

I breathed out deeply, "Reality. How, Grampy, do the Thoreaus, Gandhis, Martin Luther Kings, Lincolns—along with the thousands of other unsung heroes—fit into this reality; people who were not so much interested in conforming themselves to life, but who struggled and succeeded in conforming life, 'reality' to their dreams?"

"They are the exception." Grampy's response was terse.

"Are they? And how about your father?" Words stirred on Grampy's lips. I looked at him, "Was he the exception? Or, is he, are they the rule—a picture of what the *human* being truly is—and we, all too often, the exception?"

The silence deepened. I turned my glance from Grampy to the woods, passing over the patches of snow huddled in the deepening shade of the afternoon, before settling on an old, gnarled, pine stump, encircled by shoots of green. A question rose in me, "Grampy, there is one thing I don't understand. Often, over the years, you and Dad have told me to be realistic." I paused, searched for the words, "Can it be that this famed realism, before which we bow down ever and again—short term, bottom line, unable, it seems, to factor into its equations all the costs—can it be, Grampy, that *this realism is, in truth, unrealistic for the larger society within which it operates?*"

"What are you saying, Stuart?"

I looked at my grandfather, "I'm trying to relate business—our affairs—to life, to a human world."

"Few people will argue with the ideals you are speaking about. As I keep saying, their *application* is where the difficulties arise."

I reflected, "I can understand that, Grampy....But I *also* can understand that, if there were a genuine belief in these ideals that we so devoutly espouse, the application may well be a lot easier than it is."

"The changes you are talking about take time."

I looked at my grandfather incredulously, "Whose time—the black people in the ghettos, the young Americans in Vietnam, the migrant workers in the fields of wrath?" I breathed in, "For some people, time runs out." I paused, went on, "Grampy, for many years I have thought about your comment, that what the conservatives know intuitively, it takes those of a more liberal cast of mind years of reflection to understand." Our gazes met, "When I first heard that statement, I recognized the truth in it, but I also sensed something else. I sensed that the statement, the truth was incomplete. I believe that the so-called liberals *also* understand something intuitively, something about life, liberty, and the pursuit of more than just happiness, which, *if we want to focus on the differences*, may take conservatives as long to understand."

Grampy turned to me abruptly, "Are you a Democrat, Stuart?"

A pained smile passed on my lips, "Like a number of our forebears?" I shook my head, "No, no, Grampy. I'm neither a Democrat nor a Republican, *nor* independent of the two, the jackass or rampaging elephant—the accursed dialectic." I searched for words, "I'm a republocrat, a demolican."

Grampy wrestled with my response, "Stuart, did you read my letter to Reverend Greeley?"

"I did." We emerged from the woods and continued down the hill alongside the fence. My sights passed over the pasture, settling back into the late afternoon, empty but for a large boulder that rose up in my memory. I paused, took a deep breath, turned to my grandfather,

"Grampy, what are we doing in the midst of this undeclared war in Vietnam that is killing so many of my generation—that will soon add my draft number to the lottery?" Grampy was silent. I looked at him, struggled for words, "I understand what you wrote to Reverend Greeley, but do you understand why he stood up for those students who were protesting against the war?"

Grampy stepped over to the fence. "What are we doing?" He rested his hand on the post; my eyes on the sign—trespasses. "We are stopping the spread of Communism."

I looked at my grandfather, "Do you really believe that?"

A firmness returned to Grampy's voice, "Absolutely."

I nodded, "And what about the Vietnamese people themselves? Do they have any say in the matter?"

Grampy rested his foot on a rock, "What are you driving at, Stuart?"

"Do you think the people of Vietnam should have any say in their affairs?"

"Of course," Grampy's words were guarded.

"Then," I turned to him, paused, looked into his eyes, "why, Grampy, did we ignore the vote that was held, in which the Vietnamese people clearly expressed their wish that we *not* meddle in their internal affairs. If we are going to 'make the world safe for democracy,' shouldn't we at least respect such elections, which form the basis for the democratic process?"

Grampy considered, "I don't know which elections you are referring to."

The way to cure a communist is not to suppress his speech but to argue him out of his position. If you cannot argue him out of it.... A letter from a great-grandfather to his son, upon his entering his first elective office, awoke out of my memory. I looked at Grampy, "The *ignored* election of 1956, after which Eisenhower himself agreed that we should stay out of the conflict."

"I'm not up on the details." Grampy dug at the rock with his foot, "All I know is that Communist China is involved."

"Grampy, the North Vietnamese, our 'enemies,' have been fighting the Chinese Communists for years. Few of our leaders seem to understand that, seem to recognize that, before we got involved and set up our puppet government in the south, the Vietnamese people were fighting together to preserve their own land from Communist aggression."

Grampy's sights passed up the pasture. Black–white,…the shades of gray settled around us. His voice was subdued, "The people aren't behind the Vietnam War, as they were with the World Wars."

"Despite the Tonken Bay attempt." I turned to him, "The 'powers that be' haven't yet been able to get the American public fully behind it."

"What are you saying?" He looked at me severely.

"What I'm saying, Grampy, is what you never shared with me." I paused, "The most forthright politicians, including Franklin Roosevelt, have stated that 'In politics nothing happens by accident; if it happens, you can bet it was planned that way.'…." I looked at Grampy, "In order, as many others have said, to secure our economic interests."

"Politics is a complicated business, Stuart."

"What's so complicated about using ones citizenry—'the laborer, craftsman, mechanic,' for accomplishing political goals? The leaders have been doing that throughout history. Machiavelli wrote a classic, which is required reading in most political science courses today, about the ways in which rulers hold firm to the reigns of power."

"What are you suggesting, Stuart?"

I reflected, "Grampy, do you remember last spring when you and 'Uncle Bobby' were talking about the Pearl Harbor investigation that you were involved in during your time in the Senate?" I paused, went on, "I asked what you believed happened, and you said you couldn't speak about it." I looked at my grandfather, "Why?"

Grampy dislodged the rock into the ditch. "The issue was top security."

I searched for words, "I thought you played a central role in getting the Admiral, upon whom the blame had been laid, a fair trial— which proved that he was not guilty after all."

"I did."

"And…? Was the responsibility laid on anyone for the deaths of all those who were serving their country? Where did the investigation lead?"

Grampy turned away, "Some things are better left unsaid. . . . Those who are aware of these matters know how they sometimes play themselves out. Those that are not, probably wouldn't understand."

I turned to him, "And what about justice?"

Our gazes met, "Justice? . . . Perhaps, in such cases, Stuart, justice is not in our hands. You spoke of 'higher laws.'"

Grampy was silent. We walked on, my reflections tracing the puddles, "And so that story, too, was never told." I breathed in deeply, "That's how we honor our dead—a conspiracy of silence. The ruse goes on, as we bite our lips, sing our anthems, and insist that such transgressions don't exist in *our* country, 'the land of the free and the home of the brave.'" Pain, anger, sadness, a deep sadness filled me.

"It takes two to fight, Stuart." A disquiet filled Grampy's voice.

"I know." I looked at my grandfather. "When, Grampy, are we going to stand up for our right *not* to fight back, as your boss, Eisenhower, himself stated when he looked back over his military career?"

The puddles widened; our steps carried us ahead, together/apart. I glanced off down the field to tides of blue. Memories arose with a tune, another melody that had accompanied me through my childhood years of innocence.

* * * * *

France, Paris, left, . . . right, on through an early spring day. My path had led me through the Tuillerie Gardens to Paris's famed forest, the Bois de Boulogne. The ripples widening, parting, further parting the ebbing backdrop of silence. I sat back into the bench, tucked away beneath the spreading boughs of a willow. Before me a pond—silent and still—rested in its reflections. My gaze searched its surface. I lifted my concertina from the bench. The melody stirred—soft, distant, touched by a strain of sadness. I sang the words quietly, as an old man of single arm and crutched leg made his way along the path.

> *Underneath the lantern, by the barrack gate,*
> *Darling I remember, the way you used to wait;*
> *'Twas there that you whispered tenderly,*
> *That you loved me.*
> *You'd always be, my Lili of the lamplight,*
> *My own Lili Marlene*

*The man paused before the bench, beneath the boughs of the willow...
lifted his head. Our gazes met. A memory kindled in his eyes, "You know the
song?" I nodded, rested the concertina in my lap, "My mother played it on
her accordion when we were young." He sat slowly down on the bench beside
me, leaning his crutch against his leg.*

*A tapestry unfolded—1914, winter, France, the battle front. The allies
were dug into the trenches on one side; the Germans were across the way.
The old man hummed the melody, nodded to me. I played on quietly. His
voice was distant, "Through the Advent Season we sang the tune, one to
another, across the battlefields, when the fighting, the 'business' of the day
was over. The days grew shorter and shorter. And then, on Christmas eve, a
soldier, a first, and then a second, from our side, . . . from theirs, paused, lifted
his head, rose, arose out of the dirt and mud and earth. Others followed,
stepped forward." The old man's gaze was distant.*

*"The weapons dropped to their sides. The hatred, vengeance, and pas-
sion subsided. A profound compassion arose in our hearts. Hundreds crossed
over into no-man's, suddenly every man's land, reached out, exchanged gifts
and letters, broke bread together, shared the little we had to drink, and celebrated, in the darkest night of the year, a birth within."*

*The old man looked at me deeply, "That was the real battle—to remem-
ber, despite the ambitions and intrigues of a few leaders, despite the heat of
the war, the confusion and fury, that the other person, the 'enemy,' wasn't just
the enemy. He was an individual, a HUMAN being, mortal/immortal, a
brother." My gaze was drawn to a quiet glimmer deep in the old man's eyes,
as his words settled back into a low, soft hum—*

> *. . . My Lili of the lamplight,*
> *My own Lili Marlene.*

* * * * *

"Our right not *to fight back. . . ."* The ripples spread on out, quickened
by the glimmers of the setting sun. Words, clearer, more audible, rose
up out of my depths. I turned my gaze from the pond back to Grampy,
"We're supposed to be a civilized, intelligent people. Is there nothing at
all that we can learn from these wars?"

"That one has to be strong to survive." Grampy's words came
slowly.

I turned to him, "I wonder, Grampy, if we understand what strength is?" I looked at my grandfather, "Do we understand what George Washington, the father of our nation, meant when, upon leaving office, he warned us, in his "Proclamation of Neutrality," about staying out of foreign entanglements?"

"Times change, Stuart." The weariness weighed Grampy's words.

I looked at him. "I realize that, Grampy. But, do basic principles change, including those essential to our survival?" Our gazes met, "Washington wasn't suggesting isolationism, but rather that America's real mission was to promote peace by example, by getting our own house in order first."

"It would be nice if it were that simple, Stuart. The world, however, has changed a great deal since Washington's time. Things are a lot more interrelated; our 'house' has grown considerably since our country first began."

I nodded, as my eyes lifted to the Big House, which rose up in front of us into the early evening. Above it Old Glory—the stars and stripes—kept their eternal vigil. I turned to my grandfather, "I'm not saying it's simple, Grampy. I'm just asking if we've given such peaceful 'tactics' a real try, if our foundations have grown with our house?"

Grampy's steps slowed down. The bend in the grove of pines approached. *Drivers take care, 31 grandchildren. . . .* My eyes rested on the family sign. The ranks—children seen *and* increasingly heard—had swelled over the passing seasons. We, the younger generation, had come of age in the sixties, when little in life, it seemed, was pure—democracy or otherwise. My gaze passed up to the barn and paddock. Rickety, like her aging master, Janie still held the fort.

Grampy paused in front of the sign, our shadows glancing off to the side. A gentle breeze shifted in the trees, as the words passed silently across his lips. . . . *here and there.*

Our steps led us on up the driveway to the circle. Grampy lingered by the island of roses, encircled by its slate border and swath of spring grass. A thought came to mind. I glanced over at Grampy, who paused with Penny by the front door, "Is Easter tomorrow?"

He reflected a moment, "Yes."

"Easter?" I walked over to them quietly, "I don't remember celebrating it at Cat Bow...." I turned to Grampy, "I'm not sure I know what it really means."

"It was that holiday which meant the most to your Grandmother Bea. The Unitarian Church doesn't make a big thing of it." Grampy considered. "We celebrated it regularly in the earlier years and a couple of times when you were young and your Grandma Jane was well." My gaze lifted over the budding island to the end room on the north wing, its curtains discreetly drawn. Grampy's voice was quieter, "It has to do, Stuart, with lilies, flowers, the blossoming of spring...." Grampy's eyes rested on the flush of roses, their tender bloom rising up out of the tangle of thorns. "And about our resurrection from the dead." I looked at my grandfather. He was silent.

If you are going to go.... Summer, autumn, winter—a first year, a second, fourth, sixth, a seventh year had passed, and spring was upon us once again, anew. The Lord of Cat Bow turned and headed into the Big House.

* * * * *

Grampy hung his hat and coat on the vestibule hook, before pausing for a moment in the entrance room. Leaning against one of the abandoned love seats, he turned to me, "I'm going upstairs to put up my feet."

"Grampy, you wanted to show me a passage from a book?"

Grampy reflected a moment and, then, told me to follow him into the Pine Room. We passed through the living room—tables, chairs, a sofa edged with cushions—and continued on down the hall, by the row of closets, and into the Pine Room—framed with its galaxy of captains of industry, politics, and a soothsayer or two."

Grampy stopped in front of the far bookshelf, his hand moving over the titles, before resting on an old volume, which he took down. I watched him as he leafed through the pages, until he came to a marker. His eyes passed over the words before turning to me, "This was written by the first successful Republican candidate for the presidency." Grampy handed me the book. "Have a look; you may understand more of what I was saying on our walk." Grampy's tone was tired. He paused, then added, "It's one thing, Stuart, to question and criticize. It's another to step into the arena, where one's hands are cut, scraped, and soiled."

Our glances met. Over his shoulder, his cartoon likeness, Secretary Weeks, glanced out at me from his coliseum dungeon. I nodded. Grampy turned and headed upstairs.

My steps led me over to the sofa beside the fireplace. The house was quiet. I sat down, my eyes lowering to the page:

> *You can not strengthen the weak by weakening the strong;*
> *You can not keep out of trouble by spending more than your*
>   *income;*
> *You can not help small men by tearing down big men;*
> *You can not help the wage earner by pulling down the wage payer;*
> *You can not establish security on borrowed money;*
> *You can not further the brotherhood of men by inciting class hatred;*
> *You can not build character and courage by taking away a man's*
>   *initiative and independence;*
> *You can not help men by permanently doing for them what they*
>   *could and should do for themselves.*

Abraham Lincoln. I reflected and then turned the pages, my eyes passing over other passages by Lincoln—some familiar, some less so— until they stopped on the text of his Second Inaugural Address. Cousin Ned's words about Martin Luther King—dreams/nightmares—awoke within me, bringing back glimmers of a lobster bake from an earlier summer season. I read the lines to myself:

> *On the occasion corresponding to this four years ago, all thoughts were anxiously directed to an impending Civil War. . . . Neither party expected for the war the magnitude, or the duration, which it has already attained. Neither anticipated that the cause of the conflict might cease without, or even before, the conflict itself should cease. Each looked for an easier triumph, and a result less fundamental and astounding.*
>
> *Both read the same Bible, and pray to the same God; and each invokes His aid against the other. It may seem strange that any man should dare to ask a just God's assistance in wringing their bread from the sweat of other men's faces; but let us judge not that we be not judged. The prayers of both could not be answered; that of neither has been answered fully.*

The Almighty has His own purposes. "Woe unto the world because of offenses! for it must needs be that offenses come; but woe to that man by whom the offense cometh!" If we shall suppose that American slavery is one of those offenses which, in the providence of God, must needs come, but which, having continued through His appointed time, He now wills to remove, and that He gives to both North and South, this terrible war, as the woe due to those by whom the offense come, shall we discern therein any departure from those divine attributes which the believers in a living God always ascribe to him?

Fondly do we hope, fervently do we pray, that this mighty scourge of war may speedily pass away; yet if it be God's will that it continue until the wealth piled by bondsmen by two hundred and fifty years' unrequited toil shall be sunk, and until every drop of blood drawn with the lash shall be paid by another drawn with the sword, as was said three thousand years ago, so still it must be said that the judgments of the Lord are true and righteous altogether.

I breathed in.

With malice toward none; with charity for all; with firmness in the right, as God gives us to see the right, let us strive on to finish the work we are in; to bind up the nation's wounds; to care for him who shall have borne the battle, and for his widow, and his orphan—to do all which may achieve and cherish a just, and a lasting peace among ourselves and with all nations.

I rested the book on my lap. "Malice,...charity," Lincoln's words echoed on within me, as my glance lifted to the musket above the fireplace. Yes, it took the avenging angel of a civil war, and the sacrifices of a Lincoln, Colonel Cross and thousands upon thousands of other Americans, for us to realize that we couldn't own LABOR—slaves, *human* beings.

And LAND, the second traditional element of the economic process? It had taken the destruction of all too much of the forests of northern New England for us to realize that we can't simply "own" land, our very foundation, if that ownership carries with it—as it so often did—the privilege of exploiting our common resource, the rape of the earth. Other ties, less restrictive and more creative, more responsible, are required: stewardship, community land trusts, and the National Forest System that Great-Grandfather had helped to establish.

In a more reflective moment, Great-Grandfather's vision led him up the White Mountain trail, "As he climbs through the hardwoods and Hemlocks into the Spruces and Firs and through the Gnomewoods into the Fir Scrub toward the summit, he finds no more boundary posts. He realizes that as a citizen, he is joint owner not only of the mountain but of the whole range."

I lowered my gaze back down at the book. And CAPITAL? The third traditional element of the economic process and bulwark of the opposition that manifested itself in the labor and land issue? What was it going to take before we realized, along with Ben Franklin, that we can as little "own" capital, as we can possess—take possession of—those very realms from whence our ideas originate? I thought back to an internal dialogue that had arisen in me during my time in France, a response to the refrain that was often voiced overseas: *The American just chases the buck....*

> *And what's behind the buck?*
> Once upon a time, a gold standard...
> *And what's behind the gold?*
> Originally the sun...
> *And what's behind the sun?*
> *What is the American really chasing?*

The Pine Room was silent. I paused, listened. Are we able to decipher any longer the words inscribed on our almighty dollar, *In God we Trust?* A verse from our national song, forgotten, forsaken, passed across my lips: ...*America, America, may God thy gold refine, till all success be nobleness and every gain divine.* I took a breath. When will we Americans awaken from, and to, our dream?

My glance lifted to the photos—statesmen, military leaders, tycoons—that lined the far wall, before resting on the old "Communist" Marshall Tito, sharing a good laugh with Grampy. The argument

appeared over. Politics aside, they had found a common cause. Two
bulls, . . . the cow was conspicuously absent. I lowered my eyes again to
Lincoln's words, returning my searching gaze over the page.

> . . . It may seem strange that any man should dare to ask a just
> God's assistance in wringing their bread from the sweat from
> other men's faces; but let us judge not that we be not judged.

I breathed out, closed my eyes. *The better angels of our nature.* . . . Yes,
Godfather Abraham, how do we give them wings?

* * * * *

I was tired as I settled into bed that evening in the War Room. Pulling up the quilt, I leaned back against the headboard. In front of me on
the opposite wall, a First World War gas mask hung absently from its
hook. Beside it over the dresser, a helmet leaned into the shadows. My
gaze turned to the boots, picture, and plaques, their luster faded with
the years, before lowering to the worn journal on my lap. I took a deep
breath. The conversation during my walk with Grampy had rumored
within me through the late afternoon and into the evening. "The Great
War," so it had been. The first of two world wars—followed by smaller
and seemingly more manageable conflicts in Korea and Vietnam—its
glories had been sung and recited in many a tale and tune, which, over
the years, had etched themselves in my young and receptive mind. I
opened the volume. The 'long, long trail-a-winding' led Grampy to the
battlefields of France.

Sept. 4, 1917

Dearest Bea,

> *We are well on our way by this time, and thus far the trip has been all
> that could be desired. Our quarters are much better than I dreamed
> we would have, and the men in the regiment are also well taken care
> of—comparatively speaking, of course.*
>
> *I assume you know that Captain Fish was very suddenly taken
> away from us, thus leaving me in command of the battery. I and every-
> body else were mighty sorry to see him go, but of course I would be a*

*peculiar individual if I did not welcome the opportunity to take charge
for a while. We are having 1–2 lectures a day in the assembly room,
and all together my time is pretty well taken up. Endicot Putnam is well
and riding steerage, as are a number of no less lights.*

*We had a lecture this morning from Doc Miller, who told us all the
possible ways there are to be killed on the battlefield. His main point
seemed to be that if he had us at a hospital in Boston, he could probably
fix us up, but that we couldn't look for much assistance on the front.
Yesterday someone came down with a wild rumor that they were bet-
ting 5–1 on Wall St. that we would never reach France. Tom Saunders,
Mac, and I immediately pulled out our life preservers, inspected them,
and figured which rail we would go over. We've been inspired though by
a Captain on board who was in the Canadian artillery. He had both
legs shot off on the "Somme" and is now going back with his wife and
is going to try to get into the French aviation. Can you beat that for
guts?*

*Well, Bea dear, there isn't much I can say at the present. Take
good care of the kid now, and don't let her forget she has a father.
Give loads of love to Mother and to Dad, and save a few for yourself.
Affectionately,*

                                                                Sin

I turned the pages of the old journal, letters, fragments, passages,
one after another, followed Grampy's footsteps over the Atlantic—the
drum beats quickening as we went.

                              * * * * *

                                                    October 25, 1917

Dearest Bea:

*We are on dry land again, though a lot farther away than before. We
have been rising at 5:15, walking two miles and shooting all morning
until 11:00. Then two miles walk home and lunch. At 1:30 lectures
commence; some days we have three, an hour each, and other days
only one or two. After all this, supper is at 6:00 and several evenings
we have had lectures for an hour or two.*

I get terribly lonesome for you at times, but there is no sense

in it, and I don't mean to speak of it or to have you think for an
instant I am trying to complain.

A smile touched my face. Complain? Not us red-blooded
Yankees. I wondered, did it take the distance and deprivations
of war for Grampy to realize the deep love he felt for Bea? The
stiff upper lip was resolute.

When I think of others who are giving up much more than I am,
I realize how selfish it is to think of myself. So don't think that I
am not satisfied, for I am, and naturally I wouldn't be in any other
place at present of my own choosing, than right here ready to knock
the germ out of Germany (that's fair for a novice, what?).

When I get home, we'll all have such a party that the town will
stand aghast.

Most of the boys, that is the officers, would like to see the war
over. I wouldn't write this to anyone else, however, for they might
think we all had cold feet. Such is not the case, I assure you, and
while no one is hunting for trouble, I guess you will find the good
old 101st F.A. there when the whistle blows.

Most the letters I censor have a bunch of X's for kisses, so I guess
I will adopt the custom and send you a few. You can distribute them
as you see fit.

Well, Bea, I used to think that I loved you at home, but it wasn't
anything to the way I do over here.

> *Lots of love to you all,*
> *Sinclair*

PS. I am raising a mustache, and the barber has given me 6 months
more to keep my hair, so you see what's a poor fellow going to do?

> *Dec. 18, 1917*

Dearest Bea,

I feel very guilty for not having written you for so long. My only
excuse is that I was on the go last week just about every second.

We had a field inspection etc., and it meant a lot of extra work. You should see us all in our helmets. We are a very different crowd from the one you saw at Boxford. The men have changed a good deal and begin to look like real soldiers now. We have been doing a good deal of digging lately, and I have been down in the trenches and dugouts digging with the boys in order to get toughened up a bit. Everybody is in great spirits, and all I believe are much more warlike than when they first hit this dismal hole.

The last few days have been cold as ice, and the wind has been blowing a gale. When we go out for a drill, we look like a bunch of Teddy bears. First the big helmet and on top our steel helmet, with a strap under the chin, then a good woolly muffler, one of Burberry's best "French Warms", a pair of wristers and mittens....It's not too bad, except that we can hardly move. When we get to the front, I fear we'll make pretty good game for the Boshe. Well, here's hoping I'll be around to answer your next letter. Keep them coming. They mean a lot.

> Good night. Loads of love.
> Sinclair

* * *

July 28, 1918

Dearest Bea,

I have, as I anticipated, had no chance to write for the last 2 weeks. Our last 2 nights at the position were sleepless ones, on account of false gas alarms and a raid both nights....We were billeted every night in the prettiest French towns. The people were fine, especially the kids. One place where we stopped for lunch, there was the prettiest girl about 10 that I ever saw, but she wouldn't come near me. She snuck up and dropped a big bunch of violets in my hand and then beat it for all she was worth....

You will be pleased to hear that we are enjoying a good rest, which we were certainly all of us ready for. I received your last letter and was glad you knew where and how the 101st F.A. were shar-

ing in the 'show'. It was a wonderful experience, and, having come through o.k., I can say I wouldn't have missed it for a good deal.

The enemy crossed the Ourg, and we are after him. At present we have our position in a woods, which the infantry cleared yesterday PM. I have never seen so many dead Boshe and Americans. The former outnumber ours by about 3–1 here. There is plenty of salvage and souvenirs galore. I got a belt off one with the buckle which has on it, "Gott mit Uns," and we have equipped ourselves with everything we need. It is very evident here that our artillery fire was effective....

I glanced across the bedroom to the cabinet and its dusty relics, before finishing the letter:

You can imagine what it was like when I tell you we covered 40 kilos, in addition to firing about 3,000 rounds per gun. One day we were going from 8 a.m. to 6 p.m. without stopping—that was when the boys were trying for the crest on the north.

It was wicked the way the Boshe came over and machine gunned us. They came over mostly around sun down. One night, five came about 500 meters over the battery, and believe me, the old iron crosses looked larger than headlights on a machine at night. The Huns must have suffered very severely, from the numbers lying around. In one place, I counted about 50 dead within a 100 meter circle, and so it went. We picked up some pretty good trophies, but they are hard to lug about, and I didn't keep a great many. Did father ever get the shoulder straps I sent him in June. They will be quite historic some day, I think.

Everybody you know is well, although there are few of the old crowd left. There are several calls I think it would be nice if you made on the families of some of our men. The following Newton boys were killed, Sgt. _____, Pvt. _____, and I would like to suggest that you go and see their family. Sgt. _____ was one of the finest men I have ever seen, and he went like one too. He was our next choice for a commission and would have made a bully officer. The latter was our orderly and a mighty fine boy. I certainly was awfully sorry that we lost him....

I suppose when you get this you will be making plans for the latter part of the summer. I hope you will arrange to go to Mt. Prospect with mother for a month or so. I dare say, Dad will be in Washington, and she will probably be glad of your company, rather than none. Good night, dear Bea.

Loads of Love,
Bud

* * *

Oct. 21, 1918
At the Front

Dearest Bea,

You will think nothing of me for not having written before, but I have been fighting a tough war lately, and its been about impossible. It's perfectly bloody weather now, cold, rainy, and mud miles deep, and campaigning in the open isn't what it was in July, by any means. For instance, the night we moved into this position, we marched 20 kilometers in the pouring rain and were up all night trying to get the guns into position on a high hill. Everyone was sopped to the skin, and it was a hard job. We have to carry all the ammunition up the hill by hand and are working to get enough for the 'show', which we hope will start soon. The Huns, moreover, shell us here day and night, and the countryside is the worst shambles I've ever seen.

Shaking my head, I thought of the "troop" of business leaders that Grampy was to lead back to Germany after a second world war— "shambles upon shambles"—whose recommendation would contribute to the establishment of the Marshall Plan. The tone of his report was characteristically matter-of-fact. The conclusion was reached not so much out of "sympathy" for Germany and its people, but rather because it was in America's best interests that stability is returned to the country, so that it would not "go communist."

Lying out in this weather gets to the men. . . . Sunday night we had a good baptism of high explosives and gas. A lot of my men have got sick, a number wounded, and twenty-two gassed in our last position, which leaves me mighty short.

Footsteps sounded in the hall. I glanced at the clock on the table, as the door opened. 10:40. Grampy looked in, "You're still up?"

I paused, lifted the journal, "I'm doing a little reading."

Grampy glanced at the familiar cover and then at the shelf, before nodding, "Get some sleep." He started to close the door again.

"Grampy...." Grampy turned, lifted a tired glance to me.

"You *really* were in the war, weren't you?"

"For a good two years."

Grampy's gaze was distant, mine searching. I looked at him. My thoughts returned to Paris, the Bois de Boulogne, and a lingering melody that had journeyed across the waters, "Can I read a passage to you?" Grampy looked at me. I lowered my gaze to the journal and turned the page:

The night before we moved out of our last position, the Boshe put over the worst concentration I've ever dreamed of. From 9 PM until 2:30 AM, they threw them like rain—high explosives, gas (Arsenic Mustard and Diphesgene) and about everything they had. I sound more or less of gloom, don't I? Nevertheless, I am mighty well and in good spirits. We are all tremendously pleased with the way things are going. The peace talks rather got us for a day or two, but we got over it. It affected the men somewhat. Lots of them are afraid now that they'll get bombed off before peace is declared. And it is demoralizing, unless you put it right out of your mind, which I try to do. I guess it has got the Huns much worse than ourselves, though.

I looked across at Grampy. He leaned quietly against the door frame, his eyes lowering to the floor as he listened to his words.

I trust you will excuse the paper—everything is muddy and dirty, and I am especially so. Moreover, my paulin leaks, and we are generally uncomfortable. You should hear the choice language hereabouts. I often wonder if I will ever again become as "Mook" Boyer says, "gently nurtured."

Well, loads of love to you, and I hope you will appreciate the difficulties of writing. Affectionately,

I paused, lifted my eyes to my grandfather, "*Sin—clair.*"

The room was silent. I rested my head back against 101st F.A. Battalion of the 26th Yankee Division above the bed board, "Grampy?" Grampy looked up at me. I considered, "What did you mean when you said that you wondered if you would ever again be 'gently nurtured?'"

Grampy reflected long, lifting his eyes about the war room—helmet, gas mask, boots.... Our gazes met, "Often over the years I've thought of the morning in Washington when Bea and I were coming through the Wardman Park's revolving door." A tenderness, susceptibility touched Grampy's voice, "As it swung around, Ed Smith, an eminent Senator of the day, stood before us.... I introduced Mr. Smith to Bea. Taking off his hat, he held her hand in his and, after looking at her intently for a long time, turned back to me and said, 'Now I know why you're decent.'" Grampy paused, searched for words, "'Gently nurtured'... Your grandmother understood what I meant. We grew up together; she was the oldest and dearest friend I had."

Our glances parted. I took a breath, "Grampy...." I drew a piece of paper out of my notebook on the side table, as the refrains of a whippoorwill flitted through my memory. Grampy's eyes rested on me. "Where do Eisenhower's words, your Chief Executive and Commander in Chief, fit into this story:"

> *Every gun that is made, every war ship launched, every rocket fired signifies, in the final sense, a theft from those who hunger and are not fed, those who are cold and are not clothed. This world in arms is not spending money alone. It is spending the sweat of its laborers, the genius of its scientists, the hopes of its children.... This is not a way of life, at all, it is humanity hanging from a cross of iron. THERE WILL BE NO PEACE UNTIL THE PEOPLE OF THE WORLD STAND UP AND ASK FOR IT.*

The silence deepened with our gazes. I searched for words. "I often feel as if some kind of spell, bewitchment, enchantment has been cast over our land.... How is it that this American Dream of ours all too often ends up as a nightmare for so many?"

Grampy's eyes lifted above me to his battalion spread out over my head, "I am familiar with those words of Eisenhower.... They are not surprising to anyone who has been in battle." My eyes sought his. Something stirred in his voice, "No one in their right mind wants war, Stuart. But, it hasn't been something that we've been able to do away with. The impulse is deeply ingrained in humanity." Grampy's reflections deepened, "There are similar words that have stayed with me over the years, spoken by another great leader, the former Secretary General of the United Nations. Malik quoted from the New Testament to make his point about the 'powers that be'":

> For we wrestle not against flesh and blood alone, but against Principalities, against Powers, against the rulers of the darkness of this world, against spiritual wickedness in high places.

I nodded, breathed out, "What's gotten into us?..."

Grampy rubbed a yawn with the back of his hand, as he lifted his gaze out the War Room window. Mine followed his up to the still stars that filled the encircling heavens. Cast in the glow of the hall light, Grampy was silent. Memories of his evening visit to our cabin seven years earlier welled up out of the depths. "None of us, Stuart, can do the job alone. Probably the most important thing one learns in war, as perhaps nowhere else, is that we need one another." Our eyes met, "What I and your father have been unable to accomplish in our lives, may be your generation's job to carry on as best you know how. The important thing is to step into the ring." Words lingered about his mind. His voice was quieter, "... to honor while you strike him down, the foe who comes with fearless eyes."

Grampy's glance rested on me, "Goodnight, Stuart."

"Goodnight, Grampy." He turned, stepped out into the hallway, and closed the door.

I breathed out, set the diary down on the bedside table, "GOTT MIT UNS." A worn buckle rested on the top of the dresser. Turning off the light, I settled into bed with the image of my grandfather in heart and mind—dressed to the hilt with rifle, bayonet, gas mask, woolly muffler,... and a lingering question: *"I wonder if I will ever again be gently nurtured?"* Easter dawned. "GOD WITH US."

12

LEAVING

Love is swift of foot,
Love's a man of war
And can shoot
And can hit from far.

June 15, 1968

Dear Friends,

I have some news to impart to you—and to my other close friends. I wish I might look you in the eye as I tell my story, but I guess I can't do that—right away, at least.

Jane's situation, as far as we can figure, had it's tenth anniversary last January, and soon after the doctors got after me and insisted that I make some change in my living arrangement.

Following their orders—I went to California for a short stay—fell in love with a delightful lady whose roots tie in with the Weeks' family as far back as 1885.

Result—I am now working on some changes in my life—involving, first, a divorce, and then marriage to Alice ("Teenie") Requa Low of San Francisco.

Jane is bedridden, completely helpless, and has been for several years—can't speak, read or write, feed herself, or turn in bed. She literally has no mentality whatsoever, and is suffering from advanced

Alzheimer's disease from which there is no return.

She has had perfect care for these many years, without which she could not be here today, and of course this care will be continued at the hospital here in Lancaster.

After our marriage, Alice and I will come back to Lancaster where my old friend, Bishop Sherrill, plans to come to conduct a Service of Blessing.

All this seems good to my children and to a handful of old friends with whom I have discussed the matter—so I plan to proceed accordingly. My best to you.

Faithfully,
Sinclair

The Lord of Cat Bow bowed demurely in front of his bride, lovely if no longer blushing. She took his hand, rose, and waltzed gingerly across the living room floor with him. None of us had seen such a smile on Grampy's face in years. Yes, our grandfather had gone and got himself married! It was hard to believe. But, there they were, Grampy, Teenie, and her miniature schnauzer, Tippy Toes—a formidable trio, all kicking up their heels across the old living room rug.

We had sensed something was in the air, but we couldn't have been more flabbergasted by the news. "What would you think about your grandfather getting married?" Dad, who once again had been summoned to Lancaster for a heart-to-heart, put the question to us with a perfectly straight face. "What!" It was a surprise, to say the least, to have your father break the news to you that your "own grandpa" was getting married. An old cookout melody raised a smile on Nat's lips. But, so it was. At seventy-six, Grampy hadn't given up on love. He was prepared to give it one more try, turning West this time to California and a woman named Alice, more fondly referred to as Teenie, who shared in common with Grampy two previous marriages that had been cut tragically short.

Given their ripe years, the courtship had been short and sweet. Yes, Teenie had taken loving aim, and her gentle arrow had hit its mark:

Darling,

I will be with you—God willing—very soon. So there is no point in telling you about the mundane things happening here abouts. So, we skip all "you and me" things, and I'll send you a few excerpts from a book I love.

"Can one stop people being hurt, and had one better? Laura asked this question more of herself than of Lilah. In her experience, all the richest and most valuable things were mixed up, somehow or other, with being hurt. Sooner or later, everything that was nice hurt as well. Love affairs hurt (like the devil). Marriage hurt. Children hurt. She half shut her eyes at the thought of children, as if to shut out Tim and Sarah and the intolerable pain of separation from them.

"And directly from being hurt, it seemed to her, sprang all the qualities she valued most, in others or in herself—courage, a measure of insight and self knowledge, and the secret sense of strength, of the indestructibility of the human spirit in the face of disasters, which is the most precious possession of them all. All of these things could only be had at a price—and cash in advance at that." (These lines made me think of you.) "The price of being hurt again and again—almost to the point of extinction. Happiness, she thought of Bridges again, was the 'flaunting honeyed flower of the soul,' but the root was pain, and the twin fruits, knowledge and strength."

Now I must pop this in the mail. Small children are coming into the house—so peace departs. More soon. If things seem difficult, remember these lines I've shared.

And so, my love, good night and God bless.

Teenie

The newlyweds weren't home for long, before we discovered that a trip was in the making to warmer climates. Apparently, Teenie nearly got cold feet on her first visit to the Northern Kingdom, after the furnace had shut down in the Big House, and the Lord of Cat Bow gallantly swept her off in his arms to the Mary Elizabeth Inn in Lancaster, where they squeezed into a trim king-sized bed. The jaunt south was followed by a trip to Ireland. The doctor's orders had not yet elapsed. Grampy had some sights to see and respects to pay, starting with the Blarney Stone, upon which, after the proscribed genuflections, he succeeded in planting a kiss—or so announced the post card that found its way back to Cat Bow.

And so it was. The chimes on the old grandfather clock were merrily tolling, as the empty place across from Grampy at the dining room table was once again filled. Yes, the Lord of Cat Bow had found his lady. Flowers bloomed on the sills. The newlyweds' happiness lasted for two precious years, before this time it was Grampy's health that began to fail.

Memo From: Sinclair Weeks

I was out walking with my Golden Retriever, who is young and frisky. Suddenly, with no warning at all, she "clipped" me in the most approved gridiron style, for which the present penalty is 15 yards—and should be more. As I spun around to land on my face, apparently my right leg got caught in a rut or whatnot on the road and didn't come along with the rest of my anatomy. End result— three fractures and one bone displacement in my right leg and ankle. Expect to be as good as new but the schedule indicates it will take about 14 weeks from 19 February, the date of the accident.

I'm not having fun, but I am sure there are a number worse off than I am at the moment. Greetings from Alice and me.

* * * * *

In the late spring of seventy-one, I made the decision to join the musical show *Up with People*, in place of my senior year in high school. The decision was a simple one. As everything seemed to be falling apart and down, I wanted to offer a hand in lifting things *up*, and I hoped to get a boost myself in the process. Amid all the turmoil, the emphasis on *people*—human beings—had become central for me.

Before I headed off to join Cast B in Warwick, New York, I paid a visit to Grampy at Cat Bow. I had taken up the guitar again over the last months in preparation for the show and had brought along an old friend of Grampy's, "Bill Bailey."

In the Big House, I found the back door open. Pausing, I looked out through the screen onto the afternoon terrace. Framed by the white picket fence and flower beds, The Lord of Cat Bow was stretched out on the lounge, a book folded open across his lap, taking a snooze with old Mother Nature. In the background, the Presidential Peaks formed a familiar backdrop beneath the clear, blue heavens, calling to mind an old tale—Montreal due North, Boston due South, Bangor due East, Burlington due West, ... by Jesus!

Opening the screen door, I walked across the lawn and sat down quietly beside Grampy. My glance rested on a cane, propped up on the side of the chair. Pulling out my guitar, I drew my fingers across its strings. The Lord of Cat Bow's eyes opened with the music. "Hello, Grampy." My greeting was returned with an ample yawn, which Grampy shook off, as he pulled himself up in his seat.

I was taken aback by how much Grampy had aged since my last visit three months earlier and, searching for words, asked him what he was reading. Grampy's eyes lowered to the book, "It's a collection of old Revolutionary War sketches." He was silent a moment. Then, he turned the book over and picked up where he had left off, reading aloud:

> *Ethan Allen, the leader of the Green Mountain Boys, was a fiery old Vermonter, who preserved his spark right up to his last day. Late one night, as the end appeared to be near, his doctor entered his room, a dire look on his face, "Colonel, I fear the angels are waiting for you."*

My eyes rested on Grampy.

> *Allen, who was as unabashed by the thought of angels as he had been by the presence of the British at Fort Ticonderoga, turned his gaze on the doctor and, pulling himself up in bed, proclaimed, "Waiting are they ... waiting are they? Well god damn 'em, let em wait!" The Colonel had spoken his last words.*

Grampy lifted his gaze from the book down across the field to the Boat House on the lake. Leaves rustled through my memory on a gentle Indian Summer breeze. Grampy turned his sights on out over the countryside to the Presidential Peaks that arched the horizon. A stillness lay over our Northern Kingdom. My eyes rested on The Lord of Cat Bow. Seventy-seven, almost seventy-eight years old, Grampy was slowing down, and he knew it.

"How are you, Grampy?"

"I'm okay." He glanced at me and, then, away, "I'm still in one piece."

"How's Teenie doing?"

"Other than an ache and pain or two, nothing serious." Grampy motioned to the Big House. "I believe she's taking her afternoon nap."

"She hasn't adjusted yet to the fresh air."

"Either that or my snoring."

I smiled. Grampy looked out to the distant peaks, resting his head back against the chair. His voice was quieter, "Do you know, Stuart, how the Presidential Mountains got their names?"

"No," I shook my head, glancing out over the spring countryside.

Grampy reflected, "In the summer of 1820, your great great great uncle, Major John W. Weeks, set out with a party of men—'distinguished characters,' as referred to by their guide, old Ethan Crawford—for the base of Mt. Washington. At that time, Washington was the only mountain that had been named by the settlers. After a dinner of trout at Crawford's cabin and a few tall tales, the party turned in to get a good night's sleep for their climb the next day."

Grampy added a yawn to the story, "Up early the next morning, the gentlemen packed up their provisions for the climb, which included a couple of bottles of 'O-Be-Joyful.' Their plan had been not only to name, but to anoint, the neighboring peaks, and the drinks were brought along for the baptism." I nodded quietly as Grampy picked up the pace, "By midmorning the expedition arrived at what your Great Uncle John referred to as 'a beautiful pond of clear water, distant one mile from the apex of the hill.' This was one of the earliest references to the 'Lake of the Clouds.' After refreshing themselves with the cool mountain water, which to a man they found delicious, the party continued on to the summit."

A faint smile touched Grampy's sleepy face, as he gazed up at Mt. Washington, "I often think of that crew, leaning back into the clouds as they named the peaks, Adams, Jefferson, Madison, Monroe, in descending order of height, and drank healths to each—before topping off the ceremony by lifting their glasses in a hearty toast to the Creator."

"Did they make it down in one piece?" Grampy's smile reflected over my face, as my sights shifted from "Jacob's Ladder" to the Ammonoosuc Ravine.

Grampy turned back to me, "Their account reports that, after resting in the sunlight, they betook themselves back down the trail, stopping once again at the pond to drink of its waters—apparently at considerable enough length so that some of the party became quite blue."

My gaze descended with the climbing party back down to the terrace. 'All this and heaven too'—a recollection returned to mind. "Grampy?" He turned to me. "Do *your* thoughts turn to the angels?"

The smile passed over The Lord of Cat Bow's quiet face, still pale from his nap. He closed the book, "Now and again." A deepening breath lifted his chest. "At some point, everything in life, including life itself, draws to its end."

"How do you feel about that?"

"Old age?…It's exasperating."

This time I was silent. Grampy turned back to me, "My walks have gotten shorter; the stories that always came quickly and easily seem to have lost their endings. Even familiar names elude me." He rubbed his hand vacantly over his cheek, "As you come face to face with that ultimate reality, it's a test of one's faith."

"How are you holding up, Grampy?" My question surprised us both.

"I've been thinking a good bit lately about a correspondence I've had over the last year with an acquaintance of the Jewish faith. He sent me a passage from the Talmud, which speaks of the significance of the age in which one dies." Grampy reflected, "From what I've understood, if one dies before the age of fifty—that is referred to as death by *kareth*—one is cut off for certain sins. At sixty, death comes by *the hand of heaven*. At seventy, it is the death of the *hoary head*." Grampy paused. "At eighty, 'the age of great strength,' it is the death of *a vigorous old man*."

"What does 'great strength' mean?"

Grampy considered a moment, then opened the book again, leafing through the pages until he came to a letter, which he drew out of the folds:

Jan. 26, 1969

Dear Sinclair Weeks,

I now know that there is no age limit to the curiosity of man, and your query as to what I mean when one lives past 70 "with great

strength" is an answer that all Jews know who have read or studied
even a little bit....In further explanation of "great strength," I recall
in my readings the fact that Rabbinical Philosophers of old have
declared "great strength" alludes to the right hand of GOD, for with-
out that the existence of all life is problematical.

While most Jews know the meaning of "great strength," there is
nothing in Judaism that prohibits non-Jews from enjoying the same
help. Sinclair Weeks is living with "great strength!"

> *Most Sincerely Yours,*
> *Dan*
> *Daniel I. Reiter*

"'The right hand of God....'" I looked at Grampy. "How do Unitar-
ians feel about such matters?"

"All in one; one in all." Grampy reflected, "Regardless of your faith,
Stuart, life has its challenges, any way you look at it."

* * * * *

The screen door opened behind us. Grampy sat forward in his chair
and, seeing Teenie, arose with me to greet her.

"Hello, Teenie." I reached out a hand.

"I'm glad you made it, Stuart." Teenie leaned forward. I gave her a
kiss on the cheek, before passing her on to Grampy, who had a warm
hug ready. They swapped a yawn, as I pulled up a lawn chair, which
Grampy eased over beside him. "May I join you?"

Grampy nodded, "Of course. We're just catching up."

"Men's talk?"

"We've just been discussing the old Rabbis . . . and angels."

Teenie nodded thoughtfully at Grampy, as she took a seat, her
glance passing over the terrace, "It's a lovely afternoon."

I looked at her, "How are you, Teenie?"

Teenie opened her hands in light, free gesture, "Taking everything
into consideration, I'd say I'm doing pretty well. Would you agree,
Sinny?"

Grampy smiled and took his wife's right hand in his, "We're
managing."

"Most of our socializing these days is with the doctors." Teenie glanced over at Grampy, "But I guess that's to be expected when, together, we tip the scales at one hundred and fifty years plus." I smiled. "They are a kind lot, though, and assure us that we still have a few more years on the face of this beautiful earth." Teenie's gaze passed down the field to the Boat House and lake, "One thing I haven't been able to get your Grandfather to do, though, is to fill me in on all the family lore. One of your cousins, Stuart, told me that you used to have lobster bakes on the lake in earlier days." I nodded.

"Where did you get the lobsters?"

"Grampy imported them."

"Like me." Teenie smiled and rubbed Grampy's hand, "It sounds like a tradition we should renew." Grampy's thoughts were distant. "And how are you, Stuart?"

"I'm fine, Teenie."

"Did your mother say you are going to spend the next year with *Up with People?*"

"Yes. After my time in Paris, it's hard to think of confining learning to a classroom."

Teenie reflected, "I saw the show—oh, it must be two years ago now."

"How did you find it?"

"It was remarkable. I've never seen so much energy in my life, nor such a reaction from an audience. It was really quite an uplifting afternoon." Teenie turned to Grampy, "I remember, in particular, being moved by the concluding song. Its words escape me now, but its theme, I believe, had to do with roads which come together."

I considered, "I only saw the show once, just before Mom took me to the airport earlier in the spring. I think I was already half way over to France. My memories are pretty much like yours—people, a lot of people on stage, and a lot of energy."

"Why did you decide to join, Stuart?"

I looked at Teenie, "I'm continually seeking a balance." I paused. "These last years haven't been easy on my generation either." Grampy's eyes rested on me. "I don't know, perhaps I'm looking for another road, as you described. Thoreau spoke of marching to the beat of our own drum."

"What will you do about school?"

I smiled, "I'm taking it with me."

"You are?" Teenie raised her eyebrows.

"That's part of the package. A year of high school or college is included."

"You mean you not only put on the show and perform it, but you continue your studies, as well?"

I nodded.

"It sounds like you won't have any time to get into trouble."

I reflected, "I guess that's part of it."

"Where will you be traveling?"

"We'll put the show together in Warwick, New York. Then, we'll tour the States for a few months, before going overseas to Europe, beginning in Belgium. We return for Christmas, and I'm not sure of our program in the new year."

"Where do you stay when you travel?"

"In host homes."

"That's right. I remember the daughter of a friend had a few members of the cast with her." Teenie considered, "So you are going to have quite a family over the next year."

"Yes, but I've been well prepared."

"I can imagine." Teenie turned to Grampy. "What do you say, Sinclair?"

Grampy rubbed his chin, "I thought we might join him on the road."

Teenie laughed, "Wonderful. I think we'd make quite a team, dancing across the stages of Europe!"

I turned to Grampy, "When I'm back at Christmas, I'll put on a special performance for you."

Grampy's eyes rested on me, "I'll hold you to that." I nodded.

Teenie pointed to my guitar, "Can we have a preview?"

I glanced down at it, "Sure, though I can't guarantee we're in tune. I've just taken the guitar up again after my months in Paris, so I'm a bit rusty."

"So are we; we'll sing along with you."

I lifted up the guitar, "Do you have a request?"

Teenie looked at Grampy, "What is your wish, darling?"

Grampy turned to me, "Do you know, 'Won't You Come Home, Bill Bailey?'"

"You introduced me to him."

"Great, he's an old friend of mine, too," Teenie clapped her hands. I started in:

Won't you come home, Bill Bailey.... Won't you come home.

Grampy and Teenie picked up the tune together, patting their hands on Grampy's lap:

I've moaned the whole day long. I'll do the cookin', darling.

Teenie smiled at Grampy:

I'll pay the rent.

Grampy shook his head:

I know I've done you wrong.... Remember that rainy evening, I drove you out, with nothing but a fine tooth comb? I know I'm to blame, well ain't that a shame. Bill Bailey won't you please come home!

The afternoon wore melodiously on with the deepening greens in the spring field. The tune brought back memories. Other requests followed—favorites of Grampy's, of Teenie's, which I did my best to resurrect on the strings.

The sundial followed its orb faithfully into the horizon. A light gray hue touched the late afternoon. Teenie considered for a moment. "There is a lovely tune that many of your generation have been singing these days." She turned to me, "Where have all the flowers gone?..."

I nodded, "That's a protest song against the war, Teenie."

"Is it? It's quite beautiful." She thought a moment. "I'm not sure I've heard more than the first verse. Do you know it?"

"Yes, I've learned it over the last few years."

She turned to Grampy, "Let's hear it. We've had enough of wars."

Grampy's and my eyes met. "The floor is yours now, Stuart."

I nodded, tightened my E string:

Where have all the flowers gone? Long time passing.

Teenie joined in:

Where have all the flowers gone?

Grampy turned his sight down through the fields, to the swelling tides of the lake, as I sang on.

Long time ago.
Where have all the flowers gone? Young girls have picked them ev'ry one....

The image of a young French girl, handing Captain Weeks a shy bouquet of violets, stole my breath for a moment:

When will they ever learn? When will they ever learn?

Teenie looked at me; I continued:

Where have all the young girls gone?
Long time passing.
Where have all the young girls gone?
Long time ago.
Where have all the young girls gone?

Teenie glanced at Grampy, I at them both:

They've gone to young men every one.
When will they ever learn?
When will they ever learn?
Where have all the young men gone?
Long time passing.
Where have all the young men gone?
Long time ago.
Where have all the young men gone?
Gone to soldiers every one.
When will they ever learn?
When will they ever learn?

I paused. Teenie lingered with the melody, "Does it go on?"

I nodded.

"Play." Teenie gently gripped Grampy's hand, resting on the book. Ethan Allen's words returned to mind.

> *Where have all the soldiers gone?*
> *Long time passing.*
> *Where have all the soldiers gone?*
> *Long time ago.*
> *Where have all the soldiers gone?*

Teenie waited for the lyrics and, then, joined in again; her voice was quieter:

> *They've gone to graveyards every one.*
> *When will they ever learn?*
> *When will they ever learn?*

The evening settled gently upon us.

> *Where have all the graveyards gone?*
> *Long time passing.*
> *Where have all the graveyards gone?*
> *Long time ago.*
> *Where have all the graveyards gone?*
> *Gone to flowers every one.*
> *When will they ever learn?*
> *When will they ever learn?*

I glanced out across the countryside, as I rested my hands on the strings of the guitar.

"Is that the end, Stuart?"

I looked at Teenie, "And the beginning again; it depends on what one gets from the song."

Grampy and Teenie were quiet. My fingers touched the strings of the guitar, searching for a melody, happy/sad. I looked at my grandparents, "I have a request—if that's okay?"

"Of course." Teenie nodded, "If we know it."

"It's a song we've sung over the years, but I've never found all the verses."

Teenie looked at me, "What is it called?"

I paused, considered, "I'm not sure of its title—'All Night, All Day?'"

Teenie smiled and turned to Grampy, "Yes, we know it well." Teenie picked up the melody, while Grampy listened quietly.

All night, all day, angels watchin' over me, my Lord.
All night, all day, angels watchin' over me.

Day is dyin' in the West,
Angels watchin' over me, my lord.
Sleep my child and take your rest,
Angels watchin' over me.

All night, all day, angels watchin' over me, my Lord.
All night, all day, angels watchin' over me.
Children sleep, the moon is high,
Angels watchin' over me, my Lord.
You're safe, and love is nigh.
Angels watchin' over me.

All night, all day, angels watchin' over me, my Lord.
All night, all day, angels watchin' over me.

Now I lay me down to sleep,
Angels watchin' over me, my lord.
Pray the lord my soul to keep.
Angels watchin' over me.

All night, all day, angels watchin' over me, my Lord. . . .

Teenie hummed on quietly to the end, "There is another verse, but it escapes me at the moment." I looked at Teenie, nodded.

Reaching for his cane, Grampy rose, "Thank you, Stuart."

I looked up at him, "Thank you, Grampy."

Holding onto Grampy's hand, Teenie stood up beside him, "Will you join us for supper?"

"I appreciate the invitation, Teenie, but I have to get going. I still have a lot of packing to do before I'm off."

Grampy followed the stone slabs toward the door. Teenie joined him, taking my arm in her other hand, "We're glad you stopped by."

I looked at them. "Yes, I wanted to see you both before Christmas and the snows set in."

"Hopefully, we'll be gone by then to warmer climes."

I looked at her.

Grampy held the back door open for us, before bringing up the rear. I followed Teenie in and on through the dining room to the entrance room, darkened by the aged floorboards and paneling.

"I almost forgot," Teenie paused and reached into her skirt pocket. "I found a little poem, Sinny, in one of the house scrapbooks, that I copied down and wanted to share with you both." I put down my guitar, as Teenie unfolded a piece of paper. Grampy leaned back against one of the attendant love seats. Adjusting her glasses, Teenie stepped over to the small window by the phone, to catch the departing beams of light:

> *I count my gardens by the flowers*
> *Never by the leaves that fall*
> *I count my days by golden hours*
> *Not remembering clouds at all*
> *I count my nights by stars not shadows*
> *I count my life by smiles not tears*
> *And with joy on this my birthday*
> *I count my years by friends not years.*

Teenie glanced over at Grampy, cast gently in the aged glint of the entrance room. "Your birthday is coming, Sinclair, seventy-eight." She moved over to Grampy, leaning against his shoulder into the gentle shadows of the love seat. "You have many friends." Grampy gave her a soft kiss on the cheek.

"You'll be in my thoughts on your birthday, Grampy. I'll see if I can dig up an old glass of 'O-Be-Joyful' from on high."

Grampy smiled. I walked over and gave him a kiss goodbye. He slapped me gruffly on the back and, then, rested his hand gently on my shoulder. "Take care, Stuart."

I looked at him, "You, too, Grampy."

Teenie stepped forward. I gave her a hug, before collecting my guitar and heading out the door. They followed me, lingering on the doorstep. I opened the car door and paused, my gaze passing up to the barn. Cat Bow was quiet. The playhouse and apple orchard were set off a ways from the beaten track, as the echoes of small grandchildren had scattered with the years. My thoughts searched for the forgotten verse.

As I got into the car, Penny and her dainty companion perked their heads up from the garage and tip-toed over to Grampy, who had stepped across the driveway to the circle. Settling into the car, I pulled slowly out of the driveway. Raising my eyes to the rear-view mirror, my glance rested on Grampy, astride the budding island of roses. I waved. Grampy raised his cane, returning my farewell—before lifting his gaze up through the enfolding limbs of the old elm to Bill Rines house and beyond. I watched my grandfather, until he was out of sight. . . . *No, by Jesus, I don't know how a person could be much more in the middle a things.*

A smile tugged tenderly at my lips, as I glanced ahead to the Presidential Mountains that filled the horizon, gazing down from their nocturnal peaks upon our temporal Northern Kingdom. The melody played on in my mind, while above the peaks a budding crown of stars brightened the heavens.

All night, all day. . . .

THE ENDING

I'm a pretty weak reed now. The doctors don't want me traveling far and wide any more. I'm pretty much staying put and hoping to stretch out my few remaining days, but I must confess I'm getting pretty tired of this illness and don't seem to be able to eat my way into the middle of the pie anymore. Guess I'm losing my appetite for life.

Sinclair Weeks, Letter to Carlton Ketchum, Sept. 25, 1971

THE ENDING

None of us is born the same,
We don't know why; it's the way we came.
Every heart beats a little differently,
Each soul is free to find its way,
Like a river that winds its way to the sea.
For life is a journey,
And there are many roads beneath the sky,
And there are many good people,
Who don't see eye to eye. . . .

THE MELODY FROM our *Up with People* show that afternoon lingered in my mind, as I followed my steps through the still Belgium night, down along a winding, winter path to the banks of the river. Pausing at its edge, I found a resting place on a large, bare rock and turned my gaze out into the river's reflections—currents that flowed silently on amid the tides of moonlight.

The letter I had received earlier in the day from home brought news, both inevitable and unexpected: *Grampy isn't well. He has been transferred to a nursing home in Concord, Massachusetts.* The family didn't go into detail. It was left to me to read between the lines.

I glanced out over the river. Having to leave his beloved Cat Bow meant not only that Grampy's condition was serious, but that his roots were being cut from the very soil that had nurtured him. I pulled the collar of my coat up around my ears, as I struggled with the aching feeling of emptiness that welled up within me. The currents flowed on through the small medieval town of Huy that had spanned the centuries. Above the town, a small range of mountains, which had harbored a concentration camp during the First World War, formed an imposing backdrop in the night. For the last three days we had been graciously hosted by the inhabitants of Huy. In thanks, we had not only performed for public audiences in the town theater, but, as was our custom, we had reached out to those who were unable to come to the performances.

My thoughts returned to our show that afternoon in the local old folks home. As we walked in, nearly fifty strong, an elderly nurse welcomed us and led us down a long, pale corridor, to an open common room at the far end. Entering the room, we were greeted by an array of distant expressions. Older people, many in wheelchairs, a number adrift in beds that had been rolled in for the occasion, others, perched in chairs, occupied the space—yet their presence was distant. We quietly set ourselves up at the far end of the room and went over our program, before a guitar led the soloist into our first song:

> *Good night I said to my little son,*
> *So tired out when the day was done.*
> *Then he said, as I tucked him in,*
> *"Tell me, Daddy, what color is God's skin?"*

The rest of the cast joined in with the chorus:

> *What color is God's skin? What color is God's skin.*
> *I say it's black, brown, it's yellow, it is red, it is white.*
> *Every man's the same in the good Lord's sight.*

Our words stirred echoes in the hall, eliciting little response from those gathered. As we proceeded, however, the atmosphere slowly warmed up—the music prodding faint reactions, hands gently tapping the arms of chairs and wheelchairs alike, slippered feet reaching for the floor. We did three numbers from our show and, then, started into an old Flemish folk song that we had learned during our tour. *Wel Anne-Marieken, waar gaat gij naar toe?* ... The tune, more familiar, appeared for a moment to stir our audience. Moved, we watched smiles awaken on aged faces, words rumor on dry lips. A few of the older folks sought to clap their hands to the beat, while others feebly nodded their heads. As the reactions from the audience grew, our hearts and voices were lifted.

At the conclusion of the last number, we went up to the old folks to greet them and wish them well. Everybody in the cast was visibly moved, as our hosts reached out to clasp our hands in an attempt to express their appreciation. *Up with People....* An old woman struggled to pronounce the words. I nodded, *Leve de Mensen.*

Before I headed out, I noticed an elderly man, bent over in his wheelchair at the back of the room. Our glances met, drawing me over to him. He smiled up at me sadly, as if apologizing for his condition, and beckoned me closer. As I leaned down, he took my hand in his. *Thank you....* The old man struggled to clear his voice, before continuing in broken English, *Thank you for bringing us these moments of happiness.* I stood in front of him, unable to move, while tears unexpectedly gathered in my eyes.

* * * * *

The currents flowed on through the moonlight, lit now by starry glimmers that had dipped down into the watery reaches of the river. The frail, bent body of an old man settled in my reflections. Lifting, straightening itself up, his/Grampy's gaze rose to meet mine. Smiles,... tears flowed gently down my cheeks, surging up with a tide of feelings that quietly overwhelmed me. Taking a deep breath, my thoughts returned to a letter Dad had shown me the evening before I left. Clearly moved by the occasion of Cat Bow's farmer, Bill Rines' funeral, Grampy's words revealed a side of our father and grandfather that our sire was not often given to express:

> *Dear Sin,*
>
> When I walked into the church today with you three boys by my side, I had the most mixed emotions probably ever assembled.
>
> Sadness with respect to the occasion—pride that the Weeks family was able to add so significantly to the mourners gathered there. Turning many plans on end, changing all kinds of arrangements—all complicate life, of course.

However, all this is paid back many times and in many ways to
those whose thoughtfulness has been placed on the scales.

Thank you three so very, very much. This means more to me than
you think.

Aff'ly,
Father

On, the currents flowed, through the night. I lifted my gaze up along
the darkened flanks of the mountain, up beyond the prisoner-of-war
camp that we had visited the day before, up—on up into the heavens,
near and far. My thoughts journeyed back to my visit with Grampy
seven months earlier. The fading image in the rear view mirror filled my
mind. *The middle of things....* I breathed in. It never occurred to me, as
I drove off, that that would be the last time I would see Grampy at his
beloved Cat Bow.

Gathering my thoughts, I rose from the still rock. Christmas was
just six weeks off. The concluding words from our show settled in my
mind:

> *... You and I are different from our brother;*
> *Could that be why we need each other*
> *As we go along?*
> *Everyone is partly right,*
> *And everyone is partly wrong.*
>
> *Not every man can sing your tune;*
> *From where he stands, there's another view.*
> *With every turn we're learning more,*
> *And perhaps we'll find*
> *That the walls we build are only in the mind.*
>
> *There are many roads to go,*
> *And they go by many names.*
> *They don't all go the same way,*
> *But they get there all the same.*
> *And I have a feeling, that we'll meet some day,*
> *Where the roads come together, up the way.*

* * * * *

Winter came, and the roads led back again to America, Boston, Concord.

"Grampy has changed a good bit. Don't be surprised, Stuart, if he doesn't recognize you at first." Dad's words settled into my mind, as I pulled into the parking lot of Rivercrest Nursing Home and turned off the key. Off to my left, the banks of the Concord River rose up into the still winter afternoon.

Collecting my guitar from the back seat, I crossed the lot, brushed by a thin veil of snow, and followed the walkway into Rivercrest. At the front door, I was greeted once again by a nurse, who took my name and then led me down a long corridor of clean, white walls, interrupted by plants and bright, cheerful pictures. I followed silently.

Pausing at Grampy's doorway, the nurse knocked and, then, nodding kindly, turned and headed back down the hall to the reception area. I listened a moment before stepping forward and slowly opening the door.

My eyes rested on an old man dressed in pajamas, with a familiar plaid bathrobe tied limply around his waist. He was sitting silently in a large chair in the corner of his room, his gaze drawn out the window. Beside him, vases of flowers bloomed on the sill. My glance lowered to the table in front of his chair. A single rose bent over a tray full of cold lunch.

"Grampy?..."

The old man didn't move. My eyes followed his out the window and across the still white landscape, etched by the river. Placing my guitar by the bathroom door, I walked over to him and, taking a quiet breath, placed my hand on his shoulder. Slowly, Grampy turned and lifted his countenance—tender, susceptible, straightforward—to mine.

"Hello, Grampy." I hesitated a moment, then, leaned over and gave him a warm kiss. He lifted his hand in a faint greeting and looked at me for a long moment before speaking quietly, "You've come back."

I nodded, "Yes, it's Christmas."

"Christmas...." The word rumored on Grampy's lips.

I took a package out of my coat pocket, "I haven't yet tapped Captain John Weeks' O-Be-Joyful spring, but I did manage to get my hands on some good German chocolate for you." Grampy's eyes searched mine questioningly, before lowering to the chocolate in my hand. "Something to sweeten your diet." A pained smile touched Grampy's face. I placed the box of chocolate in his hands. He stared at it absently, before letting it fall onto his tray. Grandma Jane passed through my mind. "I trust, Grampy, they've allowed you a couple of vices these days."

Grampy gazed at me searchingly.

I reached a hand to him, "What do you say, Grampy?" His own greeting had become unfamiliar. I looked at him silently. The changes from our June visit were striking. Thin and wan, the color had withdrawn from Grampy's cheeks, leaving his lips dry and chapped. As he turned his vision beyond me to the door, I glanced into his eyes, silent, listless. "How are you, Grampy?"

"Tired." His voice was distant, his eyes heavy.

I nodded, as my sights fell on a commode. Beside it, a host of pills crowded Christmas cards on the bedside table. Above, on the wall, a stout cherub leaned back into its spruce wreath—a worn evergreen halo.

I pulled up a chair beside Grampy, "How are the angels?"

A searching look touched his face. I paused and then placed my hand on his in his lap. "Grampy. . . ?" The word stirred memories. He listened. I searched his face, "Do you remember the story you used to tell me about the comely woman who walked into the White House one day and announced that she wanted to have a look at President Lincoln?" Our glances met. Grampy was silent. I continued, "Taken aback by the simplicity of the visitor's request, Secretary Wells led her to the president's office." Grampy's eyes lowered to my hand in his lap. I paused, went on, "The woman stood in the doorway, as Lincoln rose from his seat behind his desk. 'What can I do for you, M'am?' the president asked. The lady merely repeated her words, 'I just wanted to have a look at you, Mr. President.' Lincoln bowed kindly." My eyes rested on Grampy, " 'When it comes to the business of looking at one another,' the president nodded, 'I must say that I have the distinct advantage.' "

I was silent. Grampy raised his gaze inquiringly into mine, touched suddenly by tears, "Did you read that passage I gave you in the Pine Room, Stuart?"

I wiped the tears, "Which one?"

"The one by Lincoln."

"Yes...." I nodded, "Yes, Grampy, I read them all."

"Good." Grampy's glance lowered to the tray of food and slender rose. The room was quiet. We sat by the window, searching for words, memories, hopes, a familiar melody—until a knock returned to the door. An orderly walked in, greeted me, and motioned that it was time for Grampy's supper. Rising, I glanced at his plate and then, excusing myself, stepped back.

* * * * *

I took a short detour home through Concord Center, turning up Monument Street by the Colonial Inn and continuing out to the old North Bridge and Minute Man National Park—the destination, Grampy had recounted, of many a weekend outing, by horse and buggy, for homemade lessons in history during Grampy's youth.

Pulling into the empty parking lot, I turned the engine off and made my way across the street. A full moon brightened the evening, casting shadows in and about the trees. At the top of the path, I paused. In front of me, framed by the still December evening, the rude wooden span of the old North Bridge reached across to the opposite bank of the river. On the far side, gathered up by a still enclosure of trees, the Minute Man statue, musket and plowshare in hand, in balance, kept its eternal vigil. My gaze rested once again on the scene, before I followed the Redcoats trail down through the snowy corridor of pines to the bridge. Beneath its arch, a moist patchwork of snow and ice forded the river. I lingered a moment at the rail of the bridge and, then, mounted its crusted planks.

At the center of the bridge, I paused, and looked down at the chilled blue-black waters that cut a corridor through the ice. Tucking my hands into my coat pockets, I raised my sights upstream. Memories of earlier seasons and of a child, young to the world, returned to mind. Following his steps down through the field behind his house, the boy paused at the bank of the river. For long moments he stood still, leaning into his reflections as the waters flowed by. An outer current was visible on the surface, a current, I had come to realize over the years, that flowed through my own family—business, politics, worldly affairs. I watched through the seasons of my youth. There was another current, below the surface, flowing in the opposite direction—another stream, less visible, but no less a part of our American life, Concorde. I stepped back. My gaze continued on upstream, beyond my vision, to the river's crest and an old folks home, gently cast in the setting sun. Yes—the words welled up within me—yes, at the end the soul always returns to its source.

Afternoon passed on into evening. I turned, returned up the crusty path to the parking lot. Off to my right, the Old Manse, home of the Hawthornes and, before them, a family named Emerson, edged the winter field. 1775: a political *revolution*, the "shot heard round the world." Fifty, seventy-five years later, the reverberations grew. My eyes rose to the upper corner bedroom of the Old Manse, the view looking out over the battlefield. An *evolution*, a call to cultural independence arose out of the small New England hamlet, in the form of an aspiring essay, "Nature." And today, a twentieth century? I searched for words: *involution*, a turning in to those deeper tides that ebb and flow within us?

That evening, after a quiet supper, I slipped up to my room and sought out a passage in a book I had been reading by Odell Shepard, *Pedlar's Progress*, on the life of a lesser-known Concordian and father of four little women, Amos Bronson Alcott. My visit to Grampy moved within me.

This book will be written out of the assured conviction that America has always been, is now, and throughout her coming centuries will continue to be, profoundly idealistic. That she has never been exclusively so, of course, I am aware; but neither, I think, has she ever been quite the crude, coarse and Mammon-minded country of the conventional interpretation.

Founded upon a thought, grounded upon a book, lineally descended from ancient prophets and modern dreamers, she is at heart still passionately dreamful and prophetic, given to spiritual rebellions, to the never ending wars of intellectual independence, and to migrations of the mind that ignore horizons.

The common mistake about her has been the headlong haste in which she has set her young strength to her preliminary task. Not her foreign critics alone, but even her sons and daughters have been too deafened, even deceived, by the uproar of her mere preparations. Too easily and too soon have they concluded that America delights in uproar for its own sake, that she foresees and desires no final goal, that she lives for purposeless activity alone.

Although this is an error, it may become truth. Preoccupation with the means of living has for too long postponed our consideration of life's ultimate values. Things unquestionably first in the order of time have already come, for too many of us, to seem first in the order of importance. There is a question how long we can safely continue to ignore the nobler half of our national memories and nature. So central and inherent an idealism as ours can never be wholly lost, indeed, but it can be, and already has been, distorted, deceived, and put to sinister uses. Little by little forgetting our birth in the spirit, more and more doubting the dream that has led us thus far on, we face even now the danger that always confronts a people who do not really know themselves....

I closed the book, as words rose up out of the gathering backdrop of silence: *Are* Gandhi, King, Thoreau, ... Great-Granddad the exception, Grampy? Or, are they the rule—a picture of what we, the *human being,* truly are? Winter, spring, summer, autumn—and winter once again, longing on into spring. The tides welled up within me, breaking the surface, falling from my eyes, down, down, down, rippling gently on across the stream of time.

Christmas that winter lacked a good bit of its cheer. Instead of going north to Cat Bow, we gathered at Aunt Frannie's and Uncle Woof's home in Westwood, Mass. What had always been a joyous occasion was muted by Grampy's absence. Halfway through the evening, we paused and drank a toast to our sire. Then, excusing ourselves, the party broke up, and the families headed home.

The rest of the vacation was equally restive. I had little desire to look up friends or partake in the Holiday festivities. Instead, I went to see Grampy twice more. But, with each visit his gaze was more distant, his reactions fainter. The intervals between our words lengthened, until only an ebbing silence connected us.

On my last visit, before heading back out on the road, Grampy and I sat silently by the window, together/apart, as the shades of dusk settled over the wintry landscape. And, then, I leaned over and picked up my guitar. Grampy lowered his eyes to the instrument, a glimmer of recognition kindling. "I found that last verse, Grampy, when I was on the road." I drew my fingers across the strings:

> *All night, all day, angels watchin' over me, my Lord.*
> *All night, all day, angels watchin' over me.*

Grampy looked up. I sang on:

> *Day is dyin' in the West,*
> *Angels watchin' over me, my Lord.*
> *Sleep my child and take your rest,*
> *Angels watchin' over me.*
>
> *All night, all day, angels watchin' over me, my Lord.*
> *All night, all day, angels watchin' over me....*

I paused, as the melody stirred on Grampy's lips:

> *Children sleep, the moon is high,*

I lowered my voice:

> *Angels watchin' over me, my Lord*
> *You're safe and love is nigh,*
> *Angels watchin' over me.*
> *All night, all day, angels watchin' over me, my Lord.*
> *All night, all day, angels watchin' over me.*

Grampy continued on, his voice silent, searching:

> *Now I lay me down to sleep,*
> *Angels watchin' over me, my Lord.*
> *Pray the lord my soul to keep.*
> *Angels watchin' over me.*
>
> *All night, all day, angels watchin' over me, my Lord.*
> *All night, all day, angels watchin' over me.*

If I die before I wake,

Grampy grappled with the words. My voice picked up, carrying his:

Angels watchin' over me, my Lord.
Pray the Lord my soul to take.
Angels watchin' over me.

All night, all day, angels watchin' over me, my Lord.
All night, all day, . . .

Grampy paused abruptly and looked up at me: "Bea. Where's Bea?" Our gazes met long and long, before a faint smile touched Grampy's lips:

Angels watchin' over me.

I breathed out, wiped my eyes, and carefully placed my guitar down on the floor. Grampy settled back into his chair. Drowsiness filled his eyes, until they slowly closed, and sleep came gently over him, drawing his vision within. I looked at my grandfather long and long. Then, as shadows darkened the room, I stood up, leaned over the rose, and gave him a kiss. At the door, I turned one last time and quietly bid my grandfather *adieu*.

* * * * *

CROSSING THE BAR

Sunset and evening star, and one clear call for me!
And may there be no moaning of the bar, when I put out to sea;
But such a tide as moving seems asleep, too full for sound and foam,
When that which drew from out the boundless deep turns again home.
Twilight and evening bell, and after that the dark!
And may there be no sadness of farewell when I embark:
For though from out our bourne of time and place, the flood may bear
* me far,*
I hope to see my pilot face to face, when I have crost the bar.

Alfred Lord Tennyson

I stared out the window of the plane, as the sun sank into the horizon. Mom's phone call earlier that morning still rung in my mind, "Stuart, we've got some sad news for you. Grampy is dying." I listened silently and then responded, "I'm coming home."

As the plane journeyed on into the darkening night, Mom's words echoed on within me. "Dying,"... the word was suddenly invested with a reality greater than I was able to comprehend. I settled back into the seat, my head resting against the window. I realized how much I had grown up over the last years and how my relationship with Grampy had grown also. To the simple love that I felt as a child for my grandfather, had come other qualities, difficult to put into words, and yet, no less real. Over the seasons of my youth, Grampy had changed from a kind of St. Nicholas figure—a goodly, if somewhat remote, presence—to a staunch patriarch, the Lord of Cat Bow. Indeed, for a precious year or two, Grampy had something God-like in him, to which my cousins and I looked up with a mixture of awe and reverence.

> Give ear, ye children, to my law,
> Devout attention lend,
> Let the instructions of my mouth
> Deep in your heart descend....

So it was. Among Grampy's files was a 151st Psalm, which, on occasion, he had called forth. But the immortality, I discovered, had its human side, as well—the smiles, their tears. In my early teens these glimpses—tender, straightforward, susceptible—drew me closer to Grampy, as he became a source of wisdom and experience. In my middle teens, as the sixties unfolded, the more human side drew us suddenly apart—as his mortality, as mine, was set in ever-sharper relief.

I breathed out, gazed out the window of the plane through the star-strewn heavens. And now with Grampy's approaching death, I sensed that another change was before him, before me. Threads from our conversation the spring before on the terrace of Cat Bow returned to mind. As the infirmities of old age became more pronounced, I found myself struggling to understand who Grampy was. The more the question grew in me, the less significant became all the honors and tributes and titles that had been bestowed upon him—until they all fell to the side, leaving me with the groping memory of a frail old lord, wrestling quietly with his beloved angel. *When the going gets tough?...yes, the tough get going.* I leaned back into the seat, closed my eyes.

* * * * *

At the top of the ramp, I caught sight of Mom among the faces of the crowd. As I approached, a sad smile touched her lips. Taking a deep breath, I hugged her, as she said, "Grampy died quietly a few hours ago, but he wasn't in pain."

The ride home was quiet. More memories, reflections, and halting words. To my question about how Dad was taking it, she paused, and then answered, "He is heart-broken." Tears returned to my eyes, to hers, as she went on to say that there would be a memorial service in Cambridge tomorrow, followed by a smaller, more intimate ceremony at the grave site in Lancaster. In accordance with Grampy's wishes, he would be laid to rest beside Bea, with whom he had begun his journey.

As we pulled into the driveway, I was surprised by the lack of excitement I felt at being home again. We walked into the house, finding Dad alone in the study, standing in front of the fireplace. As he turned to welcome me, I was struck. I had never seen my father cry before. And it hurt a little more.

* * * * *

The family ranks gathered the next afternoon at Harvard's Memorial Church, joined by friends and associates who had come to pay their last respects. Greetings were quietly exchanged. Some faces were familiar, 'Uncle Ned,' 'Uncle Bobby,' Mina, and Grampy's devoted secretary, Mrs. Murdock, stirring in me halting smiles of recognition. Others, elder business associates, fellow laborers in the political vineyards, and former comrades in arms, were less so. Alone or in groups, the guests filed up the granite steps, through the large paneled doors, and into the church, where they followed the red-carpeted aisles to seats in the chaste wooden pews.

The family joined them, Uncle John and Teenie leading the way, as they filed in from Appleton Chapel, to take their places in the reserved seats at the front of the church. And, then, as the doors were closed, a silence settled over the congregation, turning our attention, young and old alike, to the altar. I closed my eyes to stem the flood that welled up within me.

The minister, Dr. Rhys Williams, arose, stepped forward and unfolded the text that he had prepared, *Upon all who enter this world rests the command which we may not fail—for the path of life leadeth from dawn until the setting sun and all must walk in this path....* Beside me, Mom's hand came to rest on Dad's left hand, his right hand reaching into his coat pocket for a handkerchief, which he lifted to his eyes. Mine, blurred, glanced off and up, rising through legions of names carved in marble cataracts upon the walls—Harvard sons, who had given their lives in two world wars—rising up to the arched Georgian windows and vaulting roof, ... seeking, searching, closing around the tide of tears.

Notes from an organ lifted us to our feet; a hymn rose from the congregation, "Lead Kindly Light." Nat shifted the hymnal in front of me, my eyes following the printed words, my voice silent. Then, as the congregation took their seats once again, Uncle Bish stepped up to the pulpit, his tall, angular, goodly frame cloaked in a gown. Another passage was read, my mind reaching for the words, slipping off, and then back again, *But those who look to the Lord will have new strength. They will grow wings like angels. They will rise and not be weary....*

I paused, looked up. The Lord's Prayer followed, and, then, a second hymn, followed, in turn, by passages from the New Testament and Old—words both foreign and familiar. *Who shall ascend into the hill of the Lord? Or who shall stand in his holy place?...* I bowed my head, repeating the words of a bedtime psalm that Mother had said with us over the seasons of our youth. *He that hath clean hands, and a pure heart: who hath not lifted up his soul unto vanity, nor sworn deceitfully. He shall receive a blessing from the Lord, and righteousness from the God of his salvation.*

As the last hymn ended, the minister remained standing. Looking out across those assembled, he paused and, then, spoke, *Before the unknown we must stand with bowed heads and hearts of awe. From mystery to mystery we pass, trusting that mystery which overarches life. Let us carry his courage with us, so that we may be able to hope till hope creates the things it contemplates. This is to be good, courageous, and free. This alone is life, joy, victory!*

At the conclusion of the service, friends lingered, drew nearer, stepping forward to reach out a hand, an arm, an embrace. Smiles gave way to tears. I stepped back to the side of the church. To my right, an older man looked on quietly. Our gazes met. He walked over to me, "Are you one of Mr. Weeks' grandchildren?" I nodded. He paused, "Your grandfather was the captain of my unit during the war." He struggled for words, "He stood by me not only at the front, but afterward when we returned to the States and had to pick up life anew." The man reached out a hand, I took it, shook it, thanked him for his words, turned right, turned left....

Off to my right, a middle-aged lady was holding Dad's hand. "I never knew Mr. Weeks, but my father worked for him for many years, and one of the last things he made me promise, before he died, was that I would attend your father's funeral." Dad nodded silently. I looked down. "Please give my respects to Mr. Weeks' family." She turned and departed.

As the family made their way out of the church, my glance rested on Teenie. Words of the duet we had sung together on Cat Bow's flowery terrace the spring before rumored on my lips. Yes, the ranks had thinned; Captain Weeks had gone, gone to graveyards ....

The day was long and exhausting. And yet, sleep eluded me that night. After the others had turned in, I sat up in the study, leafing through a folder of papers that Dad had laid out: a rich and varied patchwork, which included letters of condolence, obituaries, and personal testaments—straight-forward, tender, ... susceptible—that Grampy's last years had drawn forth from him. A fire kept me company, burning quietly in the hearth.

On top was a memorandum:

In the event I drop by the wayside, I list below a few items I would like to see attended to.

I should like my remains to be cremated and my ashes taken to the Summer Street Cemetery in Lancaster, alongside Bea—and Jane if she predeceases me.

As for funeral arrangements, I think as a particular matter that neither my remains (nor ashes) need be brought to Boston for services. However, I do suggest that there be some memorial services at the First Church in Boston—Unitarian (Dr. Rhys Williams).

As for this service, I think there need be no bearers, and the time

selected ought to be such as to give people from a distance—assuming
there are any—an opportunity to get themselves to Boston for the service.
I have no suggestions as to the service, save my desire that 3 hymns be
sung:

1) *Lead Kindly Light*; 2) *Abide with Me*; 3) *Nearer my God to
Thee.*

Otherwise, the family and Dr. Williams can set up the program,
except for my wish that there be no eulogy of any sort. I do like "Crossing
the Bar" by Tennyson.

There need be no services in Lancaster, save those customarily held at
the graveside—although, because of the fact that presumably there would
be a number of people come to the graveside, the service there might be
a little longer and cover a little more ground than would normally be
expected at such an internment.

I may simply add that I should like very much for my son-in-law,
Reverend Henry Sherrill, to have some part in either or both of the
above services.

Sinclair Weeks

As usual, Grampy covered all the bases—right to the very end. I
reflected, turned to the Congressional Record and to a tribute from
Edward Brooke, who had followed Grampy's footsteps into the U.S.
Senate:

The Death of Sinclair Weeks

*Mr. President, the nation and the Republican Party are diminished by
the passing of Sinclair Weeks, who died yesterday, fittingly enough in
Concord, Mass.—where American patriotism had its beginnings.*

*Sinclair Weeks was a patriot and a public man, in the best sense
of those overused words—always committed to a cause in which he
believed, always caring, always giving of himself.*

*He was a versatile man, a wise man, a good man, who never lost
his zest for and love of politics and business. He cherished his family.
He gave unstintingly of his time and talents to Harvard, Northeastern
University, and—in the last years of his life—to the University of New
Hampshire. . . .*

It is comforting to know that the Weeks tradition of and for public service has been and will be carried on by his children. The trail of constructive and imaginative political action, which their father and grandfather blazed, will, I know, continue to be an inspiration to the children, grandchildren, and great-grandchildren whom Sinclair Weeks leaves behind.

* * * * *

War, politics, business, . . . the sons. The generations beckoned. I reflected, turned the page. Senator Brooke's words were followed by more recent passages from Grampy's diary, which offered less familiar glimpses of Sinclair Weeks. If Grampy became more conservative in his old age, he, like so many of his fellow human beings, appeared also to become more philosophical:

I like business because it is competitive. It rewards deeds rather than words and requires that those involved focus on the tasks at hand, instead of getting carried away by how things should be. It undertakes to give people what they want and not to reform them. There is a lot of hypocrisy and sentimentality in life, and business is honestly selfish. It doesn't deal with a lot of pretenses, but promptly penalizes mistakes, laziness and inefficiency, while rewarding those who work hard and apply themselves.

. . . At home I observed New Deal locusts devour many economic treasures essential to American success—even for survival. Those conditions spurred my reaction. From 1936 on, I tried so hard to defend American business. In that aggressive role I later was selected by President Eisenhower to head his Commerce Department—the statutory champion of private business and the promoter of profits and jobs. In its defense I endured with pride the "slings and arrows" of hostile union bosses, Ivy League radicals, left-wing pundits, and business-baiting politicians.

In my term as Commerce Secretary, I had the satisfaction that I helped spur the economy to the world's then highest peak of prosperity, to start history's biggest public works project—known as the Interstate and Defense Highway System—and to give the public all-time record benefits by the Department's competent service agencies. All this the

Eisenhower administration brought to the American people, and peace too.... Despite obvious flaws in both myself and my calling, ours has been a life-long love affair.

A wane smile touched my face, as I thought about Grampy's words and our walk through the spring afternoon—puddles, reflections drawing us together, moving us apart. The business of business?... *What is the American, what are we really chasing?* My gaze rested in the flames.

* * * * *

More pages followed: an excerpt from a correspondence relating to Senator Joe McCarthy; a passage from Grampy's diary on another correspondence he had had with the Kennedy family, followed by the exchange of letters; and, lighter of touch, a similar bipartisan sentiment found expression in a letter Grampy wrote to a New Hampshire gentleman and democrat, who had managed to capture the Governor's office.

April 20, 1950

Judge Lawrence G. Brooks
First District Court of Eastern Middlesex
Judges' Lobby
Malden, MA

Dear Judge Brooks:

I must apologize for not sooner responding to yours of March 27th, but I've been on the road most of the time and have had no opportunity until now to sit down and write you.

    I'm afraid I cannot, as you suggest, "speak out locally about Senator McCarthy," and, of course, knowing McCarthy, I must naturally disagree with your reference to him as a "blackguard." I do not, of course, approve of people going into a deal like this one of McCarthy's without having the evidence to back up what they say, but McCarthy is certainly no blackguard, regardless of what effect his actions may have on the Republican Party. McCarthy is just mad, in my opinion. In the Marine Corp., he fought his way from one foxhole to another all the way from Honolulu to Okinawa, and now he sees China and probably the rest of Asia handed over to the Communists and the things he fought for and saw his friends die for falling one by one, and he just doesn't like it....

From the standpoint of our country, if McCarthy and a few more, even though at first they may not be able to produce the evidence, can sooner or later cause a few more communists to be rooted out of our State Department, they will, by their "martyrdom," (as political figures) have done their country a service, even if they do politically fall by the wayside. And, after all, that is more important than the success or failure of any political party.

I am sorry that it would seem you and I are in the opposite corner on this one, but, I dare say, it must be so.

Sincerely Yours,
Sinclair Weeks

* * *

Although of different political faiths, I had often been in touch with this famous Boston business genius, Joseph Kennedy, over the years. One of my latest contacts was when his son Bobby had been assassinated. I was deeply moved because, among other reasons, I knew his son, Bobby, played on the Milton football team with my son, Bill.

So I sent the oft-bereaved parents a letter of sympathy. Joe was unable to reply, but his wife, Rose, did, thanking me in her own long hand.

June 7, 1968

Dear Joe,

You will, perhaps, be surprised to hear directly from me, but, in the appalling situation in which you and your family are enmeshed, I can't refrain from sending you a few words which I hope will provide comfort.

Strangely enough, my first thoughts on receipt of the tragic news went to the letter President Lincoln wrote Mrs. Bixby when she had laid five sons on the altar of freedom. This letter of President Lincoln's is, by every conceivable test, one of the classics.

I hope I may not be considered presumptuous enough to compare the two, but I would remind you that your boys, too, died in defense of their country and for its best interests as they saw these best interests.

I am sad beyond measure to have to address these lines to you and can only hope that the good Lord will comfort and support you and your dear wife as you reflect upon these things.

Faithfully Yours,
Sinclair Weeks

* * *

Governor John King
State House
Concord, NH 03301

Dear John,

Thanks much for the photo, which I just received—taken on our terrace lawn. If you ask me, the two of us are a pretty handsome pair. We look good together in the picture, and it's just a pity that we are separated by that unfathomable gulf known as politics. Thanks again for everything.

Most Sincerely Yours,
Sinny

* * *

Tucked in between the letters was an unexpected passage that Grampy had copied into his journals:

Ill fares the land, to hastening ills a prey,
Where wealth accumulates, and men decay;
Princes and Lords may flourish or may fade;
A breath can make them, as a breath has made;
But a bold peasantry, their country's pride,
When once destroy'd can never be supplied.

* * * * *

I paused.... My gazes turned to the flames in the fireplace, before settling on an envelope, containing earlier letters of condolence following Bea's death, along with a note that Grampy had written to Uncle Woof, a rare glimpse into the depth of the loss he had felt for Bea.

Dear Woof,

I have been writing letters steadily for a month and am still at it. This has resulted, I dare say, in my neglecting you and very unjustifiably so. Your two letters arr'd and were much appreciated. This, as you understand, has been a cruel blow, and I just can't seem to understand it at all. We had had thirty wonderful years together and to think of going on alone is just about all I can take. Really the whole thing is like a bad dream from which it seems I must awaken.

I breathed in, read on:

Last Sunday I went down to the cemetery, and I just couldn't take it all in or seem to realize what I was doing. The children are wonderful, but even with the whole family around it's terribly lonely.... Your mother knows and those who have been thro' it, but you have to lose your life's companion to really understand what it all means. I'm trying to readjust myself. The doctor wanted me to come back here and get my summer off as planned, and I'm glad I did. It was a bitter pill to come up here again, and I didn't relish it at all, but I'm sure it was the thing to do.

> *My fond wishes to you,*
> *Sinclair*

I rested Grampy's letter on top of the others, as I closed my blurring eyes. Words rose up within me: *Could it be, Grampy, that the reason why you said so little about how you felt over the years with respect to Bea, your bride, to matters of the heart was because you weren't sure you really wanted to know yourself?* I wiped my hand over my cheeks and glanced down at the last page in the pile—a poem of author unknown. Smiles, tears....

> *We can call the young fellow named Weeks,*
> *One of nature's most lovable freaks,*
> *For the older he's grown*
> *The better we've known*
> *That he never will join the antique.*
>
> *His parents baptized him as "Sin"*
> *(With a "clair" that they later threw in)*

If he feels he is game
To live up to his name,
He'd jolly well better begin.

That syllable "clair," you can tell
(If you're French and you know how to spell)
Means "luminous," "bright,"
"Reflecting the light"
And it sums up the guy pretty well.

* * * * *

The next morning, we gathered around the breakfast table, before heading north for the burial. The meal was quiet, as Grampy filled our thoughts. After we had eaten a few minutes, Dad suddenly broke out laughing. Surprised, we looked at him, inquiringly. Dad's laugh settled into a tender smile, "Your Uncle Bill told a wonderful story about your grandfather yesterday, after the service." Dad paused, wiped his mouth, continued, "During the last few days in the nursing home, Grampy rarely moved or talked. He had had enough of all the pampering and refused the food that was offered to him. This made things difficult for the male nurse, whose job it was to see that Grampy ate. One morning, after many futile efforts, the nurse got a bit exasperated and, putting down the plate, called Grampy to task: 'Mr. Weeks, why don't you eat?'" Dad shook his head. "Grampy, who was sitting back in the chair beside his bed, was silent. The nurse tried again, still with no luck. Finally, privy to Grampy's political leanings, an idea came to mind. Bending forward, he issued Grampy a challenge: 'Mr. Weeks, you are behaving like a democrat. Are you a democrat? Mr. Weeks, I think you have become a democrat!'"

Dad looked at us, "The room was silent. And, then, the curtains parted for a brief moment, as your grandfather opened his eyes, sat up straight, and exclaimed in a firm, clear, voice: 'NOW I'VE HEARD EVERYTHING!'" Dad paused, wiped his eyes, "Those were the last words anyone heard Grampy speak." Tears streaming freely down our cheeks, we all joined Dad in his laughter.

* * * * *

The family gathered quietly around the large boulder with the letters, "WEEKS", set into it, in the hillside burial plot in Lancaster. Behind the boulder, a hedge extended its evergreen embrace, rising up to a
slender birch, whose wisps of branches reached out into the afternoon.
Stillness lay upon the day. Before us on the ground, Bea's gravestone,
adorned with three, simple, intertwining, ivy leaves, rested back into the
years—"Feb. 4, 1895–July 10, 1945."

> *Thine be the quiet habitations*
> *Thine the green field's blossom*
> *Sown amid smiles of saintly recognition*
> *As sweet and tender as thine own.*
>
> Whittier

My eyes lingered on the inscription, carved in its marble face, as a
thought came unexpectedly, to mind: What was it like, Bea? What did
you feel? Grampy's letters to you from the front, I've read. And your
responses, . . . sitting at home with a new-born child, wondering if your
husband would ever return? A first war. What was it like when a second
war followed, and your oldest son, John, stepped forward, following in
his father's martial footstep; followed in turn by Dad, dismissing the
motherly advice you offered. Wife, mother, grandmother—what, Bea,
did you feel, as those tears welled up in your eyes? Life/death. . . .

I turned to the place that had been prepared beside my Grandmother's grave. Together again. A mound of dark, frozen soil was piled up over
the broken snow. Beside it lay the casket. My gaze came to rest on it.

Slowly the family rounded the circle, huddling close together to
share the sparse warmth. The minister waited till all were quiet and,
then drew a text out of his coat pocket. His eyes rested on it for a
moment, before he lifted his head: *Trust the dreams for in them are hid-
den the gate to eternity, for what is it to die but to stand in the wind, melt
into the sun. . . .*

I looked at the minister, as the words released a quiet tide of tears
in those family members, who had managed to contain themselves at
the more public memorial service the day before. Uncles, aunts, cousins,
and young great-grandchildren, their eyes moist, blurred, directed their
gazes toward the casket on the bare, snow-strewn ground.

I breathed out. I had no tears left. Instead, in their place, another feeling awoke, unexpectedly, within me.... *And what is it to cease from life but to feel the breath from restless tides that it might rise and expand to see God unencumbered.* The minister's words came to my ears, as I quietly stepped back from the family. Turning around, I lifted my gaze out over the sloping valley, the quiet snow-decked fields, merging with the hushed forest that flowed on, rising over the hills and mountains of our Northern Kingdom. My breath deepened, my glance lifting on up into the blue firmament.

Sunlight bathed the afternoon. From deep within, a smile gently broke across my face, as words from one of Bea's condolence letters that I had read the night before filled my mind: "It's hard to understand, Sinclair, why these things have to happen. But, somehow I know you will lift up your eyes to the hills you and Bea so loved and draw the strength to carry on."

... *World without end.* The minister closed his text.

* * * * *

A sunbeam lit the Pine Room. I lifted my eyes from the small, gold-framed photo, nestled in the nook of Grampy's desk. Among the shades of gray, the fleeting smile passed across my lips. Above Bea's picture, my glance settled on a passage by Abraham Lincoln, its words now etched in my memory:

> *If I were to try to read, much less answer, all the attacks made on me, this shop might as well be closed for any other business. I do the very best I know—the very best I can; and I mean to keep doing so until the end. If the end brings me out right, what is said against me won't amount to anything. If the end brings me out wrong, ten angels swearing I was right would make no difference.*

"Amen," the word broke gently on my lips. I turned, my eyes passing over a longer letter from a father to his son that reigned in silence over a dwindling herd of elephants.

> ... *So, in the final analysis, Sinclair, you have to make good on your own account. That I am sure you will do if you follow the above precepts and*

any others, which your common sense will indicate. Good luck to you.

Father

The lines receded into the passages of a life. Grampy's desk was clear. The letters, notes, and concluding affairs had been attended to and laid to rest. A time to stand, yes, and a time to step aside....

I turned. The Pine Room was still, quiet, abiding. My glance passed slowly over the chairs, sofas, a cobbler's bench, and empty, cocktail tray. On the far windowsill, Christmas cards had been replaced by passing tidings of another season. Bookshelves edged the sills, filled with old volumes, passages for posterity—great-grandfathers, grandfathers, fathers, and sons.

I walked over to the fireplace, pausing before the musket and powder horn that kept their eternal vigil above the flames—still now for six months since Grampy's departure for Rivercrest. Nursing Home. Running my fingers along the top of the fire screen, I closed my eyes, as a flood of memories rose up within me—spring, summer, autumn, a late winter's eve arrival: *What do you say, Grampy?...* Dad paused for a moment in the hallway behind me, before climbing up the stairs to collect his suitcase. I listened, until his steps faded away, then turned toward the door.

The gallery of photos and cartoons filled my gaze: friends, family, business and political associates, a retiring general, royalty and rabble-rousers, lords and ladies, a debonair cat, downcast hound and—I nodded my head—the cantankerous old donkey, peering over the shoulder of an emphatic soothsayer, profits, prophecies,... and "a cheerful note from the cartoon bird?" More memories, recollections, anecdotes returned to heart and mind. As I started out the door, my glance fell on the picture of a young bright-eyed soldier, drum sticks poised, ready to strike up the beat.

In the hallway, I paused before the Telephone Room and then stepped on out to the greenhouse, retiring into the seasons, its flowers gone, bereaved, its shelves empty but for a faint scattering of pebbles. *I count my garden by the flowers, never by the leaves that fall....*

My gaze passed on down to the pond, stirring reflections of a summer paddle the year before with a new friend. As our canoe passed the

Davidge's cabin, the forest line ended, and the view rose up through the field to Cat Bow. "My God, what a place!" Startled by Betty's words, I looked up at the Big House and farm. For the first time I saw Cat Bow not with my eyes alone, but with the eyes of a forthright friend.

"Who lives there?" Betty turned to me.

"My grandfather." The words rested on my lips.

"That's an amazing home." Betty's voice was quieter. I nodded, reflected, wondered why I had never before been able to see the farm through other eyes, never recognized that the Big House, my little universe, *was*, indeed, big. For me, it had always been Cat Bow, Grampy's home, and the place where we spent our childhood and young adult years.

"What a fortunate man." She turned to me.

I was silent, as my thoughts went to the Lord of Cat Bow, resting back onto the lounge chair into the afternoon, a book in his hand, slipping down onto his lap—enfolding fleeting passages of a life. Grampy, the ailing lord, nursing with his fiery old Green Mountain brother, Ethan Allen, an all so ancient, all so mortal wound. Our paddles dipped into the lake, dissolving the scene in a swirl of blue.

The ticking of the grandfather clock roused me from my dreams. Stepping back, I looked up at its venerable old face, etched with roman numerals and its large bronze hands. Ten to four—the rest of the family were gathering their bags.

I turned from the doorway, following my steps down the corridor to the north wing of the house and the large, sprawling boudoirs that harbored strained echoes of unfulfilled love. I paused on the threshold of Grandma Jane's room. The hospital bed had been moved out to provide space once again for the pair of old spindle beds, with their comforting quilts and goose-feather pillows that had offered welcome repose in less pained hours.

My steps led me back down the hall, past the rows of closets, F, P, J, S, W, B, glimpses of childhoods past, and on into the living room. Grampy's old rocking chair leaned back into the years. Across the way, tables, benches, chairs, congregated about the large living room rug, which edged the entrance to the Summer Room, boarded up, its wicker throne gently vanquished.

My steps carried me on into the dining room. In front of me, the old maple table filled the center of the room, bare but for a pair of hushed candles, which flanked the pewter centerpiece. I paused a moment and, then, stepped forward, resting my hands on the back of the chair that sat before the fireplace, at the head of the table. At the other end of the table, an empty chair seated maternal memories—Teenie, Grandma Jane, Bea—framed by the stalwart old hutch. The bell sat silently on the centerboard. My thoughts journeyed back over the seasons, as my gaze rose to an embattled scene on the wall,

> *Spirit that made those heroes dare,*
> *To die, and leave their children free,*
> *Bid time and nature gently spare*
> *The shaft we raise to them and thee.*

I glanced out at the sun porch, with its view down over the hayfield, before opening the swinging door into the pantry and kitchen. Clean and neat as ever, my eyes passed over the old soapstone sink, the stove, empty of pots, and across to the counter. A cookie jar, tucked into the corner beside the windowsill, harbored crumbled memories of earlier days and festive seasons. All was silent. Aprons hung from their hooks on the back of the larder door. Dora and Cynthia had moved on to other settings, following the kindly footsteps of old John Crawford.

In the back hall, I rested my hands on the wooden banister, glancing out through the woodshed, laden with succulent smells, to the garage, before I continued around and up the stairs. Glimmers of sunlight spilled into the attic playroom on my right. In the center of the room, cobwebs gently clasped themselves about the swing. Behind the swing, the rocking horses leaned back into the shadows of the eves.

I paused, walked on down the hall. The door opened to Mina's room on my left, neat and tidy, now as before.

The hallway led on to 'Uncle Ned's old quarters. The sawdust had been swept up; only memories lingered. Across the hall, a spy hole peeked out at me from a neighboring door. Inside, Dad zipped up his bag. Footsteps sounded from the far end of the hall. I looked up. To my left, nature prints, snatches of wit and wisdom, and pictures of kith and kin lined the walls—a great-grandmother, her son, bride, and brood in poised silhouette. At the far end of the hall, the carpet paused at Grampy's door, gently closed, before curving on down to the War Room.

Opening the door, I stepped in and glanced about: boots, gas mask, helmet. My eyes settled on an old buckle on the dresser, the words echoing across my lips, before I raised my gaze to the mirror. Eight, almost nine years. . . . a life itself had passed. The war was over. One . . . two. . . three . . . four . . . the old Westminster chime sounded our departure. Young girls—soldiers—graveyards. . . . I turned and headed down the stairway.

At the bottom of the stairs, I started toward the Entrance Room and, then, lingered in the back hallway, listening, reflecting, stepping over to the backdoor. Opening it, the dream from the night before filled my mind—*The boy ran out of the door and across the terrace, his arms opening wide, his steps carrying him down through the waving field of grass, carrying him with great, free strides, arms outstretched, in sweeping curves by figures in the golden, sunlit field. "Stuart!" A man with a lawyer's coat reached out to the young boy, called him over. . . . On, around, the boy's strides broadening, by the first figure, the second, the investor's tie, leaning forward, reaching out, beckoning, . . . on down the field and around a third figure, the business man's vest, calling, waving, . . . by and on, head raised, arms free, outstretched, carried in great widening strides.*

"GRAMPY!" The boy looked ahead in the field. A figure was waving to him in the goldening field of grass. "GRAMPY, you're back; you're here!" The boy ran toward him, nearer, nearer, nearer. . . . "GRAMPY!" The old man lifted his arm . . . and slapped the boy gruffly/gently on the back, pushing him forward, "Keep going, son."

On, the child ran, arms widening, strides lengthening. . . . down through the field to the Boat House, wrapped in a smoky haze, and the blue expanse beyond. The dream, yes, the dream. . . . Open your eyes, Stuart!

The vast shining snowfields of the distant peaks gazed down from the heights. Washington, Adams, Jefferson, Madison. . . . Beneath the ever changing guise of the seasons, the peaks were the same, ever the same, rising up joyfully—joyfully—over our aspiring kingdom into the encircling rounds.

I leaned back against the doorway. My eyes rested on the sun-dial, cloaked in melting snow, as a verse flowed through my mind, *...Enshrined in a perfect domain.* I turned and, closing the terrace door quietly, continued back through the dining room to the Entrance Room. Mom and Brad were quietly zipping up their suitcases. Nat brought his bag out to Dad, who was packing up the car. Bea's footsteps made their way down the hall. The family was quiet. I collected my coat from the back of the faithful old love seat and put it on, before lifting my eyes above the volumes of books to the aged owl, perched silently atop the shelves. Our gazes met. I lingered a moment and, then, picked up my bag and followed Bea, Brad, and Mom out the door.

Pausing on the doorstep, my glance followed the road up to the barn. Its two wings—framed in by the empty paddock, bereft of its sire—reached out loyally to the Big House. To the left of the barn, the sheds, turkey coop, and a snowy glade silently enclosed the barnyard. To the right, the road led on up to Bill Rines's house, pausing on the crest of the hill, before climbing further up to the Bill Weeks' house at the edge of the tree line. Beyond, Mt. Orne carried my vision on up into the heavens. *Thou must penetrate the portal where thine angel thee perfects....*

The afternoon sun had begun to warm the day. I continued over to the car, lifting my bags and placing them in the trunk with the others. Bea settled up front with Mom and Dad. I squeezed in beside Nat and Brad. *If you're going to go....* Summer, autumn, winter, spring—returning anew, ever anew. Dad paused a moment, his glance drawn back out the window and, then, started up the engine.

As the car drove around the circular driveway, my gaze rested on the island in its midst, empty but for rose bushes that broke through the melting crust of snow.

We called him *Grampy*. A smile—tender, susceptible, straightforward—a tear touched my lips. The family was quiet. The car continued on down the drive. To our left, the old elm lifted its enfolding boughs up, up, up...with a happy/sad melody, over our Northern Kingdom.

I took a deep breath. In front of us, on both sides of the road, white fields of snow spread out, engulfed in sunshine. Birds darted off the roadside fence, rising with their songs into the dawning afternoon.

Leaning my head against the window, my gaze fell on a second sign, nestled in the grove of pines. Its words passed across my vision:

DRIVERS CAUTION ANEW,
GREAT-GRANDCHILD NUMBER 9
NOW IN VIEW!

President John Adams wrote that the great grandfathers study war, so the grandfathers can study politics, so the fathers can study business, so the sons can study history and literature. The author's forbears have served in state or national office for the last eight generations. His great-grandfather, John Wingate Weeks, was the secretary of war in the Cabinets of Harding and Coolidge, and was also responsible for the landmark environmental legislation known as the Weeks Act. The author's grandfather, Sinclair Weeks, the "Lord of Cat Bow," was a U.S. senator and secretary of commerce under Eisenhower. The author's father, Sinclair Weeks Jr., was a business leader. Stuart Weeks has directed his creative energies into the cultural sector, as a writer, educator, and founder and director of The Center for American Studies in Concord, Massachusetts.

In this capacity, he has hosted programs for over 1,000 international leaders, introducing them to American culture through the historic window of Concord. Stuart has hosted the radio show *Of, By, and For the People*, authored the column, "Uncommon Sense," and is currently completing, with two colleagues, the transcription, editing, and preparation for publication of Ralph Waldo Emerson's yet unpublished, complete masterwork, *The Natural History of the Intellect*. A father of four, Stuart and his wife, Juliane, divide their time between Concord, Massachusetts and the Granite State of his forbears.